Go Fish Australia is a comprehensive guide to fishing throughout Australia — inland, around the coast and underwater. It is a companion book to the TV series of the same name shown on ABC-TV and produced for the Australian Recreational and Sport Fishing Confederation Inc.

Richard Allan is the pseudonym of a retired Sydney businessman who is a dedicated amateur fisher, the author of Fishing and Fishing Tackle and a regular broadcaster of fishing reports on ABC Radio.

GO FISH AUSTRALIA

ALL YOU NEED TO KNOW ABOUT FRESHWATER
AND SALTWATER FISHING –
A COMPREHENSIVE GUIDE FOR EVERYONE

Compiled by Richard Allen for the Australian Recreational
and Sport Fishing Confederation Inc.

Published by ABC Enterprises for the
AUSTRALIAN BROADCASTING CORPORATION
20 Atchison Street (Box 4444) Crows Nest NSW 2065

Copyright © Australian Recreational and Sport Fishing
Confederation Inc., 1988

First published 1988

All rights reserved. No part of this publication may be
reproduced, stored in a retrieval system or transmitted
in any form or by any means electronic, mechanical,
photocopying, recording or otherwise, without the prior
written permission of the Australian Broadcasting
Corporation.

National Library of Australia
Cataloguing-in-Publication entry
Go Fish Australia

ISBN 642 53090 4.

1. Fishing—Australia. I. Australian Broadcasting
Corporation. II. Allan, Richard, 1932-

799,1′0994

Illustrated by Richard Pieremont
Designed by Deborah Brash
Set in 11/13 Plantin by Midland Typesetters
Printed and bound in Australia by Macarthur Press, Parramatta, NSW

Front cover photos: Fred Jobson, Rod Harrison
  Richard Allan, Barry Wilson
Back cover photos: Shane Mensforth, Barry Wilson

Foreword

This is not just another fishing book full of rigid how-to-fish and tackle-rigging directions which can mystify and confuse even the crustiest lifelong fisher. It is a practical and easy-to-understand guide for those of any age setting out to fish anywhere in Australia.

The book is also one very important element of a new written and visual adventure of exploration and learning for Australians, *Go Fish Australia*, developed over three years by the Australian Recreational and Sport Fishing Confederation (Inc.), the peak national organisation working for and representing this country's 4.5 million recreational and sport fishers.

But the book and the other elements of the *Go Fish Australia* concept—the television series and the instructional videocassette versions—are not, by any means, only for that one-third of the Australian population already experiencing the joys and wonders of fishing and fish. As those who will thrill to the visual elements of *Go Fish Australia* and who explore the pages of this book will appreciate, fishing is not simply using hook and line to separate fish from water.

Whether pursued from the armchair in book and video, or more actively on lake, stream and big bluewater, from rocks or beaches or in the estuary, fishing is the vehicle for a total learning experience. It is a doorway to uncomplicated fun and enjoyment in the outdoors with family and friends, to all the natural and many of the physical and social sciences, to the intricacies and mysteries of the still uncounted myriad life-forms which share the planet with us beneath that one great boundary between two worlds—the water surface.

No one can ever learn or experience it all but every fishing outing teaches something and enriches us in some way. For me, it always emphasises the complexity yet fragility and vulnerability of the environment and ecological life support systems of the natural resource on which fishing depends—the fish themselves. It follows, too, that the quality of the fishing environment is in great part a measure of the quality of human life.

In this book you will share the feelings, experiences, knowledge, skills and ideas of people who have already opened doors down the Australian fishing corridor. One overriding impression emerges from their collective work: a love of fishing and fish and a concern that the Australian fishing environment, with its precious fish species and stocks, is preserved.

And that brings us back to the *Go Fish Australia* concept. The concept elements—the television series, the instructional videocassettes and this book—are all educational in intent and, I think you will agree, entertaining and fun.

I dedicate this book to my ten-year-old son, Gerard, and all his peers, that they may Go Fish Australia with a new appreciation of the world-class natural fishing resources Australia possesses, with an awareness of the need for preserving these resources and with a commitment to continuing the type of work on which the Confederation is embarked—to raise the quality of fishing as a satisfying and rewarding sport and recreation for all our youngsters who come after us.

Graham Pike
President
Australian Recreational and Sport Fishing Confederation Inc.
PO Box E243, Queen Victoria Terrace, ACT 2600

In appreciation: Many thanks are due to ESSO Australia Ltd for its generous support of the *Go Fish Australia* concept; to the Australian Sports Commission which provided the initial grant to make the entire project possible; and to the members and associate members of the Confederation—Australian Anglers Association, Australian Casting Association, Australian Fresh Water Fishermen's Assembly, Australian National Sportfishing Association, Australian Underwater Federation, Game Fishing Association of Australia, and Native Fish Australia (members); Amateur Fishermen's Association of the Northern Territory, New South Wales Recreational Fishing Advisory Council, Queensland Sport and Recreational Fishing Council, and the Western Australian Recreational and Sportfishing Council Inc. (associate members).

Contents

Preface (xi)

The Lucky Fishers' Country (xiii)

Tropical Queensland 1

Small-Boat Fishing 1

Gamefishing in the North 5

Coastal Rivers and Estuaries 8

Subtropical Queensland and Northern New South Wales 13

Fraser Island 13

The Bribie Banks 15

Brisbane and Environs 18

Byron Bay to Noosa — Rock and Beach 22

From Granite Tops to the Barwon 25

The Manning to Noosa 28

New South Wales Mid-North Coast Offshore 32

Crowdy Head to Ballina 34

New South Wales Central Coast — Rock and Beach Fishing 38

Lord Howe Island 40

Gamefishing North of Sydney 43

The Hawkesbury River 46

Western New South Wales, Victoria, and South Australia 51

Victoria and the Riverina—Native Species in the Inland Rivers 51
Out on the Darling 54
St Vincent and Spencer Gulfs—Small-Boat Fishing 56
Fishing Along the Bight 59
Adelaide to the Victorian Border—Rock and Beach 60
Trout Fishing in South Australia 62

South-Eastern Australia 65

Sydney Harbour 65
Botany Bay 70
Sydney Rock and Beach 72
The Illawarra to the Victorian Border 76
Small-Boat and Light Game 81
The New South Wales South Coast—Rivers and Estuaries 85
ACT and Environs 88
The Snowy Mountains and the Monaro Region 91
The Victorian Coast—Surf and Rock Fishing 95
Victorian Coastal Rivers and Estuaries 99
Western Port 101
Port Phillip Bay 105
Trout in Victoria 113
Victoria and Tasmania—Gamefishing 115
Tasmania—Rivers, Bays and Estuaries 118
Rock Fishing in Tasmania 122
Tasmania's Wild Trout 124

Western Australia   129

Inland Fishing in the South-West   129
Perth to Albany – Beaches, Estuaries and Bays   131
Perth to Albany – Saltwater River Fishing   136
Small-Boat Fishing   138
Gamefishing   142
Esperance to Cuvier – Rockfishing   145

Northern Territory and North-West Western Australia   157

Estuary and River Fishing   157
Small-Boat and Light Game   160

The Environment   164

Estuaries and Bays   164
Native Freshwater Recreational Fisheries of Eastern Australia   166

Australia Underwater   175

Queensland Down Under   175
Spearfishing in New South Wales   177
Victoria Underwater   178
Abrolhos Island Adventure   180
Underwater Western Australia   182

Rigs and Safety   185

Hooks   185
A Bit About Berley   187
Small-Boat Safety   188

Preface

This book is the result of an idea expressed by the president of the Australian Recreational and Sport Fishing Confederation during the organisation's first year. While the then executive members of the Confederation were still comprehending that they were responsible for representing all fishers to the Australian Government and in the community generally, Graham Pike suggested that the Confederation might try to produce a few film documentaries or videocassettes, with an educational slant, on the value of Australia's fishing and fish and the fragility of the fishing environment. I doubt if any member at the time imagined that the idea would result in a national television series and instructional videocassettes becoming available, together with this book—all under the title of *Go Fish Australia*★.

I have found enormous enjoyment in compiling the book and contributing to it and I am grateful to all the contributors for their co-operation. Many will be familiar, their names often appearing as the authors of articles in fishing and outdoor magazines (and on a book or two). Others may be less well known and a few are new.

All have a common interest—a love of fishing. They have fished for most of their lives and the experience and knowledge they provide within these pages will help newcomers, the casual enthusiasts and even long-term anglers to enjoy their fishing more.

Fishers have as many ideas and opinions as there are fish to catch (and authors on the subject are no exception). For that reason I can exempt myself—and the Confederation—by use of the disclaimer that the ideas and views of the contributors are their own and do not necessarily represent those of the Confederation. However, I will add that it is unlikely that such a collection of fresh, basic information on fishing around Australia has ever been available in a book that is easy to take wherever you travel.

There are some gaps; there will be those who will find a particular area has been overlooked. In a book of limited size, there is only so much space—and Australia is a very large place. The protesters can blame me, but I feel that a reading of material on an area surrounding an omitted locality will provide information applicable to the missing waters and fish species.

Neither the writers nor I will guarantee the catching of a fish. There is no single best method of catching fish. They are contradictory in their behaviour, frustrating, perplexing and often downright unco-operative despite the efforts of the most experienced fisher. If fish were easy to catch then a major part of the attraction of the sport, recreation, pastime, relaxation or whatever you wish to call fishing, would disappear.

While it is called both an art and a science, fishing is neither; but it gives a freedom to experiment as much as both these. It's as old as mankind but as new as tomorrow and there is still much to be learnt about it for those with enthusiasm and an inquisitive mind. Very often the measure of the pleasure of fishing is not the size of the catch but the discovery of something new about fish, their habitat or seeing or experiencing an occurrence which could only happen because you are fishing.

Now, Go Fish Australia and enjoy it and appreciate how much fun it is. And appreciate the Australian outdoors and scenery and climate – and care about the environment and most of all, about the fish.

Richard Allan
Wandandian 1988

* *Go Fish Australia* is a name registered by the Australian Recreational and Sport Fishing Confederation (Inc.). The *Go Fish Australia* concept is generously supported by Esso Australia Ltd.

The Lucky Fishers' Country
Ron Calcutt

In a world in which human populations are exploding, and all forms of wildlife associated with land and sea are diminishing at a similar rate, the tyranny of distance has become something of a blessing for Australia.

We populate a small part of the fringe of a huge continent, most conveniently located in a part of the world that allows it to intrude into both the great cold-water oceans to the south, and the teeming tropical seas of the equatorial belt to the north.

Although Australia has not been favoured with those natural elements required to produce the most prolific fisheries of our planet—huge rivers and a wide continental shelf—its position of isolation has thus far protected a great deal of what is a very good fishery, and our own relatively small population has only had a noticeable effect on fish stocks close to the few heavily populated areas.

The distance from the world's great population centres that has plagued Australia since the time of the first settlement now works for us in a number of surprising ways. Our remoteness, and the untouched wildness of so much of our continent, make us the envy of the civilised world. We have that thing that is rapidly becoming one of the world's most precious assets—an abundance of natural environment.

The Australian fisher has always taken that environment for granted. This is the Lucky Country, and in the Lucky Country you have lucky fishers. We have some of the world's best big-game fishing, and magnificent stream fishing ranging from the ice-cold trout streams of the high country to the steaming mangrove creeks of the tropics.

All along the coastline we enjoy a seemingly endless string of beautiful surf beaches, and more productive headlands than most people could hope to explore properly in a lifetime.

Although we don't have the equal of the world's great rivers, the rivers we do have are still, in the main, healthy, life-supporting systems that fish very well.

In years to come, the anglers of the world will come to fish Australia, but we won't have to go anywhere to enjoy some of the world's best sportfishing—it exists in our own back yard. And as the years go by, and over-fishing, over-polluting, political upheaval and so on make the other great hotspots of the past less and less desirable, so our home waters will become more and more valuable.

I have the earnest hope that more and more Australians will sample, and come to treasure, our

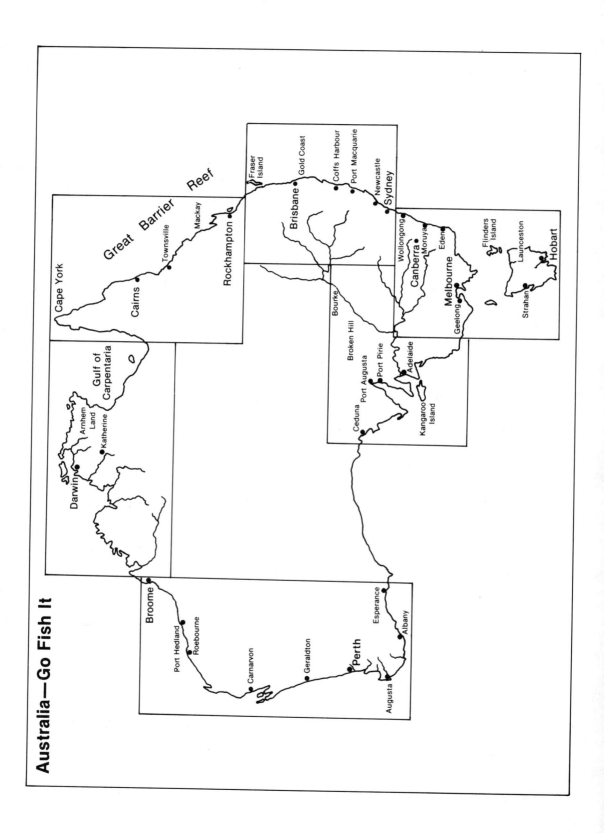

fishing. The more of us who come to know and care about it, the greater our chances of keeping its quality intact.

We have great sport fisheries still waiting to be discovered along much of the west of the continent, and to the north there are vast mangrove systems riddled with creeks, many of which have still not seen a boat. Even at some of our favourite holiday spots, such as Coffs Harbour on the New South Wales north coast, the Continental Shelf is yet to be explored, and it is one of the few spots along that coast where the shelf turns close inshore.

In this book, some of Australia's best sportfishers write about the fishing they know best and their favourite parts of the country. They will take you where enthusiasts spend dozens of hours at sea, tirelessly working to produce an unbroken berley slick, staring down that slick in search of the first flash of colour that will announce the arrival of the world's most feared marine predator – the great white shark.

You'll join them in the humid silence of a remote creek, where the stillness is shattered by the heart-stopping surface strike of a big barra; or knee deep in a cold surf at night, probing for just one huge, trophy-sized jewfish. Or perhaps you'll find your version of heaven on the high cliffs of Western Australia, watching a balloon break free as a big Spaniard tears away with the bait.

There's all of that, and much, much more, waiting for you when you Go Fish Australia.

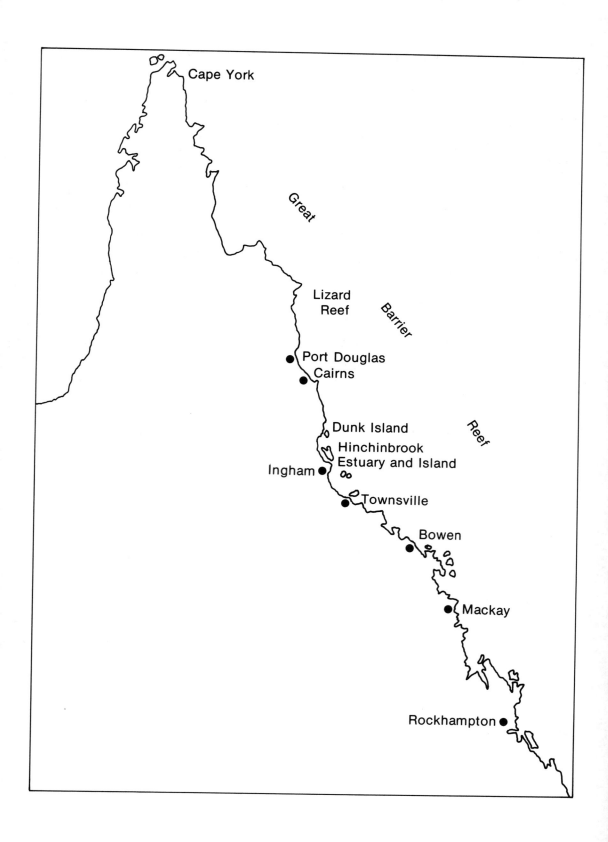

SECTION ONE

Tropical Queensland

SMALL-BOAT FISHING
David Donald

The hundreds of islands, reefs and headlands inshore of the Great Barrier Reef form the primary domain of the tropical small-boat fisher, contrary to the common belief that the outer reef is the most widely used. The waters of this vast area are protected from the ocean swells by the reef, but are subject to the effects of the trade winds and the tides. The characteristic Barrier Reef 'chop' which results can under certain circumstances become quite uncomfortable, even dangerous. It pays to be well prepared and aware of local conditions.

Boats used range in length from 3.5 metres up to 10 metres with the most common being 4 to 6 metres. The majority of craft are of fibreglass or aluminium construction and are usually outboard powered. A minimum of safety gear must be carried depending on the size of the boat and, although not required by law, a marine radio is usually fitted to vessels operating more than 10 kilometres offshore.

The boat size generally dictates the area fished with only the larger craft heading well offshore. In some areas it is possible to use the protection offered by the islands and inshore reefs to travel fairly long distances in relative safety, so a check of local charts and boat ramp facilities will be rewarding in a new area.

A chat with local tackle-shop or coastguard personnel can often be very useful.

The Popular Species

Probably the most sought-after fish in this area is the school or 'doggie' mackerel closely followed by its larger relative the narrow-barred Spanish mackerel. Both species are taken all year round but each requires its own specific angling method. Sometimes, these two mackerels will be found side by side but generally they travel in separate schools.

Doggie mackerel are usually found close inshore and are regularly taken by land-based anglers as well as those with only the most basic 'tinnie'. The fish average from 1 to 2 kilos but can weigh as much as 4 kilos and their fast and furious initial run should not be underestimated on light tackle. Best bait for doggies is Western Australian pilchard although greenback herring and anchovies are popular in some areas.

Lures such as Wonder Wobblers, ABU Tobys, Gibbs Crocs and small Halco barramundi spoons are widely used and may be cast or trolled. The weight of the lure should be suited to line size, for example, a 20- to 28-gram lure with a 6- to 8-kilo line.

Doggies will be found around headlands and sea walls, even in the lower reaches of estuaries when the water is clear. All islands and inshore reefs usually fish well for these mackerel at some time of the year, and in a few areas they will school up in specific bays and reef areas. In central Queensland, the best months for doggies are August, September and October, while areas further north usually come good at the end of the wet season.

Doggies should be bled, and gutted immediately on capture, stored out of the sun and put on ice as soon as possible, as should all fish caught in the tropics. They are excellent eating.

The Spanish mackerel are glamour fish of the tropics and why not! They grow to a large size, are capable of scintillating bursts of speed and are great eating. Spaniards range right throughout the tropics from close inshore to the outer reefs. Generally, they prefer the deeper waters around the offshore islands and reefs, particularly where there are tide rips or a convergence of currents.

Popular baits such as pilchards, garfish, pike, wolf herring and small mackerel can be fished under a float, trolled or floated out while drifting. Lure trolling is also very popular with the large-size Bomber, Rapala and C lure models and the Halco barramundi spoons being most widely used. Large surface poppers, Maverick Taipans and XOS-sized wobblers, are favoured by those who prefer lure casting.

Big Spaniards have no respect for faulty or cheap fishing tackle and should never be hindered in their ability to run. Only top-quality reels with smooth drag systems should be used along with strong, well-made rods and a line from 10- to 20-kilo breaking strain. Their bony mouths make sharp hooks a must, while their bulk necessitates carrying a substantial gaff. They are the tropical small-boat fishers' staple—a visit to the north is not complete if you don't catch at least one.

Light-game anglers in the tropics have a host of other pelagic species available apart from the mackerels. These include queenfish, trevally, cobia, tuna, sailfish and marlin—a potpourri of world-class gamefish sure to test the skill of even the most accomplished angler.

The pugnacious and high-flying queenfish is generally found close inshore, sometimes in large schools. Voracious feeders, the queenfish will rise to all types of bait or lures and once hooked usually provide a tussle characterised by spectacular jumps, sizzling runs and dogged resistance.

Trevally, on the other hand, lack the 'spectacular' style of the queenfish and save all their energy for the 'dogged resistance'. They inhabit all areas of the tropics from the shallow sandflats to the deep reefs. Big fish are often found over shallow reefs or along the edges of drop-offs. Again, all types of baits and lures are successful although the heart-stopping strikes associated with casting surface poppers means these are fast gaining popularity.

The hard-fighting black kingfish or cobia are often hooked while you are mackerel fishing and are easily mistaken for a shark by the inexperienced. In spite of their 'sharkie' looks, they are excellent to eat.

Various species of tuna inhabit both inshore and offshore waters with the mackerel tuna and longtail tuna being most common. Both these species respond best when lures are cast into a feeding school from a boat manoeuvred upwind. Neither is favoured as a table fish although longtails are quite acceptable.

The recently discovered billfish grounds off Cairns, Dunk Island, Townsville and the Whitsundays provide areas accessible to small-boat operators interested in this specialised form of light-tackle gamefishing. Small black marlin and sailfish usually turn up in winter and spring and appear to move south as the year progresses. The Cape Bowling Green (Townsville) area, in particular, is easily reached by small boats from a local boat ramp close to the Cape.

The vast area of reefs in tropical Queensland means that angling for bottom species is widespread and extremely popular. Sophisticated tackle is not required—the handline still reigns supreme. Lines of around 20- to 30-kilo breaking strain are favoured for the shallow reefs, up to 50 kilos in the deeper areas. Short heavy rods and deep-sea winches are preferred by some of the regulars.

Deep holes off headlands and the close inshore reefs sometimes fish well for black jewfish and fingermark bream plus the occasional estuary cod. On the shallow coral reefs, sweetlip, coral trout, parrot and cod prevail although a veritable species smorgasbord is more than likely the case. Deeper areas are the domain of the red emperor and scarlet sea perch but again other species invariably turn up in the catch. Regardless of the season, in the tropics all fish, even reef species, should be bled immediately upon capture and placed on ice as soon as possible.

Tackle and Rigs

Small-boat anglers use a variety of tackle from the most basic to the highly tuned rod and reel combinations of the light-tackle gamefisher. However, the following three combinations are a good starting point.

1. A lure-spinning/pilchard-tossing outfit—a heavy barra type of rod 2.5 metres long coupled with a large, good-quality threadline reel capable of holding 300 to 400 metres of 8- to 10-kilo line. It will cast unweighted pilchards and lures up to 60 grams and also will double as a light trolling outfit.
2. A trolling outfit—a jig stick-type of rod 2 metres long coupled with a good quality overhead reel capable of holding 400 metres of 15- to 20-kilo line. It can also be used for light reef fishing.
3. A reef outfit, which could consist of a 200-metre handline from 20- to 30-kilo breaking strain, but a heavy 1.8-metre rod coupled with a large Alvey or overhead reel capable of holding 300 metres of 25-kilo line is preferable. At a pinch it can be used as a trolling outfit.

The basic three-ganged 4/0 hook rig is most popular for pelagic fishing (unweighted) and for shallow reef fishing (with light sinker). A 50-centimetre wire trace of slightly heavier breaking strain than the line used is favoured when surface fishing with bait or lures.

Variations of the ganged-hook rig or two single hooks (as acceptable under gamefishing rules) are used when trolling baits. The conventional deep-sea rig can be used for most reef fishing.

Hazards, and Safety Measures

Although protected from the open ocean swells by the outer reef, the inshore waters of tropical Queensland are subject to the prevailing trade winds and tidal forces. The combined effect of a strong wind opposing a tidal flow constricted by adjacent reefs or islands can cause dangerous sea conditions although the effect is usually somewhat localised. More common is the characteristic Barrier Reef 'chop' featuring low steep swells at short intervals. Travelling any sort of distance in a small boat in a moderate 'chop' can be very uncomfortable.

It is always advisable to check the prevailing weather before putting to sea and to keep abreast

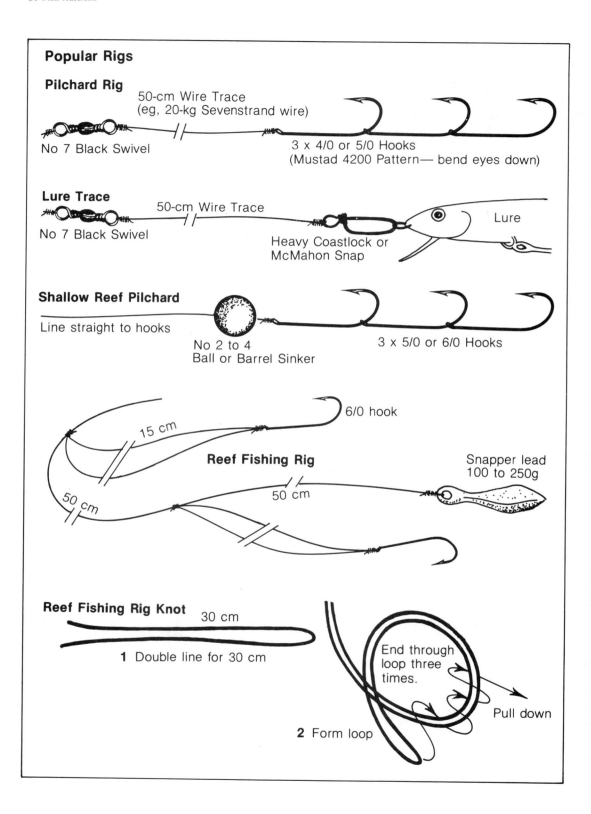

of local conditions by monitoring coastguard radio transmissions. A marine radio, then, is an important item to carry. It can also be used for positional reports, in the event of breakdown or for emergencies.

All small boats operating in Queensland waters are required by law to carry certain items of safety gear depending on the size of the vessel. Interstate visitors trailering boats to the tropics would be well advised to make sure their gear meets local requirements before going to sea. Boating and Fisheries Patrol officers make regular checks.

Tides affect the accessibility of boat ramps in many areas so a long and sometimes messy delay can be avoided by checking local conditions. The Official Queensland Tide Tables contains a comprehensive list of boat-ramp facilities and accessibility throughout Queensland as well as detailing the year's tides.

GAMEFISHING IN THE NORTH

Peter Goadby

The names, Cairns, Lizard Island, Great Barrier Reef, immediately conjure up in the minds of millions of fishers around the world the area with the deserved reputation as the world's best black marlin fishery. The best, not only for sheer size and weight of the marlin, but also for strike-rate action from big marlin. Where else in the world do anglers and crews regularly tag and release this fish over 454.54 kilos (in old measurements, 1000 pounds or the 'grander') as well as virtually all their estimated fish under this weight.

More thousand-pound marlin are weighed in or tagged and released in the approximate 220 kilometres from Lizard Island to Cairns in an average three-month season than had been weighed in during the whole history of billfishing prior to the establishment of this fishery.

Despite the weighing and tagging each year of upwards of thirty black marlin in excess of 454 kilos, plus all the other smaller black marlin, this area is not just a giant black marlin fishery; it is also a world-class fishery for the whole gamut of tropical pelagic speedsters, jumpers and deep fighters.

Striped marlin are very occasionally taken during the black marlin season of September to December. Blue marlin also occasionally show up where the black marlin are taken close to the outer Great Barrier Reef, but have been taken more frequently in the first quarter of the year on reef 140 kilometres or more east of the Great Barrier Reef.

Sailfish are present in the openings of the offshore reefs and around many of the inner reefs and shoals right through the year, but particularly from July to March. Some big tanguigue, more commonly known as narrow-barred Spanish mackerel, are in residence on all the reefs and around the rocky islands; the main season for the schools of these speedy fighters with the razor jaws is August to November. The biggest tanguigue, 20 kilos up to 50 kilos, are resident fish that have taken a section of reef or island as their home, and apart from the sharks, are the dominant predator.

Barracuda, two species weighing to 40 kilos, fit in generally with the tanguigue timetable and locale. The tackle-testing trevally of various species abound in most localities, with usually the heaviest giants coming from the corners near the openings of the outside reefs.

Scaly mackerel or shark mackerel, one of the black marlin fishers' prime bait, are taken on both inner and outer reefs and shoals along with another prime-bait species and light-tackle battler, the kawa kawa or mackerel tuna. Mahi mahi (dolphin fish) and wahoo are caught but not sought by the marlin anglers during the black marlin season. There is no doubt that both in size and quantity, they are part of a world-class fishery. These species are present in the water outside the outer reef right through the year and offer superb sport on light tackle in their own right, instead of being a nuisance as bait choppers and time wasters during the black marlin season.

The dog tooth is potentially the biggest and heaviest of the tuna species in these waters, although yellowfin and big-eye tuna also grow to 90 kilos or more and are taken at this size commercially. Dog tooth and yellowfin are generally found outside the passes between the reefs, with big-eye on the deep reefs, and around reefs jutting from ocean depths outside the main reef systems.

Occasionally longtail tuna grow to at least 40 kilos on the outside of the reefs with schools of this species close in along bays, headlands and mainland islands. Skipjack or striped tuna show up with the school yellowfin in October and are excellent as live or dead bait for marlin. As well, they are tough scrappers on light tackle. Spotted and broad-barred mackerel move through the inshore reefs and mainland islands that are the home of the spectacular and acrobatic queenfish. The mackerel species—in body shape, method of fighting and jumping—resemble the beautifully coloured mahi mahi or dolphin fish of the ocean current.

All these species along the with 'bombie' dwelling coral trout are taken by trolling or spinning, casting, jigging and even with saltwater fly. Spinning, bait-casting and fly tackle are also used for the bonefish and pompano (a relative of the scad or yellow-tail) that are in some reef-island lagoons, and for the barramundi and threadfin salmon that inhabit the estuaries, the headlands and coastal streams.

To all these can be added the bottom reef-dwelling species of all sizes from giant cod and groper perhaps up to 200 kilos and the myriad of colourful species. Red emperor and others provide sport as well as food at night, as do coral trout and various emperors during the day.

Virtually all the International Game Fishing Association world records for black marlin are held by fish from the Lizard Island/Cairns area. Many of the visiting anglers are top light-tackle fishers who respond to the challenge of the fish and records on light line rather than the 60-kilo outfits favoured by many. Black marlin fishing in this area is predominantly with fresh, dead, and less often live baits. Skilled crews take pride in the knowledge and magic that turn a dead 1-kilo to 8-kilo bait into 500 kilos of very active and brightly coloured black marlin.

The success from skilful rigging of live and dead baits for the marlin that aggregate on the reefs behind Cairns and Lizard Island means that this world hotspot remains an area of bait fishing rather than lure fishing. Lures and fast trolling have proved their worth in many of the world's billfishing areas, but this trend has not generally shown its worth on the big black marlin of the Great Barrier Reef.

The heaviest marlin caught on a lure (by Jay McDonough) was around 400 kilos—an outstanding catch by world standards, particularly as so few boats have dragged lures in the Cairns/Lizard Island area for the big blacks.

The success of baits, particularly fresh dead baits, with the marlin weighed or tagged and released in these waters, creates a need for a stock for each boat of both swimming and skipping baits. Kawa kawa, bonito, striped tuna, large scale tuna, shark mackerel, tanguigue, and milkfish are the most popular and successful skipping or splashing baits, usually trolled on the starboard outrigger. Most boats run their swimming baits from the port outrigger.

The prime swimming bait is a smaller close relative of the scaly mackerel, commonly called scad. Other baits used as swimming baits are smaller sizes of scaly mackerel, smaller tanguigue, queenfish, and occasionally milkfish. Rainbow runners of various sizes are also chosen by some crews as either skipping or swimming baits. Crews on most boats start the season with boat refrigerators and ice boxes filled with reserve stocks.

Despite this, there is usually need to top up and replace baits as they are taken by marlin, for which they are carefully rigged and trolled, or by other fish.

Anglers and crews in the Lizard Island/Cairns fishery are fortunate that all bait species can be caught at or near the islands or the outer reef fishery grounds. Kawa kawa and large scale tuna can be fished for when trolling out to and in from the marlin grounds. These species plus queenfish and tanguigue are also caught around nearby islands, reefs and shoals along with the equally prolific, but not popular barracuda and various trevally species. Scad are caught in the openings between the outer reefs.

Some skippers and crews consistently produce big marlin for their anglers by slow trolling live kawa kawa, queenfish, and skipjack, or striped tuna or rainbow runners. Slow trolling and deep running of these live baits out from the passes between the reefs as well as along the productive ridge sometimes provide marlin when faster trolling of dead baits is not giving action.

Live baiting is often productive when the combination of higher temperature water and light or no wind sometimes causes the marlin action to be slower than usual. There is, of course, the problem of unwanted sharks and even tuna, and members of the razor-toothed species taking live baits caught, rigged and trolled for marlin. The number of toothy critters as well as marlin in these offshore waters makes it imperative that each boat starts its fishing day with plenty of baits.

The challenge of the black marlin in the area is widely regarded as the epitome of gamefishing, with fish so big and powerful that any mistake by anglers, weakness in boat skipper and/or crew, or tackle, could mean loss of a fish that is every fisher's dream.

World-record tiger, hammerhead and carcharhinid sharks of various species, along with occasional makos, are there for the capture.

This area is also the world centre of black marlin tag and release and this has greatly increased knowledge of the fish. The tagging and release and recaptures have taken place on all sizes from juveniles of 10 kilos to giants over 460 kilos. Black marlin tagged in the Lizard Island/Cairns area have been recovered in many areas thousands of kilometres away. Many have been recovered one, two or three years later, back where originally released.

Small fresh baits, mullet, garfish (ballyhoo), are also generally used for the juvenile black marlin and sailfish that give so much action and sport particularly in the July/August period. Soft plastic skirts are often used over the head of the trolled baits. Along with billfish, they are also cut and smashed by a whole range of fish.

Minnow-type lures, particularly those that can be trolled at speed such as the Elliott, bibless and 15-centimetre banana-shaped lures, and those by Rapala, are successful when trolled or cast on bait casters or used on spinning tackle.

Any lures used in these waters must be rugged and practical, and pretty as well, designed to catch the eye of the fisher! The hooks, rings and all hardware on the lures must be heavy and able to stand up to big fish. Spoons, particularly the Drones are also popular and successful. Small 7-gram feathers, nylon jigs, small plastic squid or Christmas-tree types are popular and successful for smaller species, as are small Knuckleheads.

Swimming and diving lures are rigged on light 60- to 70-kilo cable wire and the non-active types such as feathers or jigs on light piano wire. Lead-head jigs are used for jigging as well as casting and take a bewildering number of bottom-dwelling species. Saltwater flies and small lures are successful on bonefish and permit pompano, while the threadfin salmon and barramundi and other inshore species are generally sought with small Elliott and Rapala minnow types and Nilsmaster Spearheads and Invincibles.

As is general in most tropical areas, the main action comes at the times of low and high tide.

Fishers vary in their preferences for moon phase, but one thing is sure, whether preferring heavy tackle from a fully equipped game boat, or a dinghy and outboard, or the shore itself, this is truly one of the world's great fishing areas.

COASTAL RIVERS AND ESTUARIES

Alan Zavodny

Fishing the coastal regions in the tropics differs to a fairly large degree from fishing the southern inshore regions of the Australian continent.

Notably, however, the bream and whiting scene of the north is one facet of fishing that remains a constant form of angling right around the country. The techniques for bream and whiting vary little regardless of where these are caught. Although anglers and rigs from one region to the next may have some variations in the approach to these species, they are in the main caught on the same baits, maintain similar habits, are found in the same type of terrain and are common during the same seasons all along the Australian coastline.

In the tropics, the bigger predatory fish of the river and estuary environment offer anglers a unique challenge found nowhere else in Australia.

This group of fish is widespread, containing several different species such as the mangrove jack, spotted-scale sea perch, Moses perch, threadfin salmon, queenfish, trevally and tarpon. Though these are the main species encountered, many anglers all over Australia have captivating dreams about what has become this nation's most famous fish—the barramundi.

The barramundi is a magnificent sporting species, among the best in the country, and as a table fish it has few equals. Regrettably, this fact has led to heavy commercial pressure on the species, resulting in the barramundi now being far less common than it was in bygone years. Pressures of fishing throughout the country have made the angler's quarry harder to catch and tropical Queensland is no exception.

Although scarcer these days, the barramundi is still very much a fish anglers can target. With the correct approach, an angler can still catch one of Australia's most famous species.

Today anglers must study the fish they intend to catch; understanding the fish's habitat and ecology is the first step to ensure fishing is successful.

The inshore predatory fish of the north have one common factor, an extreme weakness for live baits.

Fishing a snag in a river, or a deep hole at the mouth with dead baits will produce mangrove jacks, spotted-scale sea perch and other assorted species. However, tides and below-water terrain play a big part in successful fishing in the north.

When fish are present, if time and tide haven't induced fish to feed, an angler's dead bait could well be in the midst of an uninterested school of predatory fish. A live bait introduced into the same situation will almost certainly tempt a number of the school of fish into striking sooner or later, regardless of time and tide.

Barramundi have a distinctive preference for live baits, to such a degree that dead baits will seldom produce the species.

No doubt it's far simpler to slide a knife along the side of a baitfish, or place a strip bait or a whole dead prawn onto a hook, than it is to catch and pin a live mullet onto a hook. However, obtaining live bait is not all that difficult, once the angler learns a few basics of bait catching.

A cast net is the simplest method of catching mullet, herring and prawns for live bait. All river and creek predators will gladly succumb to any of these baitfish, with big bream and javelin fish also showing a distinct liking for live baits, especially the prawns.

A little bit of solid practice with a cast net, which can be bought from fishing tackle stores

Mangrove jacks lack the brute size of their related cousins the spotted scale sea-perch, however the species offers anglers a unique challenge: no fish that lives in the inshore environment is more cunning or wily than the mangrove jack. (Photo Alan Zavodny)

along the North Queensland coast, will lead to easy bait catching for the amateur fisher.

The best non-commercial live-bait tank on the market is a 40-litre plastic rubbish bin. For small punts and the shore-based angler the 22-litre version is easier to handle. Bear in mind the bigger bin will accommodate far more live baits, which can make the effort of handling the larger version viable.

Equipped with a clip-on battery-operated aerator, the bin will keep a supply of 20 to 30 live baitfish and prawns healthy. Keeping live bait healthy depends on the handling of the bait supply. Minimum handling, which is done gently and carefully, will keep the fish and prawns alive longer.

A warning to all anglers: the summer months will see marine stingers in shoreline regions — anglers must wear protective clothing when in the water chasing bait. Check with local authorities as to just what is safe clothing for wading beach areas. Crocodiles live in the north, and a definite threat exists to any person who enters water in the more remote Cape York and Gulf regions. National Parks and Wildlife, and Boating and Fisheries Patrol officers will advise anglers what are safe and unsafe practices.

Generally, the more isolated areas in the tropics produce the best fishing; however, the more densely populated areas still offer anglers far better fishing than can found on the southern section of the continent.

River and creek systems, piers, rock groynes or breakwaters in and around North Queensland centres like Rockhampton, Mackay, Bowen, Ayr, Townsville, Ingham, Innisfail, Cairns, Port Douglas and Cooktown will provide anglers with excellent fishing.

The best advice for anglers fishing these bases for the first time is, check out the tackle shops in the larger centres. Local advice is offered willingly and freely and is the best way for anglers to make a start in the right direction in a new area. Furthermore, if staying for a period in one area, the tackle stores can direct visitors to angling clubs, who have among their ranks some of the best anglers in their region. A personal introduction to a friendly club member is a catch guarantee.

Undoubtedly boats offer an angler the best chance of getting among the fish. 'Tinnies' of 3.5 metres are ideal for the river and estuary systems of North Queensland, with bigger boats offering anglers added comforts. Craft of 5 metres are big boats for this type of fishing, but not so big as to be out of the class. These big boats offer anglers good offshore fishing and since many of the river systems can be entered from the sea, anglers with craft around the 5-metre mark can have the best of both worlds.

Boat anglers will be most successful again if they have gained an insight into the area they intend to fish, just as in the case of the shore-based angler. Shore-based anglers in the 'know' will often fare better than boat anglers who leave their fishing entirely to chance.

Barramundi are a seasonal species which lasts for three months on either side of the year. The September-October period sees the start of the barra season, with the March-April months seeing the last of the fish being caught. The average size of barra caught these days is around the 3- to 6-kilo mark, with an occasional big barra up to 20 kilos still being taken each year.

Spotted-scale sea perch are commoner during the same months as barra, along with mangrove jacks and Moses perch, the last two being caught during most of the year.

Spotted-scale sea perch caught in rivers and creek systems average around 2 kilos, with fish up to 4 kilos not being overly rare. Sea-run specimens caught off headlands and rock out crops, away from the inshore system, are generally larger. Here the fish may average around 4 kilos, with 6- and 7-kilo specimens not at all uncommon.

The mangrove jacks and Moses perch which are taken are usually a little less than 2 kilos.

Threadfin salmon, trevally and queenfish caught in rivers and estuaries generally weigh in somewhere near 3 kilos. Gulf and Cape York systems will often produce these fish weighing twice as much. Big threadfin salmon around the 15 kilos mark can be caught here, providing anglers with a fight which few fish are capable of. Barramundi in these locations also tend to be larger and are found normally in greater numbers.

Eight-kilo line is standard tackle for fishing the coastal inshore areas. Threadline or overhead-type reels in good condition, with a functioning drag, will handle practically any fish anglers will hook.

Hollow glass or carbon-fibre rods up to 2.5 metres long, designed for easy casting, with a bit of pulling power, are ideal for this kind of fishing. They also will allow anglers to fish lures, to which all the fish primarily dealt with in this section will readily respond.

Kirby or Limerick hooks in the 4/0 to 6/0 size will take all the predatory species in the north. Barramundi have a massive jaw structure that would be better suited to hook sizes no smaller than 6/0. An assortment of sinkers up to 56 grams is the basic lead requirement for this kind of fishing.

Though many fish in the inshore environment are sharp toothed, none requires the use of wire traces. Monofilament traces around 20 kilos will do and will prevent bite-offs and line frays occurring.

Off piers and rock walls, along banks where depths increase, near fallen trees or similar snags, streamlets forming during a low tide, and deep holes or gutters are all areas where anglers can find fish.

Take time to study the area you intend fishing and learn as much as you can about the species you intend to chase. A bit of effort will lead you to some good fishing and perhaps even a big prime barramundi.

The *Lutjanus* group of fishes are confusing due to a variety of common names given to members in tropical Queensland. Here are the common names for the group:

Spotted-scale sea perch are also called red chopper, fingermark, red bream, sea-run chopper and red snapper.

Mangrove jack are also called creek red bream, purple sea perch, dog bream, red perch and creek 'reddy'.

Moses perch are also called fingermark bream.

Note There is a closed season during the barramundi breeding season, between the first day of November and the last day of January. There is also a species bag limit of five fish per day of fishing. Visitors fishing the tropics should check with local harbour and marine offices for information on fishing regulations in the tropics.

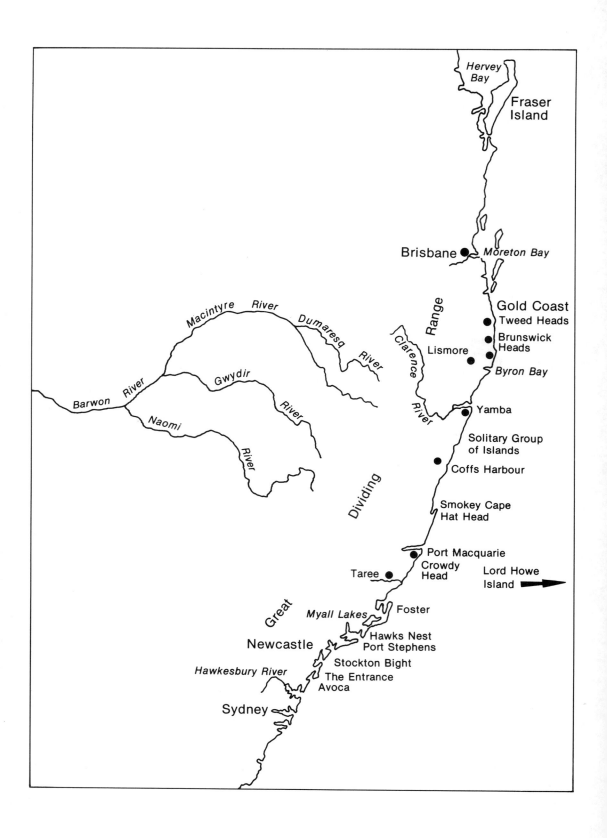

SECTION TWO

Subtropical Queensland and Northern New South Wales

FRASER ISLAND
Ted Clayton

Fraser Island is large by any standard, roughly 125 kilometres long and 184 000 hectares in area. It is separated from the mainland by Great Sandy Strait.

The island falls under the jurisdiction of the Fraser Island Recreation Board, and is managed cooperatively by the Department of Forestry and the Queensland National Parks and Wildlife Service. The northern portion is national park; commercial logging takes place in the southern section. A reasonable fee is charged for vehicle entry and camping. Permits are required and can be obtained from the National Parks Office at Rainbow Beach. The Forestry operate four developed campsites, the National Parks operate three. There are commercial campsites at Eurong and Cathedral Beach.

Access to Fraser is by large vehicular barges which operate from the mainland at Inskip Point north of Rainbow Beach, and from River Heads and Urangan in Hervey Bay. Four-wheel-drive tours operate from Noosa, Rainbow Beach, River Heads and Urangan and cater for day, safari, backpacking, fishing, and combined boat and vehicle tours.

The towns of Happy Valley and Eurong provide telephones, supplies and good accommodation. The Dilli Village National Fitness Camp is toward the southern end of the island.

Most island traffic travels on the eastern ocean beach which is a 'declared road' and is patrolled by uniformed police. Logging tracks suited to four-wheel-drive vehicles cross the island. Large areas are covered by rainforest and at Central Station campground there are beautiful forest walks of varying lengths. An excellent three-part series of Forestry maps is available from Sun Map offices. The ocean beach south of Indian Head provides easy travel. Most outcrops of rock have been bypassed by tracks. North of Indian Head at Middle Rocks and the 'Jump Up' at Orchid Beach have both been timbered.

Fraser Island fishing can only be described as superb. The western side of the island is a world of mangrove creeks and rocky ledges and wide stretches of water. The fish available include mangrove jack, cod, jewfish, snapper, sweetlip, morwong, parrot, javelin, whiting, bream, tailor, flathead and mackerel. Oysters abound and sandcrabs are plentiful. A boat can be launched but is not a necessity—there are many jetties and log ramps. In summer the mosquitoes and sandflies can be a problem.

Boats are launched from the surf beach on the northern side of Indian Head. The offshore reefs provide large catches of reef fish and mackerel. Beach fishing usually takes place in and around 'gutters'. These are deep channels created when excess water from waves drains back to sea. Most run parallel to the beach before turning seaward. A bank forms on the outside of the gutter—the water is deepest close in to this bank. Waves rushing across the bank die and deposit their froth on top of the deep water. This is referred to as 'white water', a term that is heard frequently when surf fishing. Most activity takes place under the 'white water'; baitfish shelter there and tailor and jew come to feed on them. Dart, bream, and whiting shelter and feed there.

'Pipis' are a shellfish that is common right along the surf beach and can be found by digging in the wash at half tide. They are good bait for bream, dart and whiting.

Beach worms can be caught at low tide or purchased at the townships. They are good bait for bream, whiting, dart and jew.

Prawns can be bought and will catch all surf fish. Pilchards can be bought and make the best bait for tailor and mackerel. They are used on a gang of four 4/0 hooks.

Dart are present throughout the year and provide top sport on light gear. They favour the rougher areas of 'white water'.

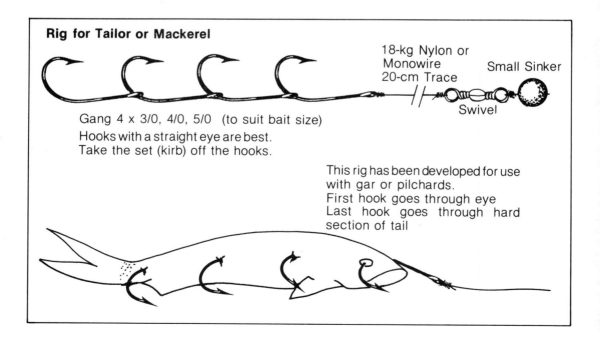

Rig for Tailor or Mackerel

18-kg Nylon or Monowire 20-cm Trace
Small Sinker
Swivel

Gang 4 x 3/0, 4/0, 5/0 (to suit bait size)
Hooks with a straight eye are best.
Take the set (kirb) off the hooks.

This rig has been developed for use with gar or pilchards.
First hook goes through eye
Last hook goes through hard section of tail

Silver bream favour white water during the day. They move in closer at night. Winter is the best time.

Whiting prefer the warm water near the shallow end of gutters. They can be easily frightened, so it is best to stand back a little from the water and cast to them. Early and midsummer is the best time.

Flathead lie close in on the beach side of gutters. They like small whiting and pilchards.

Tailor are present throughout the year, but midwinter and spring are the best time. Groups of anglers drive along the beach in search of a school; when one group is successful other groups hurry to join them until there are sometimes more than 100 people with rods fishing a single gutter. There are so many pilchards in the water that the tailor go into a feeding frenzy and literally tonnes of fish are caught. The action may go on day and night for several days.

Mackerel and tailor can be caught by casting an unweighted pilchard from the rocks and slowly retrieving it.

Snapper are usually taken from the rocks at dusk and dawn on pilchards, squid or flesh baits. The same fish will take the same baits on the western side of the island.

For most fishing on Fraser a light surf rod with a 3.5-kilo line is best. Use No 2 or 3 hooks. For serious tailor fishing a heavier rod and a 6-kilo line is normal. For jew use the same rod and a 9-kilo line.

Hazards, and Safety Measures

The greatest dangers are related to land travel. The most common accidents are caused by people riding outside their vehicle and by speed. Washouts across the beach leave steep-sided depressions that are hard to see. When a vehicle hits one the external passengers and those inside without seatbelts are seriously injured.

There are no doctors on Fraser. Getting help takes time.

Vehicles suffer extensive water damage by bogging in creek crossings. Cross at low tide. Engage four-wheel in a low ratio and do not stop mid stream.

If you are dry bogged in sand let your tyres down to 12 pounds. Reinflate them before proceeding.

THE BRIBIE BANKS
Rod Harrison

When we consider the real fishing hotspots around our coastline, we're inclined to deal with locations more remote than convenient. People pressures and the attendant crowds tend not to go hand in hand with good fishing.

But there are exceptions. Perhaps the most notable of these is the offshore fishery that lies at the back door of Brisbane, a sprawling city of over a million people, among the world's largest when its urban area, and that of its satellites, are added together.

The cornerstone of this fishery are the billfish, juvenile black marlin and sailfish which turn up at the top of Moreton Bay around each December and stay through till the autumn months. Tuna, mackerel, wahoo, mahi mahi and other migratory here-today-and-gone-tomorrow fish are also very important to this light-tackle sportfishery.

The key to the annual presence of these fish can be traced back to happenings in the mangrove fringes which, though losing ground to loose State environmental regulations that allow their wholesale destruction for development, are the nursery of the marine food chain.

Schools of baitfish, also under threat from the petfood industry, invade Moreton Bay to feed on marine life lower in the foodchain and, in turn, attract the gamefish, which prey on the baitfish as they see-saw with the tides along the top edge of Moreton Bay.

A line of undersea sand dunes that drops a sheer 25 metres in places clearly divides the bay from the open sea. It is along the seaward side of these ridges, now known as the Bribie Banks, that the marlin and other sportfish prowl when the feeding mood is upon them.

These rows of sandy banks stretch for perhaps 30 kilometres between the top of Bribie Island across to Cape Moreton. In actual fact, they form a kind of continuation of the sandy spit at the top of Bribie Island (hence their name) and run across to Moreton Island, also a sand island.

The Bribie Banks really fires when it gets scoured by the warm cobalt-tinted tongues of the East Australia current. Where the blue oceanic waters blend with the green tints of Moreton Bay, that's the place to start fishing when seeking billfish and the other sportfish that make up this summertime action.

This colour change can move some distance north of the banks on a runout tide and be right on the edge of the dunes on the run up.

On some days, when the light isn't particularly good, this blending of inshore and offshore seawaters is very difficult to pick up. Monitoring water temperatures—look for at least 21° C— and the 'gut feelings' that go with experience, are other things that count considerably in the search for fish.

There are few hard and fast rules on this ground. One is that the big fish aren't far away from the bait. If not actively feeding, they're often shadowing the schools. Locate the bait and it's a good chance you've also located the marlin and sailfish.

Of course, the bait schools are not entirely located at the top of Moreton Bay. They can be spread up to 50 kilometres to the north and perhaps even greater distances to the south, off other outlets of the bay.

But the hub of this bite is centred on the Sunshine Coast. It's a shorter run to the best fishing, launching from the many ramps in that region rather than punching almost the full length of the bay up from Brisbane.

The bait schools are signposted by sea birds, or they can be picked up on a sounder. Just how does one extract a good fish from there?

The most popular approach has been to troll the edges of the baitfish. Dead bait—mullet and garfish—seem to be preferred by the billfish, while minnow and skirted-type lures have a broader appeal.

A 20 centimetre mullet, gutted and rigged as a swimming bait with a chin sinker, is arguably the most effective bait for this fishery. Monofilament leaders give a better bait action and will take more strikes than wire.

Swimming mullet are best fished on flat lines. The constant jerking that outriggered baits are subjected to by the movement of the game poles can upset a swim bait's action. 'Riggers are better utilised with skip baits.

Garfish make superlative skip baits and can be rigged in conjunction with a small coloured squid for effect and to conceal the handiwork that went into the bait.

The usual situation on the larger boats is to tow a pair of flat-line baits—usually 'swimmer' mullet and a pair of skipping garfish using the drop-back and spread of the outriggers. The many smaller trailer boats that are fully capable of fishing these grounds settle for less elaborate arrangements.

Drag settings should vary according to the bait. Outrigger-fished baits are fished in freespool, which allows the angler to give the fish more line and the opportunity to swallow the bait, once the drop-back has been taken up.

There are the days, particularly when the juvenile black marlin are thick, when the mullet can be fished right up on strike drag. The billfish hook themselves when they crash the bait. Sometimes, however, they can be a little reluctant, tending to play with the bait before taking.

On any water, the really successful anglers have the flexibility to adjust their system according to the circumstances.

Large Spanish mackerel provide exciting fishing offshore throughout Queensland waters. This one weighed 20 kilos.
(Photo David Donald)

Generally, the marlin are more willing than the sailfish. What you've got to remember here, though, is that the little blacks are there as a kind of a weight-gain stopover – they're eating their heads off and growing fast at this stage – before embarking on the next stage of their oceanic travels. A sailfish of the same size is a much more mature animal and tends to be a bit more cautious.

Live bait is the way to bring them undone. A live yellowtail dunked amongst the bait schools will often work where straight trolling fails. Live bait can be secured by jigging the schools, or from locations inside Moreton Bay.

At times it is possible to cast live baits at sailfish feeding on the surface. This can be difficult (to say the least) with a conventional rollered game rod, and has lead to the widespread adoption of ringed-guide 4-, 6- and 8-kilo class rods in this light-tackle scene. And a specialised rig. This begins with a small double. The doubled line is then joined via an Albright knot to a 3-metre length of 50/70-kilo mono trace, to the other end of which is attached a snap. Baits, etc, are rigged on their own 30-centimetre traces, either looped or crimped via the Jin-Kai system for easy snapping onto the trace. This arrangement allows a bait to be fished in a number of ways. Covering the options, it's called.

Not every angler who fishes that radius around Moreton Bay has the opportunity to tangle with billfish. Indeed, many have to set their sights somewhat lower and take advantage of fishing in the more sheltered bay waters.

These can be very productive at times, with schools of tuna – longtails to 15 kilos – spotted mackerel, tailor and kingfish.

This action can be available at any month of the year. The tuna and mackerel are often very obvious as they crash into hardiheads and other baitfish. The various navigation buoys and platforms (the Four Beacons not far south of the Tangalooma resort) harbour kingfish, amberjacks and cobia that can provide an acid test of angler and tackle, with the winner often being the anchoring chain holding the buoy.

Poppers and small metal jigs are proven strike-getters inside Moreton Bay. High-ratio reels improve the chances of getting a reaction from the fish. Speed is a positive catalyst in saltwater lure fishing. You can never wind fast enough, sometimes.

The waters covered in this piece are also utilised by bread and butter fishers and see considerable commercial pressure. The stay-put species aren't in as good a shape as those that can move off with the oceanic currents come the winter.

The light-tackle fishery centred on Moreton Bay is a renewable resource; a great many billfish are tagged and released these days. While those baitfish schools are present, the billfish will be back with the coming of the next summer.

BRISBANE AND ENVIRONS
Ted Clayton

Families living in the Brisbane area are fortunate to have some of Australia's finest estuary and surf fishing within easy reach. The stretch of coastline from the Gold Coast in the south to Noosa in the north is all easily accessible to the day tripper. It includes a variety of fish habitats that range from large saltwater lakes and rivers with their mangrove systems and estuaries, to the deeper reefs of Moreton Bay and surf headlands such as Burleigh and Noosa.

Three islands form the eastern boundaries of Moreton Bay – Bribie in the north, and Moreton and Stradbroke in the south. Bribie can be reached via a road bridge. Moreton and Stradbroke are serviced regularly by large vehicular barges. Stradbroke has bitumen roads that connect the towns of Dunwich, Amity and Point Lookout. Moreton traffic is restricted to four-wheel-drive vehicles, but supplies are readily available at the townships of Kooringal and Combiyuro. Cape Moreton and Point Lookout provide top rock fishing. The barges cater for foot passengers. Dinghies, houseboats, yachts and gamefishing boats are available for hire throughout the area.

All of the towns can provide accommodation and camping facilities. It is an ideal environment in which to bring up children with a love of the outdoors and to develop an interest in one of our finest sports—fishing.

Species and Tackle

A newcomer to the sport does not require a big range of gear. For light estuary fishing a flexible 2-metre rod, a reel equipped with a 3.5 kilo line, some small swivels and sinkers, and some No 3 and 4 hooks will be sufficient. A 13-centimetre 'A' model sidecast is cheap, simple to use and trouble free.

To fish the surf a medium surf rod is required. The light estuary reel can be used with it and so can the hooks, sinkers and swivels. A spare spool for the reel loaded with a 5.5 kilo line will convert the surf rod for flathead and tailor fishing. For this purpose, some wire traces and 3/0 and 5/0 hooks will be required. These can be used singly or joined into gangs of four for pilchard baits.

The varieties of fish available include the delicious and plentiful whiting that crowd the shallow bay flats during the winter months and the big Spanish mackerel, cobia and jew that haunt the headlands. In between these extremes are summer whiting, bream, flathead, tailor, jew, rock cod, snapper, sweetlip, morwong, parrot, school mackerel, yellowtail king, tuna, mangrove jack and luderick. The surf provides excellent light fishing for dart and tarwhine.

The fish listed are present throughout the year, but there are seasonal events that concentrate them and make them an easier target.

Winter or trumpeter whiting school from May to August. They are caught by drifting across the estuary weedbeds. A light rod or handline rigged with a 30-centimetre trace, a small sinker and a No 4 hook is first class. Worms, prawns or strips of squid are all good baits. Three people could catch one or two hundred fish if they are that way inclined.

Drifting in the winter sunshine is one of the finest family outings.

Bream are one of the most reliable catches and can be caught from the bank throughout the year using light tackle. A long trace and a light sinker are best. Bream will take a wide range of baits including yabbies, worms, prawns and mullet. High tide is best when fishing from the bank. From May to July bream collect in large schools around the mouths of rivers and tidal estuaries to breed. Catches of 20 fish are common—an experienced angler will take 100 or more. Some famous spots are the Southport Broadwater, Jumpinpin, Brisbane River walls, Bribie Bridge, Caloundra bar and the mouths of the Mooloolah, Maroochy and Noosa rivers.

Summer or sand whiting make an appearance in late August, their numbers steadily improving in early summer and fading off as autumn approaches. Use a light rod. Experts use a trace about 30 centimetres long and slide a 4-centimetre length of red plastic tubing onto the line above the hook. Yabbies, worms and pipis are all good baits. The very best bait is a small worm known as a 'wriggler' that is dug from the beach gravel at Redcliffe and St Helena Island. Whiting are attracted to moving objects, so cast your bait out and slowly retrieve it. All of the beaches fish well but Southport Broadwater, Moreton Island and Bribie Island are exceptional.

Flathead appear in numbers with the summer whiting. A small live whiting is an excellent bait. The biggest fish will be found in the deep water alongside banks and ledges. Use a 6.5-kilo line

A prime fish for many beach, bay and estuary fishers is the flathead.

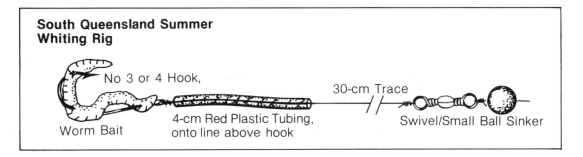

South Queensland Summer Whiting Rig
- Worm Bait
- No 3 or 4 Hook,
- 4-cm Red Plastic Tubing, onto line above hook
- 30-cm Trace
- Swivel/Small Ball Sinker

and a 13-kilo nylon trace. Use a landing net — flathead have dangerous spikes at the side of their heads.

Tailor are most plentiful in winter and can be taken in the surf, around river bars and across the estuary flats. The best bait is a pilchard mounted on a gang of four 4/0 hooks. Use a 15-centimetre trace of 18-kilo nylon. Use a small sinker, cast out and slowly retrieve. When the tailor chops keep a tight line and the fish will hook itself.

Mangrove jack are taken in the upper reaches of mangrove creeks on lures or small live fish. They shelter by logs and under overhanging banks. Use a wire trace for bait fishing. It is usually glassy calm and the bird life of the mangroves adds to the pleasure. Throw in a few crab pots.

Mulloway or 'school jew' are frequently found in the deep holes near the mouths of creeks and rivers, and can be taken on light gear using prawns or worms. Large jew weighing in excess of 5 kilos are best caught on live fish baits, and 20-kilo jew are fairly common. A sturdy line and hooks up to 9/0 are required. Coolum and Noosa Headlands fish well. The Bribie Bridge is a renowned spot.

Sweetlip, morwong, snapper, parrot and rock cod all favour the same reef areas. However, large rock cod will commonly venture well up into rivers and creeks. They can all be taken from headlands, but submerged reefs are more productive. The offshore reefs at Palm Beach, Point Lookout, Cape Moreton, Caloundra, Mooloolaba, Maroochydore and Noosa all fish well. Popular areas in Moreton Bay include Peel Island, the Rous, Rainbow and Pearl channels and the artificial reef at Cowan Cowan. Smaller fish can be taken on inshore reefs such as Reef Point at Redcliffe and the shallow reefs in Deception Bay such as Cook's Rocks and Sunken Reef. The best reef fishing is at dusk and dawn.

Snapper, sweetlip and cod like flesh baits, squid and hardiheads, morwong like shellfish, parrot prefer crabs. School mackerel are common across the bay flats in summer. Use pilchards on a four-hook rig.

Luderick school in winter but require specialised methods. Jumpinpin and Caloundra are noted areas.

Sand crabs are plentiful across the estuary flats in mid summer and are easily captured in 'tangle' dillies that are commonly on sale. Dawn is the best time.

Marlin, sailfish and tuna have become commonplace catches in the northern approaches to Moreton Bay. First-quality game boats are available for charter at Toorbul Point. No equipment is needed and the grounds are an easy hour's travel. Light tackle well suited to women and children is used.

Cooloola National Park lies to the north of Noosa. It extends roughly 90 kilometres to the town of Rainbow Beach and includes the massive headland of Double Island Point. Both towns provide excellent camping and accommodation. The entire area is a fisher's dream and includes the famous coloured sand cliffs. You can use your own four-wheel-drive, rent one, or travel with one of the many beach tours.

The beach fishing includes bream, whiting, dart, tailor and jew. Rock fishers take Spanish mackerel, kingfish, snapper and jew. There is a National Parks camping ground with water and toilets at Freshwater Creek. The nearby township of Tin Can Bay provides access to a vast estuary system that includes Tin Can Inlet and Great Sandy Strait—an area that is untouched by today's standards.

Hazards, and Safety Measures

Moreton Bay is a large body of open water and can be dangerous to small boats. If a storm is sighted head for shelter immediately.

Do not cross to the eastern side of the Bay if a westerly wind is predicted. The only shelter on the inside of Moreton Island is at the 'wrecks' at Cowan Cowan.

Ocean rocks are dangerous in heavy seas. Atherton's Rock on the south-east corner of Double Island Point may appear safe but in heavy weather the odd big sea will sweep around behind it and spill completely over.

Wear sandshoes when crossing weed beds. The risks include stonefish, bullrouts and razorback shellfish.

Blue-ringed octopus inhabit rocky estuary foreshores. They are small pretty creatures with flashing blue circles around their tentacles. Their bite is fatal.

BYRON BAY TO NOOSA-ROCK AND BEACH

David Green

The far north coast of New South Wales and southern Queensland are an overflow area. Tropical species intermingle with fish of temperate zones. It is an area where you may catch a Spanish mackerel or a yellowtail king, a painted sweetlip or a bream. As this book is intended as a guide, rather than being a lecture on species, places and rigs, this chapter will focus on planning your fishing time to maximise success on common species in the area.

If you are fortunate enough to plan your holiday in advance, preferably place a full moon somewhere in the middle of your two-week stint. You may not be able to foresee the weather, but definite planning around moon and tides will make a big difference. Look at your tide chart. The week leading up to the full moon will have evening flood tides, peaking at about 6 pm, 7 pm, 8 pm, 9 pm. These are the evenings you should fish. A few days before this, the tides will be high in the morning—5 am, 6 am, and 7 am. These are the times for an early morning beach session. Weather permitting, you can plan these long in advance.

The strip from Byron Bay to Noosa can be divided into three separate strips of coast. The northern New South Wales coast is largely unspoiled, and contains far more rocky headlands and offshore bomboras than southern Queensland.

The area from Currumbin to Point Lookout on North Stradbroke contains no significant rock platforms. The majority of fishing here, encompassing the Gold Coast and North and South Stradbroke, is aimed at common surf species, whiting, tailor, dart, bream and jew.

The next piece of coastline is from Mooloolabah to Noosa National Park. This is a very fishy stretch of water. Tropical species such as painted sweetlip and spotted mackerel are common, as are temperate dwellers such as tailor and bream.

Byron Bay to Tweed Heads

This strip of coast offers three choices of approach. These are beach, rock, and rock walls.

The rock walls in the area consistently produce big jew (mulloway) under the right conditions,

Two 'bread-and-butter' fish of New South Wales-Queensland waters—bonito and mackerel tuna: tough adversaries on light gear. (Photo David Green)

and both the Tweed River mouth and Brunswick Heads are the places to fish if you target jew. By far the most consistent method is using live bait, mainly mullet or tailor. You will need to choose a flood tide, and then fish the run out. Generally my approach would be to fish for tailor on the flood with pilchards or lures, and then put these out live. If the water is coloured by a recent 'fresh' then mullet may be more consistent.

Jews from rock walls are hard to tackle and hold on light outfits, and you'll need substantial tackle. I generally use a 4/0 Penn Senator or 7-inch (17 cm) Alvey with a 15-kilo line. You need a big gaff and a lot of patience. It is important to use a few metres of leader, usually 30-kilo mono. If you do target jew, you are looking at about one fish for twenty hours' effort, so don't expect one on your first bait.

Any recent rains that cause a bit of colour in the water will increase your average. A lot of jew are caught on lures, particularly on the Brunswick rock walls. The most popular lures are Rapala CD 18s. If you happen to visit the excellent little bait and tackle store at Brunswick Heads, have a look at the photos of huge jewies, all with big minnows fastened to their jaws. Some of these fish are over 30 kilos.

The rocks around Byron Bay lighthouse produce tailor, bream, jew and good drummer at times. One local problem at Byron is the swell size. It's a great place to surf, but the headland, the most easterly point in Australia, picks up swell easily, and budding rock-hoppers should take care. My approach to this area is to get up early and fish floating pilchards for tailor till about half an hour after sunrise, and then go on and fish either strip baits, cunjevoi or yabbies on about a 1/0–2/0 suicide, with a small ball sinker running down on to the hook. This approach will produce table fish, predominantly tailor and bream. A light beach rod and either threadline or 15-centimetre Alvey would be about right. I use 8-kilo line for this type of fishing, and on holidays my aim would be to produce a good feed of table fish in minimal time, and be home by eight.

Spinning the headland has produced tailor and bonito (both Watson's and Australian) for me. Like many northern headlands, its big pelagic fish are untapped, and for anyone who wanted to drift out a live bait, it has loads of potential for northern blue tuna, Spanish mackerel and yellowtail kingfish. There are also large numbers of big mackerel tuna in the area. Live bait may be difficult to come by, but there are often small mullet available in the corners of the beach. These can be berleyed up with bread and caught by using dough under a light float. The rocks in the area are hard and volcanic and cleats offer no benefit.

The beaches fish quite seasonally in this region. As a general rule bigger tailor and mulloway or jew run towards the middle of the year, and the bream run in biggest numbers from late March to June. The commonest summer surf fish are whiting and dart.

Many books have been written about where to fish on a beach. As a general rule, fish where you wouldn't swim. If you see rips, gutters, sandbanks and seabound channels, then these are the places to fish. The north coast beaches have far more features than the flat shallow strips of Gold Coast sand. They are generally 'deeper' beaches.

Probably the best approach to fishing the beaches is simply to spend the first few days of your holiday exploring around dawn and dusk. Look for other fishers. The choice to be made in summer months is whether to fish either worms or yabbies for whiting and dart, or to persist with pilchards and flesh baits for tailor and possibly jew. Follow the local trends. Beaches fish best on a small swell, half to three quarters of a metre being ideal. They generally are a dawn and dusk proposition, and floodtides are when you should be there.

The Gold Coast Beaches

Despite the effects of massive development and foreshore destruction, the Surfers Paradise strip produces reasonable fishing for the keen and persistent. The beach formations are generally flatter and shallower than those to the south.

Common fish encountered are bream, whiting, tailor and dart. The Gold Coast beaches, even directly in front of Surfers Paradise, support a good population of beach worms and pipis. Summer produces good whiting and dart, and once again fish early and on a rising tide. Use about a No 2 suicide or similar, and make sure you have a free-running lead with a big hole in it. This avoids clogging with sand, and makes bites much more perceptible. Fishing this way, under the right conditions, usually provides a quick feed of whiting and dart on beach worms. Places that come to mind are the Southport Spit, Main Beach in front of 'Focus', the mouth of Tallebudgera Creek and the southern end of Burleigh. If you hook a big fish by this method you have an outside chance of a school jew and an odds-on near certainty of a stingray.

The tailor season commences on the full moon in April or May. With the opening of the Gold Coast Seaway a large sandpumping jetty was built to the south of the southern breakwall.

For a few months in 1986, this jetty gave anglers access to very fishy water. Thousands upon thousands of tailor were caught. There were big jew, sharks and great trevally. The crowds grew huge, and the jetty became a pigsty. Public access was denied, police were called, and a potentially great tourist attraction was closed. For just a few months it was a fabulous spot. Now it lies behind locked gates and barbed wire. Fishers themselves are to blame.

The walls of the Southport Seaway offer good fishing. The southern wall is very difficult to fish, as the boulders are a mite too big and there are snags in profusion. Access to the north wall requires a boat trip to South Stradbroke. Under favourable conditions the end of the north wall produces a lot of tailor. Spinning here produces both great and bigeye trevally, and there is an outside chance of a tarpon. It is an excellent spot for jew.

The beaches of both North and South Stradbroke islands provide excellent tailor and jew in winter, as well as whaler sharks to two metres. For those who paddle a surfski, a small feather lure on a length of fairly solid nylon will produce tailor consistently. The locals have plenty of stories of being pulled backwards by mackerel, tuna and even sharks.

The Sunshine Coast

The beaches of the Sunshine Coast are quite deep. They produce similar species to the Gold Coast in similar seasons. The main features of the Sunshine Coast are the excellent rock platforms particularly in Noosa National Park.

One spot worthy of mention is the Mooloolabah rockwall. The western wall produces large numbers of small spotted mackerel, between half a kilo and 4 kilos. Access is simple, the sea is generally flat, and the footing is good. The most productive method I have found is to spin with small chrome spoons. Wonder Wobblers in the smallest size are ideal. Cast out only about 20 metres. Let the lure sink all the way to the bottom, then rip it back fast for 2 or 3 metres, then pause momentarily, and wind again. The fish invariably hit after the pause. Use a short length of the lightest nylon coated wire you can find, about 6-kilo breaking strain. Some people dispense with wire altogether, as the fish may be shy. The prime times are July and August.

In addition to spotties, the rockwall produces good bream and some absolutely huge flathead on live baits. It is infested with a fish ironically called a 'happy moment' or rabbit fish. The dull brown fish cause a severe sting on the slightest contact with any spine. They occasionally even eat lures and are the major hazard of nearly all Sunshine Coast fishing.

Noosa National Park is a huge area. The southern rocks, around Lions Park and Sunshine Beach, provide excellent bream fishing in winter. Strip baits, prawns and pilchards fished into any wash in the area will produce good bream. Watch out for the swell. If you are keen and strike favourable conditions, live baiting the area has produced Spaniards, northern bluefin and a lot of big yellowtail kings for our little band. Garfish can generally be burleyed up if the sea is flat.

The northern face of the National Park, with an accessible track running out to Hell's Gate, covers a lot of good ground. The rocks around the Fairy Pools produce a lot of big jew. It can be a fairly long walk carrying them out. The two bays, Granite and Teatree, produce good garfish and also yellowtail kings, as well as tailor, bream and flathead. Noosa National Park is well worth the visit, particularly in winter. Its big fish potential is untapped.

FROM GRANITE TOPS TO THE BARWON
Rob Smith

Inland northern New South Wales and adjacent areas of Queensland offer some of the most exciting freshwater fishing in Australia, both in terms of species available and environment. In the clear flowing streams in the granite belt of the Great Dividing Range, the big dams on the western slopes, and the classic reaches and billabongs of the Barwon River floodplain, there is scenery and fishing to satisfy everyone – from dedicated fly and lure sportfishers to casual anglers whose interests are tuned to relaxation and supplementing the family larder.

This region includes major tributaries of the Barwon River east of Walgett (Namoi, Gwydir, Macintyre, Severn and Dumaresq rivers), a number of large dams, and dozens of minor streams which are significant fisheries.

A varied list of native and introduced species is available. All significant native fish of the Murray-Darling—except the southern Macquarie perch and trout cod—are represented: Murray cod, golden, silver and spangled perch, eel-tailed catfish, bony bream and, in a few isolated streams, the river blackfish.

Introduced species include rainbow and brown trout, redfin, goldfish and European carp. All exotic species except carp are confined to the cooler waters of the tablelands and slopes.

The Highlands

The high country of this region comprises most of the western drainage of the New England tablelands. The streams here are the primary trout habitat. They are stocked annually from the Dutton hatchery at Ebor.

The reliable trout fishing areas are:

Namoi system — streams around and above Dungowan and Bendemeer.

Gwydir system — the upper Horton River, Gwydir River for the first 20 kilometres below the Copeton Dam wall, streams above Bundarra.

Macintyre system — above Elsmore.

Severn system — around and above Wellingrove and Dundee.

Dumaresq system — Bluff River and Deepwater River.

The better trout streams are gazetted and subject to the normal closed season for New South Wales waters.

The most productive methods are wet-fly fishing, using small winged flies and nymphs, spinning with the smallest bladed spinners and wobblers, and bait fishing with worms, crayfish and live mudeyes.

Some of the trout streams hold other species. These include catfish in all systems, Murray cod inhabit the Macintyre, Severn and Dumaresq systems; golden perch are present in the Severn and Dumaresq, redfin in the Gwydir and Severn and silver perch and carp in the Namoi (Chaffey Dam).

The Western Slopes

The waters between the tablelands and the plains are home to the popular native species — Murray cod, golden and silver perch, and catfish, though the distribution of silver perch can be very patchy. The big dams are located in these areas.

Keepit Dam: On the Namoi River between Manilla and Gunnedah, Keepit Dam is probably the most prolific golden perch fishery in Australia. Catfish are also significant in catches. Few cod are caught, though they are found in good numbers above and below Keepit. Unfortunately, European carp have been introduced into the dam as a result of the practice of using them as live bait.

Split Rock Dam: At the time of writing, Split Rock Dam on the Manilla River near Barraba was nearing completion. There is every reason to believe that it too will become an important fishery for native species.

Copeton Dam: Copeton is on the Gwydir about 20 kilometres south-east of Inverell. It is a good golden perch fishery but is more reliant on restocking to maintain numbers. Murray cod are increasing in importance here, with clear evidence of annual spawnings. Many large cod over 30 kilos have been caught. Catfish and redfin are common and trout are occasionally caught. The first liberation of silver perch occurred in Copeton in 1986.

At Bingara, 40 kilometres from the dam, a community-funded native fish hatchery has been established. Golden and silver perch and Murray cod are bred there and released into local waters, including Copeton Dam.

Pindari Dam: On the Severn River near Ashford, Pindari offers redfin, catfish and golden perch. There are some Murray cod but better populations are found above and below the dam. Silver perch were first released there in 1986.

Glenlyon Dam: On Pike's Creek in southern Queensland, Glenlyon is a reliable fishery for catfish, golden and spangled perch and Murray cod.

Coolmunda Dam: Catfish and golden perch can be caught in this warm, shallow lake on the Macintyre Brook near Inglewood in Queensland.

The Plains

At the bottom of their descent from the tablelands and western slopes, the streams develop into the wide rivers of the plains, with long, deep holes fringed by river red gums, sheoaks and willows. In flood times they overflow their banks and spread across the plains, replenishing the waters and fish stocks of numerous billabongs. These billabongs are most common on the floodplains downstream from Bonshaw, and the final sections of the Gwydir and Namoi before they enter the Barwon. The billabongs and river holes are classic inland habitat for golden perch, Murray cod and catfish. It is in these areas also that European carp are most prevalent.

The western parts of the rivers are generally quite turbid and sluggish and well endowed with snags which are a haven for the predatory species.

Techniques for the Slopes and Plains

The most popular fishing method is setlining with live and fresh baits. Top baits are earthworms, crayfish and shrimps. The reader should note that the use of live carp for bait is illegal and subject to heavy penalties. It is a practice which has led to the introduction of this pest species to previously unspoilt waters (see Keepit Dam above) and is therefore condemned. Similarly, the use of wood grubs for bait is to be discouraged because healthy riverside trees are often cut down in pursuit of them. The long-term erosion damage to riverbanks as a result of this is deplorable and will ultimately affect the fish we seek to preserve.

While the use of heavy set lines is an effective way to catch native fish, those who wish to experience the sporting aspect of fishing would benefit from the intelligent use of cord and reel and line of 5-8 kilo test with either baits or lures.

The sport of lure fishing is booming, and some of the best lure fishing waters in Australia are found in this region. The streams of the western slopes in particular are generally quite clear and as such are ideal places for lure fishers to enjoy their sport.

The principal species sought by lure fishers are Murray cod, golden perch, and redfin though silver perch and catfish do have their devotees. There are a great many lures which are successful but the basic types are deep-diving wobblers, flatfish and bladed spinners, the size being dependent on the species sought. Colours can be argued over, but you will find the fish won't ask questions if they see yellow or red! However, in hard-fished waters of exceptional clarity natural colours are often successful.

In the dams and large rivers, trolling at very low speed with deep-running lures is effective but lure losses can be high. Alternatively, the cast and retrieve method can be employed from boats or the shore.

The best times of day for fishing are early morning and late afternoon, into the night, though a number of large cod are caught around midday in the middle of summer. Generally, however, predatory fish feed more actively when the light is subdued. The best days for fishing are overcast—better still—lightly drizzling. When confronted with bright sunny conditions, concentrate on areas of cover where fish may be hiding.

Seasonal conditions play an important role in fish activity in this region. Fish are most active during the warmer months. The onset of spring is a trigger for feeding activity and this is a particularly good time to fish in the dams. Water temperatures are favourable near the surface and the fish move into relatively shallow areas (2-5 metres). As summer wears on and water temperatures rise, the fish in the dams go deeper in search of their comfort zone. Thus, in the middle of summer it may be necessary to fish as deep as 10-15 metres to locate good fish.

In the rivers, the fish are less able to go deep

in search of favourable temperatures. Therefore, in rivers which lack very deep holes, if summer water temperatures become uncomfortable, fish will seek the deepest water they can find and may stop feeding until temperatures fall.

Winter has been the traditional time for the old hands to dust off their set lines and fish the big holes of the western rivers for Murray cod. It has long been held true that the first frost of winter heralds the best time for cod fishing in the turbid western waters.

Hazards

Specific hazards to anglers in this region are:

Summer storms: These can quickly whip up dangerous chops on the big dams, and cause flash floods which can threaten camps pitched too close to rivers. Severe electrical storms are common in the period November through February.

Cold water below the dams: Water released from the depths of large dams can be extremely cold, even in mid summer.

Boating hazards: In rivers and dams, beware of subsurface rocks and timber which can snap a propeller or break an outboard motor leg: or even capsize a boat travelling at speed.

THE MANNING TO NOOSA

Warren Steptoe

Between Taree and Noosa Head is one of the most intensely cultivated parts of Australia. Once much of the area was timbered but the combined efforts of timber getters and agriculturists have dramatically altered the landscape and the character of its rivers.

Periodically, though, the rivers get their own back with floods that are legendary and which even today overwhelm massive flood mitigation works. Every year or so Lismore, Grafton, Bellingen, Taree, Kempsey or Murwillumbah features on the evening television news. To viewers from elsewhere the images of inundated homes and farms are tragic. To those born and bred in the localities floods certainly aren't a pleasure. Yet when you live with them all your life, you literally learn to live with them and, like so many of life's clouds, there's a silver lining.

Floods naturally wipe out fishing for many days but they also scour the river bed, reforming channels and removing siltation. They deposit fallen trees and other debris along the river's course creating more fish habitat. They flush out choking weed growth, such as hyacinth, allowing fishing again in reaches where you were hard pressed to find enough water to soak a line.

And most importantly of all, floods stimulate the food chain. It begins as the turbid waters subside and the saltwater species begin moving back into their estuarine haunts.

A legacy of timber getting and agriculture is river training works, attempts to make the entrances safer and more easily passable to shipping carrying timber, sugar and butter. The days of the coastal freighters are over, these having now given way to road transport, nonetheless breakwalls and training walls remain at the river mouths providing a vantage point to fish for the mighty jewfish (mulloway) at the end of a flood.

At other times 'the walls' are a feeding ground for bream, luderick and tailor – a rare instance of man's alteration to an environment actually being beneficial to fish and improving the fishing.

The other major industry between Taree and Noosa is tourism. At the Gold and Sunshine coasts in Queensland (and perhaps to a lesser extent at Coffs Harbour and Port Macquarie) this has been taken to an extreme. Elsewhere visitors on holiday contribute in varying degrees to the local economies. Significantly, even in the canal estates of the Gold Coast there is still good fishing.

The author with extreme sizes in flathead. Along most of the New South Wales coast the more common size will be somewhere in between. (Photo Warren Steptoe)

True, it 'ain't what it used t' be'; there are few places on this planet where it is. However even in a wilderness fishery, results by 'chuck and hope' fishers will give a poor indication of what is available; but if a little astute forethought is applied and some effort directed towards finding out the whys and wherefores of fishing these waters, the results are rewarding.

Bearing this in mind the New South Wales northern rivers have two things going for them: if you're prepared to do your homework, there is some great fishing available; and the area has much to offer local and visitor alike in terms of scenery, facilities (accommodation, etc) and a mild climate.

Whether the budget stretches to a high-rise penthouse, or a tent site in a park is more appropriate, or somewhere between—it's there. As a local born and bred the writer perhaps should first admit to bias but as one who also has seen more than most of this fair country, the northern rivers region owes apology to no other. Winters are cool, yet mild by Tasmanian standards; summers are hot, yet not excessively so by northern standards. Spring and autumn are very pleasant.

Each season offers various fishing options.

Bream, whiting, flathead, jewfish (mulloway), tailor, luderick, and up in the freshwater, bass (known south of the Queensland border as 'perch') are the popular target fishes, and although each is available virtually year round each has definite peaks when the best fishing is on offer.

Bream are possibly the most common catch taken, as often on rigs aimed at other fish as on those specifically intended to catch them. Winter is bream time, the annual spawning congregation in the estuaries bringing anglers together to fish the 'run'. This annual fishing bonanza occurs later at Caloundra and Jumpinpin than at, say, Port Macquarie; May-June in the south; July-August in the north. Perhaps the most famous bream runs are in the big estuaries like the Clarence (Yamba and Iluka) and the southern Moreton Bay outlet at Jumpinpin between Brisbane and the Gold Coast.

River bream are finicky feeders and fishing them on soft baits borders on an art form complete with devotees and famous practitioners. Yabbies and worms are super effective when fished on the bottom during the winter run.

Sand whiting, king of the table fish, are synonymous with summer. They're also a total family fun fish. Pumping yabbies on a sandflat; 'twisting' pipis on a nearby beach; trying to persuade beach worms from their holes in the low tide surge on the same beach all qualify as bait catching for whiting fishing almost as well as they qualify as great fun for kids of all ages.

The whiting's sandflat habitat is also often bordered by a gently sloping beach ideally suited to family fishing outings.

Being only fairly small, tackle for whiting and bream is not at all critical! The ultimate is possibly the soft 3-metre rod mounted with an estuary model 13- or 15-centimetre Alvey reel so commonly (not to mention effectively) used on the northern rivers and in southern Queensland. However, in keeping with the family fun aspect it's mainly a case of use what you've got.

Flathead or 'lizards' crowd into the estuaries in spring to breed. A few can be caught at any time of year but not in the consistent size or numbers available in spring.

Like the bream season the flathead season comes later on the Macleay and the Manning than it does at Noosa or Caloundra.

There are two basic methods found most effective. The first is to drift a boat along sandy-bottomed reaches of the rivers trailing fish baits (pilchards, whitebait, small live fish or a strip of flesh). Constant 'yo-yoing' of the line will determine whether or not a bait has been taken (success is indicated by the weight of a fish at the other end).

The second is to walk areas of extensive sandflat and tidal channel systems working water

It isn't necessary to use a rod to catch fish. Many big fish—such as this mulloway—are caught by those who use hand lines. (Photo Richard Allan)

movement in and out of the channels and flats by spinning with either lures or baits.

'Minnow'-style lures, chrome 'spoons' (such as Wonder Wobbler and ABU Toby) or the new soft plastic jigs (Vibrotails, Mr Twister, etc) are best. Baits should be hooked through the lips (vertically) or horizontally in front of the eyes so they will 'swim' when retrieved in the same manner as a lure.

Of all the fish that 'ain't what they used t' be', none is as hard hit as the tailor. Once one of the most common of fishes tailor catches have fallen dramatically enough for research currently under way to have a note of urgency.

There are still a few to be caught around the estuaries by fishing white pilchards on a gang of appropriately sized hooks in areas of meeting current; however, the cricket-score tailor catches of yesteryear are to be avoided as a matter of responsibility.

Blackfish or luderick are something of a specialist fish requiring purpose-built rods, floats and precision centrepin reels to gain best results. Nonetheless, the ubiquitous 3-metre estuary rod and Alvey reel will work well enough when the luderick are on.

Jew or mulloway have always had and always will have an air of mystique about them. They're a fish few fish for deliberately and those who do are close-mouthed. All too often when a jewie is hooked accidentally a break-off is the inevitable result. Capture of one is an event for celebration. The section of coast dealt with in this chapter is one of the best jew-fishing areas in Australia, which unfortunately doesn't make catching them any less of a waiting game.

Jew runs at the tail end of a flood have already been touched on. All the rivers from the Tweed down are likely to turn on with jew at the end of a flood. It's a case of stout tackle and a mental state of preparedness to peg a big lure or soak a live mullet or tailor until a jew comes along.

At other times, and particularly during the winter, fishing with big minnow lures (such as the largest Nilsmaster Invincible) or live baits in deep holes at slack water, or around the mouth of feeder creeks while the tide's running might just produce a jew.

The same 3-metre outfit mentioned already will also take bass from the freshwater reaches of rivers. Baits of fresh (or live) shrimps, prawns, or insects like crickets, grasshoppers and cicadas fished under a float around the fallen timber bass frequent is perhaps the most effective way of all of catching them.

It's not the most fun. That comes from using a light pistol-grip 'baitcaster' to cast various lures around the same timber.

Bass are similar to tailor in that they're not as numerous as in the past. Treat them as a bonus. A day's bass fishing adds variety to fishing one of Australia's better fishing localities.

NEW SOUTH WALES MID-NORTH COAST – OFF-SHORE

Lawrie and Julie McEnally

The mid-north coast of New South Wales offers anglers a superb mix of good fishing, excellent climate, and a wide range of accommodation. The area is civilised yet close to some wild fishing locations. It stretches from the Manning River north to the Clarence River.

What keeps the fishing in reasonable shape is the quality of the environment. While having suffered like all settled areas, the mid-north coast has been lucky to retain many areas vital for the survival and breeding of important angling species.

The other factor that ensures interesting fishing is the overlap of tropical and temperate species available. This is most noticeable at sea where fish like Spanish mackerel, cobia (black kingfish), rainbow runner, and spotted mackerel turn up very regularly. More common east-coast gamefish are also available with marlin, wahoo, yellowtail kingfish and all tuna species being common at various times throughout the year.

Other tropical visitors include mangrove jack, tarpon, cod and various species of trevally. These fish are mostly found in the large estuary and river systems.

The more common temperate species that make up bread and butter angling can be located in good numbers. Fish such as bream, whiting, flathead, mulloway, tailor, blackfish, flounder, drummer, dart, snapper, morwong and other regulars can all be found.

As a little bonus offshore bottom anglers can find pearl perch on many offshore reefs. The pearl perch is one of the greatest table fish in the world and is mostly found on reefs in the 35- to 90-metre depth range.

Other interesting captures common on the deep reefs include samson fish and harpuka. Harpuka are found in the very deep water from 90 to 180 metres. Along with the harpuka a few tasty bar cod may also be located.

The fishing tends to be rather seasonal and anglers visiting the area should take careful note of the times they choose for their holiday.

The list opposite will give an idea of the main species, their occurrence and the peak periods to look for them.

The area has a very wide range of fishing options. Almost all of them offer quality fishing. Everything from the freshwater upper reaches of the big rivers, to the rivers and estuaries, beaches, rocks and bluewater offers something of value to anglers.

If a good burst of rainfall provides a muddied 'fresh' at any time the jewfish will go berserk along the river entrances as they feast on all the bait being swept out to sea.

The Spanish and spotted mackerel are found around headlands, islands and shallow reefs that dot the area. Famous spots for these fish include Point Plomer, Hat Head, Fish Rock, Grassy Heads, Urunga, Coffs Harbour and the Solitary group of islands.

Species	Occurrence	Peak
Spanish Mackerel	January to June	peak April to May
Spotted mackerel	January to June	peak April to May
Black kingfish	January to August	peak April
Mulloway	All year	peak April to June
Marlin	January to March	peak February
Dolphin fish	October to May	peak February
Yellowtail kingfish	All year	peak October
Yellowfin tuna	June to October	peak August
Wahoo	December to June	
Striped tuna, Mackerel tuna, Bonito	All year	
Rainbow runner	December to June	
Tailor	All year (large fish May, June)	
Bream	All year	peak April to May
Blackfish	All year	peak March, August
Whiting	All year	peak summer
Flathead	All year	peak summer
Drummer	March to August	
Snapper	All year	peak April to June
Pearl perch	All year	peak early winter
Harpuka/Cod	All year	
Bass	All year	peak January, February

The best ways to catch these elusive and sometimes frustrating fish include live baiting, trolling baits and lures.

The best and simplest way to find a mackerel is to use a live slimy mackerel or tailor on an 8/0 hook with 45 centimetres of 30-kilo wire trace set 2 metres under a float. Rigged garfish and mullet trolled slowly are popular as are large minnow lures like the Rapala and Rebel range.

Greenbacked tailor from 2 to 5 kilos work the washes around the headlands and hunt along the gutters of the big beaches. Fish of this size provide superb sport for land based anglers.

The tailor are taken on the traditional ganged hooks with garfish or pilchards for bait. Lures are often worked in situations where the fish are situated well offshore and long casts are needed to reach them.

Beaches and the intervening headlands throughout this area are amongst the most spectacular in the country and many areas are open to four-wheel-drives to help anglers get access to the fish. Just watch the signs marking where you can and cannot go.

The area is well supplied with bait and tackle shops as well as boat hire for estuary anglers. These places provide plenty of good local information for visiting anglers. Accommodation to suit all tastes is also available throughout the area and the various tourist associations can help with this.

The New South Wales mid-coast is home to a lot of people and a lot of fish. It's a great area with a beautiful environment and some challenging, quality fishing.

Hazards, and Safety Measures

Be careful around river bars. Virtually all rivers between the Manning and the Noosa have a 'bar' at their entrance to the sea. Many of these are infamous with a number of fatalities occurring each year. You don't have to be attempting to cross the bar to get into serious trouble.

The small boats particularly, so suited to estuary fishing, are often anchored somewhat casually and if the tide's falling and the anchor lets go or the motor malfunctions there's no doubt where you'll finish up.

Always carry adequate anchor, chain and rope—it's your first and last line of defence and it makes fishing at anchor less of a hassle anyway.

CROWDY HEAD TO BALLINA

Ross Garven

Take the Pacific Highway north from Sydney and you will have reached the New South Wales north coast when you arrive at Taree. From here the highway as it travels northwards only occasionally brushes the coast. Thus the fishing traveller has to make numerous turn-offs towards the sea to visit the many exciting fishing areas that are available.

North from Taree the Harrington Road leads out to the delightful little fishing village of Crowdy Head. A loop road through the Crowdy Bay National Park leaves the Pacific Highway at Moorland and a gravel road takes you through Diamond Head to Laurieton. A walk through Kattang Nature Reserve to Point Perpendicular could put you on to almost any of the species available on the north coast.

The coast road continues on through headland and beach areas to Port Macquarie. At the mouth of the Hastings River, Port Macquarie is the largest coastal town on the north coast. It is built along about three kilometres of rocky outcrops and small beaches providing a great variety of fishing area for all species.

From the Pacific Highway at Kempsey a short run will take you to Crescent Head. South by gravel road are the more remote headlands of Racecourse, Big Hill and Point Plomer. Northwards from Crescent Head are the popular fish producing areas of Hat Head, Smoky Cape and South West Rocks.

Further north from the Pacific Highway, roads into Grassy Head and Scotts Head offer smaller seaside resorts with both beach and rock fishing.

The highway then touches the coast at Nambucca Heads and Urunga—both at the mouths of small rivers and both well worth a try.

Coffs Harbour, another large coastal town, has

the popular Sawtell area to the south and numerous small beaches and headlands to the north towards and beyond Woolgoolga. The various Solitary Islands can be seen from the highway through this area.

The highway now leaves the coast to travel well inland towards Grafton. Much of the coast is now part of the massive Yuragir National Park. Similar isolated coastal resorts are found within the park. The road into Wooli and Minnie Waters is well worth the effort.

Return to the highway and travel down the Clarence River to reach Yamba at the northern end of the Yuragir National Park. From here limited access is available south through the park. The trip into Brooms Head and the Sandon from Maclean will reward you with excellent rock and beach areas.

On the north side of the Clarence River, Iluka and the nearby headlands and beaches have long been known as top fishing spots. North from here two very long beaches run along the Bunjulung National Park, the first one to Evans Head, and the second on to Ballina. The beach to Ballina has good access and is well worth fishing, particularly in winter.

The Species

There is a great variety of species found along the north coast beach and rock areas. Most of them provide good eating.

The real prize catch of the region is the large mulloway, more commonly known locally as jewfish. These provide the ultimate experience in game fishing from the shore. Availability as far as time of year is difficult to predict. They can be taken at any time of year with a little more certainty around May. This coincides with the northward schooling movement of fish including sea mullet. Most are caught from the rocks with river mouth breakwalls being the most popular.

Tailor are the bread and butter fish of the coast and provide thrilling fishing when they school up and bite freely. The smaller fish appear on the beaches in the autumn and the larger fish appear during winter until they leave to spawn in August.

Bream are the standby fish. When everything else fails try the bream. This fish is very popular on the beaches at night. They are at their best from autumn to winter. Other species taken on the beach are whiting and flathead.

For those who like a struggle from the rocks, reel on at least 8-kilo breaking-strain line and do battle with the mighty rock blackfish (black drummer). Winter months through to September prove to be best.

Luderick, a relative of the rock blackfish, is also a great sportfish. This is a much lighter gear type of fishing, again from the rocks.

There are a variety of surface fish available such as the various types of tuna and the much prized Spanish mackerel. As well as with bait, these fish can be taken on lures.

Snapper and groper may also be encountered. Both are strong hard fighters. Groper are restricted by law to two fish per day.

Baits

Naturally occurring baits can be gathered or caught immediately prior to the fishing session. This ensures that the bait is fresh.

On the beach the two baits that are most widely used are pipis and beach worms. Pipis are very easily gathered. All that is needed is a bucket or container to put them in. On a rising tide they often dislodge themselves from the sand and the waves then wash them further up the beach. If this is not happening, it is a simple matter to wriggle the feet into the sand and feel for the pipis below the wet sand. It is even possible to do this while actually fishing. Find the pipi with your feet and have it ready for the next cast. You can't get fresher bait than that. Pipis are a very successful bait for bream and whiting from the beach.

Beach worms provide an irresistible bait to most fish. They do, however, require some skill to catch. Fish, either fresh or old, can be used as berley and will attract the worms to the surface. Wash the berley around at the top of the wave line and if worms are in the area they will show their heads. The catching technique varies from person to person. Most will find it necessary to be actually shown the method of capture by an experienced worm catcher. If all fails sea worms can be quite often bought from bait shops.

Cunjevoi grows on the rocks. This purple coloured ascidian lives inside a tough protective covering. A strong sharp knife or similar instrument is needed to cut open this covering and expose the soft-bodied animal inside. Cunjevoi is mostly used for rock blackfish.

Cabbage weed, sometimes called sea lettuce, grows as a green leafy plant on the rocks. Picked off carefully and hung from a small hook it provides excellent bait for luderick.

Octopus is a very tough bait used for mulloway and snapper. These can be found in rock pools usually at low tide. Beware of a small octopus with blue rings. The blue-ringed octopus is deadly. Do not touch it. Fortunately it is reasonably rare.

Yabbies can be caught with a pump on sand spits inside river mouths. They are excellent bait for bream, whiting and flathead.

Crabs are found around the rock pools and are good bait for groper and bream, and tailor and yellowtail are also useful as bait.

Other popular baits that can be found in most bait shops are Western Australian blue pilchards; garfish used whole for tailor or cut up for other species; white pilchards for bream and flathead; abalone gut for rock blackfish; tuna for most flesh eaters; prawns for bream, rock blackfish, flathead; and squid for mulloway.

Tackle and Techniques

Rods used for fishing the north coast traditionally have been long. Fixed-spool reels have been found to be suitable for most of the fishing techniques required. The sidecast or threadline-type reels are used for the lighter style of fishing for whiting, flathead, bream and tailor from the beach. Revolving-spool or multiplying-type reels are used for mulloway and spinning from the rocks.

Fishing the surf requires a very sensitive touch. The tips of the rods therefore need to be fine. The beaches in this area are often gradually sloping to the sea. A quick observation will tell if the beach has any useful formations or gutters. These occur where there is deeper water closer to the beach protected on the outside by a sandspit. Quite small versions of these gutters, even if they are not very deep, are the places for whiting and flathead. Bream and tailor like the more open deeper gutters with more movement of water, particularly if there is foamy water drifting across it from the spit. In these places casting distance can be an important factor especially for tailor.

To achieve good casting distance with a fine-tip rod, the taper of the rod should be quick so as to give a strong butt section.

Rigs for surf fishing are best kept simple. For bream, whiting and flathead lines of 3-kilo to 4-kilo breaking strain are adequate. Hooks are tied onto a trace of at least 30 centimetres and are of 1/0 size or less. The sinker is then used above a small swivel. The sinker should be kept as light as can be effectively operated. Greater casting distance, or movement of water could cause a larger sinker to be needed. For flathead the sinker can be used right down on the hook. If this method is used it may still be necessary to use a small swivel about a metre above the hook and sinker. This will help to prevent the build up of line twist.

The tailor rig is made up of the traditional four-hook gang rig and a short trace to a swivel and sinker. Line used for tailor needs to be at least 6-kilo breaking strain. This ensures that the line is able to take the strain and not break when being cast.

Flathead and whiting can be taken quite well

during daylight hours. Tailor are at their best during the daybreak and dusk periods while bream tend to be more readily caught at night.

Rock-fishing techniques for bream, tailor and rock blackfish tend to differ only in that a small round sinker is used directly on top of the hook. This makes it less likely for the rig to snag up.

Mulloway fishing from the rocks is highly specialised. Shorter stronger rods, lines of 20- to 30-kilo breaking strain and strong reels with effective drag systems are needed. Hooks up to 12/0 are used and large baits help to entice this fish.

Hazards, and Safety Measures

Great care must be taken when fishing from rock areas. Figures show a considerable number of drownings each year as a result of careless rock fishing. Failure to recognise potential danger is the basic problem.

The most deceiving situation occurs along steep sloping rocky headlands that face into deep water. A long low swell may not appear to be of any great concern in this deep water. However, when it reaches the rock face the hidden power is released and the water suddenly rises many metres further up the rocks than is expected. People fishing on rock ledges with no easy escape can be trapped by these conditions. After the wave reaches its summit the water then descends even more rapidly. A person taken down by this rush of falling water is very likely to be seriously injured against the rocks.

There are a number of safety factors that should be considered by all people fishing rock areas.

1. Other than at very protected areas, no attempt should be made to fish from rocks during rough sea conditions.
2. Fish with at least one other person.
3. Watch an area for at least ten minutes before proceeding towards the water. This applies particularly if fishing an area early morning before daylight.
4. Select good protective non-slip footwear.
5. Wear light clothing – don't wear waders on rocks.
6. If fishing for larger fish such as mulloway take a long gaff.
7. Don't rely on forecasts of slight seas to be correct.
8. Know the state of the tides and learn to recognise a rising sea.

Environment and Conservation

The north coast of New South Wales has one of the most attractive environments for fishing anywhere in the world. The mild winter climate makes this area particularly suited for fishing at this time of the year. The contrast of long white sandy beaches interspersed with rugged rocky headlands provides a great variety of fishing environments.

A great deal of the coastline has been set aside as national parks, providing natural settings and scenic backdrops adjacent to the water. The value of these areas can be maintained by responsible use of the access roads and tracks. Where access roads are provided drive on them only. Where beach driving is permitted use only the beach access provided for entering and leaving the beach. Drive only on the beach and not on the sand dunes. Respect the rights of other beach users and use your vehicle only as a means of transport to your fishing destination. Responsible use of vehicles in beach areas will help to maintain an unspoilt environment.

There is extreme pressure on the fish resources of this area. Some species have been over-fished and the stock reduced to basic survival level. Take only the amount of fish needed for immediate needs. A licence is required to sell fish.

NEW SOUTH WALES CENTRAL COAST— ROCK AND BEACH FISHING

Barry Wilson

Despite the fact that this area, which extends from the Hawkesbury River to Harrington (near Taree), is probably the most closely settled section of the Australian seaboard outside our metropolitan areas, it still provides excellent fishing. Among the reasons for this are the many estuaries and large coastal rivers which provide nursery areas for fish populations and the many offshore reefs which minimise the problems of over-fishing and pollution. The southern end is an easy day trip from Sydney. It contains some large coastal cities such as Newcastle, Gosford and Taree as well as many popular coastal holiday resorts such as Avoca, Terrigal, The Entrance, Swansea, Nelson Bay, Hawkes Nest, Seal Rocks, Forster, Hallidays Point and Harrington.

There's abundant territory to keep rock-hoppers and the beach fishers happy. The coastline generally consists of surf beaches, separated by rocky headlands. These beaches tend to become longer and the rocky headlands less prominent as you travel north—for example, compare the extensive sandstone headlands just north of the Hawkesbury River with the long beaches of Stockton Bight and the Myall Lakes National Park.

Generally, however, the area's beaches are smaller and have deeper water close in, when compared with beaches of the far-north coast. Rock shelves are more extensive also, with adjacent deep water. This makes for easier fishing conditions and anglers are often less dependent upon tides than they are in many other areas.

Rock-hoppers usually have the advantage of low, flat sandstone ledges. These are easy rocks to fish from as they allow fishers greater freedom of movement and generally provide safe, comfortable fishing platforms. Even in rough-water conditions it's always possible to find a safe protected corner in which to try your luck. This is not to say that you can overlook the fundamental safety rules which must be observed by all rock-hoppers.

You should never fish exposed ocean rocks in rough-water conditions and it's advisable to study water conditions for some time before you venture onto the rocks, taking note of how far waves wash across the rocks (if they are wet or contain fresh seawater care is needed) and of where you could exit if you were unfortunate enough to be washed in. You must remember that others may also be put at risk in trying to rescue you if you did get into difficulties. Most lives lost from our ocean rocks occur through inexperience or carelessness and it's not often that you hear of experienced anglers getting into trouble. Proper footwear is also essential and this usually consists of sandshoes or sandals (such as Kaydees) with metal plates or screws fixed to the soles to prevent slipping. Most anglers prefer to wear shorts and clothing which doesn't restrict their freedom of movement.

Holiday times are especially busy and accommodation must be booked well ahead. Popular fishing spots are often crowded with local and holiday anglers; however, with a little investigation there are plenty of areas when you can avoid overcrowded conditions. The area is well serviced by access roads and much of the coastline is now contained within the boundaries of national parks, such as Bouddi (which contains one of our first marine sanctuaries) and Myall Lakes.

The climate is ideal for the angler and fishing is a year-round activity. Winters are mild with average temperatures in the coldest month of July ranging from a minimum of 8° to a maximum of 18° C. During the summer, in January and February, average temperatures range from 19° to 27°; however, humidity never becomes as unbearable as it can be further north.

Most fishers prefer the summer months. However, at this time, later afternoon north-east winds can be troublesome and it may be necessary to fish early morning sessions. The best fishing is often available in the more settled weather of the autumn and early winter months. A spray jacket is handy for most of the year as, even in the summer, it can be cool around the rocks if you become wet with spray.

The most productive fishing is usually available in the early morning or late afternoons, especially if these times coincide with a high tide. For experienced anglers night-time angling can be very effective. A run-in tide is a good time to start fishing; however, anglers may find that some spots may fish well, or indeed can only be fished, on low tide. Most fish prefer some action in the water which produces washes (those areas of aerated, cloudy water) either giving cover for schools of baitfish and predator alike, or else washing in feed. Generally flat-water conditions are not very productive.

Some local knowledge is always useful. It's worthwhile joining one of the many active fishing clubs in the area as attending meetings may enable you to meet local anglers from whom you can possibly glean local piscatorial secrets. A contact point could be obtained either from a local telephone directory or from a sports store. Incidentally, local sports stores are also an excellent source of local information. Detailed local maps and books, such as *Reader's Digest Guide to the Australian Coast* and the *Fishing News* map series are invaluable when checking out new areas. *NSW Central Coast Fishing*, published by Gene Dundon, is an excellent book covering all aspects of angling in that area.

The most popular species caught in the area are tailor, bream, luderick or blackfish, whiting, drummer, and flathead, but many other species are common, including tuna and other pelagics. High-speed spinning for tuna had its beginnings on the Central Coast. Some of these species are present year-round but generally the best times are: tailor and bream—autumn/early winter; luderick—summer/autumn; blue groper and drummer—autumn/winter; and whiting, pelagics, mulloway and flathead—the summer months. In summary, the best fishing is available during autumn when conditions are more settled and the water is still warm.

Most local anglers utilise sidecast gear, consisting of a low-mounted Alvey reel and a light, flexible rod of about 3.4 metres. A good combination for smaller fish would be an Alvey 15-centimetre (6-inch) reel, spooled with 6-kilo breaking-strain line and a Butterworth MT4144 rod or similar; for tailor and medium-sized fish an Alvey 16-centimetre (6.5-inch) reel with 8-kilo line and an extended Butterworth FSU4120 rod or similar. Luderick anglers usually use an Avon centrepin reel (or perhaps one of the new Alvey models), with light-weight line of about 3 kilos, and a Butterworth GP3145 rod or similar; and for spinning for pelagics a super-fast threadline reel, or overhead gear such as a Seascape or Shimano Speedmasters, fully loaded with 12-kilo line and a Butterworth MT8132 rod or similar.

These are only some suggested outfits and there are many other combinations equally suitable. It's worth while persisting with the Alvey reels because of their durability; however, many anglers do use threadline outfits. It always pays in the long run to buy quality gear which will last indefinitely with proper care.

Fresh bait can be purchased in most local areas or enterprising anglers can gather their own supplies. The most commonly used baits for the species mentioned are: tailor—Western Australian pilchards or garfish; bream—cut-fish baits such as mullet or tuna, pilchards, squid, yabbies, prawns or whitebait; mulloway—small live baits such as yellowtail or tailor, large slabs of fresh fish, squid or octopus legs; drummer—cunjevoi or prawns; luderick—green weed or cabbage gathered at the spot being fished; pelagics—metal lures such as the Arrows or, on the Central Coast, a lure which can be purchased locally called the half-by-quarter; groper — red crabs freshly caught by running your hands through the growths or red weed found on low-lying rocks.

Beach fishers must learn the art of reading a beach from a suitable vantage point, picking out deep holes and gutters which could shelter species such as tailor and bream, or even mulloway — especially on a run-up to high tide. The activity of any other anglers is a good way to check out any fishing action and water conditions, such as any rips or weed in the water. As mentioned earlier it's helpful if there's some movement in the water, but if there's too much sand being stirred up fish may move out to deeper water.

Around the ocean rocks similar methods can be used before commencing to fish. Most rocks in this area have a reefy bottom close in so many anglers fish using a semi-floating bait, with a small ball sinker running down to the hook. This substantially reduces terminal tackle losses. A golden rule for all rock-hopping is to use the smallest sinker and lightest line that you can get away with. For this reason a container of mixed-weight ball sinkers should be carried, together with a small waterproof container for your hooks.

Many anglers make the mistake of believing that a long-distance cast will yield more fish, overlooking the fact that fish are often feeding close in along the edge of the rock ledges or beaches, where feed is being stirred up by tidal and wave action. Fishing such areas, especially in conjunction with berley, will often yield the best catches. The intelligent use of berley, such as soaked bread or chicken pellets, will often attract fish right to your feet, away from outlying areas of reef. This can often mean the difference between a good bag of fish and a poor outing. There are many low rock shelves which are covered with water on high tide and it's a very effective technique to fish these after dark for bream and drummer, a technique called pot-holing. This method will often provide a feed when others fail.

There's so much good territory it's hard to cover any particular area in detail. Some top spots for rock-hoppers would have to be Avoca, Terrigal, Catherine Hill Bay, Nelson Bay, the Little Gibber, Seal Rocks and Forster; and for the beach fisher The Entrance, Budgewoi, Stockton, and the area around Myall Lakes National Park contain many top spots. Throughout the area fishing is excellent, with ideal conditions for the beginner and expert alike.

LORD HOWE ISLAND
Glen Booth

For many years, Lord Howe Island, some 700 kilometres north-east of Sydney, suffered from a reputation of being a great place to catch all the kingfish your heart desired, and very little else. A few locals (and a couple of switched-on mainlanders) had an inkling of what lay in store for anglers who were prepared to avoid studiously the inshore carpet of kings and work the offshore drop-offs and canyons; but by and large, Lord Howe Island remained the slumbering giant of the Australian sportfishing scene.

This situation changed abruptly in March 1982. The commencement of sportfishing tours to the island, under the guidance of Ron Calcutt, Rod Harrison and Lord Howe Islander, Paul Beaumont, has seen many hundreds of keen anglers arrive at the island with high hopes and full tackle boxes, and leave a couple of days later with some great fish to boast about, a few stories about the one that got away, and quite often, significantly lighter tackle boxes!

There's little doubt that Lord Howe is Australia's premier kingfish location. The size and sheer numbers of kingfish make them a tourist attraction in their own right and very few visitors leave the island without catching a kingie or two. Small kings (up to 10 kilos) will hit small to medium-size deep-running minnows and skirted trolling lures all day long, while the larger specimens that are of interest to the sportfishers respond to the same lures in the larger sizes.

The deadliest method of all, however, is to drop down a live kingfish of a half to one kilo on a big hook attached to a whipper-snipper handline or a suitable stump-pulling game rod. Whaler sharks (which almost match the kings for numbers) will eat nine out of ten baits, but when that monster greenback is doing its best to tie you up on the bottom, you'll know all the bite-offs and toothy grins were worth it.

As the years go by and a more rounded view of Lord Howe's true fishing potential becomes evident, the so-called 'season' seems to grow longer and longer. January through March sees school and mid-sized yellowfin tuna hugging the drop-offs and deep-water canyons that ring the island. Trolling is the most practical and successful method used (the vast colony of mutton birds precludes the use of berley and live bait can be a bit touchy at times) and triple hook-ups are common enough to make other techniques unnecessary.

The winter months, it now appears, produce the best yellowfin tuna fishing, with the fish *averaging* 50 kilos or more and the odd fish topping the much sought after 100-kilo mark. Granted, the weather can be fickle at this time of the year, but most serious bluewater anglers would tolerate a joggly sea to have a shot or two at a big yellowfin. Once again, trolling medium to large Konahead-style lures has produced most of the fish, with the lures tucked right in tight to the white water of the boat's wake taking the majority of the strikes. Those razor-toothed oceanic speedsters, the wahoo, turn up at odd times throughout the year, although February to May are considered the peak months. When the wahoo are really on, they can exact a terrible toll on the contents of one's tackle box if the lures aren't rigged on wire, but wire has its share of technical problems and if billfish are targeted, then most anglers decide to hang the expense and persevere with heavy mono leaders.

And speaking of billfish, the island's billfish potential is only being crystalised, as return groups that have had their fill of the inshore kingfish, wahoo, school yellowfin scene, gear up with no-nonsense 24- and 37-kilo outfits, big lures rigged with two hooks, and start to work the deeper water wide of the island.

No definite billfish answers are available yet, but it's fair to say that most groups visiting the island get a shot at one or more marlin during their stay and a handful of Cairns skippers who have a nose for 'sussing out' new billfish locations are keeping a very close eye on developments at the island. A scout trip by one Cairns-based boat produced over 25 billfish up to 300 plus kilos (with much bigger fish being lost) over a one month period, so the potential is certainly there.

Blue marlin are the real heavyweights of the neighbourhood, the best fish to date being a massive 228-kilo specimen – reason enough to be fishing 24, 37 and maybe even 60-kilo tackle. There are enough fish out there to give the big guns a vigorous workout and, with the emphasis being on tag and release of any fish that can't be utilised as food, it ensures that the marlin are released in good condition.

Black marlin of between 50 and 180 kilos make up the bulk of the billfish number with striped marlin putting in an appearance from time to time. Sailfish are an occasional capture, but they're always healthy specimens in excess of 45 kilos and one pending world record sailfish in excess of 80 kilos was taken at Elizabeth Reef recently, so it pays to expect the unexpected when fishing these fertile waters.

It may sound from all this that Lord Howe is a heavy-tackle location, but the place is so rich in fish life that it's entirely up to the angler how and what he fishes for. A berley trail and a light-medium spin rod or baitcaster and it's possible to stay hooked up from sunrise to sunset on all manner of pelagics and bottom grubbers and not

Several species of tuna feed on the baitfish around the top of Moreton Bay. This mackerel tuna fell to a popper-style lure cast into a feeding school. (Photo Rod Harrison)

make the slightest bit of difference to their numbers. A casual glance at the Australian record chart reveals a number of light-tackle categories that could be filled with the right kind of approach and plenty of lures!

The island holds some fine silver trevally, many of which can be classed as 'uncatchable' on their home ground. Generally, however, a 4-kilo baitcaster will stop most fish encountered, with the light line being essential to get the big blurters to bite in the gin-clear lagoon water. A little berley helps sharpen their appetites and a rising tide around dusk will also attract small to medium whaler sharks—red-hot performers in shallow water. The lagoon also holds bluefish (a first cousin to the east-coast luderick), large schools of garfish and mullet, whiting, spangled emperor and some huge silver drummer, the likes of which are seen but not often caught back on the mainland.

The island's beach and rock fishing doesn't receive the attention it deserves, which is a pity, as it is of a quality not often found on the mainland nowadays. Blinkies, Middle and Ned's Beach (away from the fish-feeding area) produce XOS-sized salmon, dart, trevally, whiting, mullet and his highness of shyness—the much revered bonefish. Lord Howe (and Elizabeth Reef too, it appears) are probably the two most likely locations in Australia to give an angler a better than average chance of nailing a bone; all it needs is a little concentration and dedication on the angler's part.

The rock fishing is unsurpassed and a serious rock-hopper could easily spend a month on the island without scratching the surface of what is classified as good fishing water. Some of the better locations involve a bit of a walk to get to them, but the walks aren't as taxing as many of those found on the mainland and the fishing is indeed worth it.

Kingfish, ranging from 'rats' up to unstoppable, moss-backed monsters, are prolific, as are salmon, spangled emperor and trevally. A little berley, a bobby cork, or a floating bait can turn up all sorts of surprises and crab baits will produce all sorts of rock dwellers including the unusual double header.

Land-based game fanatics could have a lot of fun matching wits and muscles with the kingfish tribe, but there are a few locations that would have to be right on for yellowfin tuna and maybe even marlin off the rocks. All it needs is someone enthusiastic enough to give it a go.

So, that's a thumbnail sketch of fishing at Lord Howe Island. The next few years will see the fishing effort expanded even further, with the arrival of a 17-metre aluminium game boat to work in conjunction with *Santara* around the island and range even further afield, taking groups to Elizabeth and Middleton reefs—one of Australia's last true fishing frontiers.

Having only two serious sportfishing boats working the area with any efficiency, the place is in no danger of suffering the ravages of over-fishing or inshore netting, and strict development controls mean there are no pollution problems, so it is hoped Lord Howe Island will be a place our grandchildren will be able to visit to experience the standard of fishing we have today.

GAME FISHING NORTH OF SYDNEY
Glen Booth

Considering its close proximity to Australia's most densely populated urban area, the offshore fishing in the Sydney-Central Coast region is little short of phenomenal. Almost every weekend or public holiday, weather permitting hundreds of boats, ranging from 4.5 metre tinnies through to 20-metre full-blown luxury gamefishing rigs, push offshore to match wits with all manner of pelagics which ride the warm ocean currents.

And they catch fish too—black, blue and striped marlin, yellowfin and striped tuna and albacore, a host of shark species, from lumbering great tigers to the aggressive mako, some fine yellowtail kingfish, and when the currents and temperatures are suitable, the occasional wahoo and dolphin fish.

The continental shelf comes as close to the mainland as 25 kilometres in some places along the Sydney–Port Stephens coastline and this contributes greatly to the region's success.

Some sort of gamefishing action can be found almost all year round, but the season really kicks off in the early spring months. In years past, southern bluefin tuna put in an appearance around this time, but commercial devastation of their stocks means that catching a southern blue off Sydney is as unlikely as winning Lotto, so most of the action comes from mako and blue sharks, and sometimes an early yellowfin or two. Blues and makos are usually more prolific wide of the continental shelf, and are attracted to the baits with the aid of a berley trail. Any fish flesh will do, but tuna and mullet are preferred. Mullet are particularly popular, as they are cheap, easy to obtain and store and are extremely oily into the bargain. The bodies are put through the pot as usual, and the heads and tails are dropped directly over the side at regular intervals, where they sink rapidly to the bottom, luring the 'big biteys' up from their deep-water haunts.

Your average blue shark is a bit of a dead loss as a fighter, preferring to loll around the berley pot where they are easily gaffed or tagged. Occasionally, one will put on a bit of a performance on light line, but even a 100-kilo blue is fairly easy to control on 4- or 6-kilo tackle, so there is little status attached to killing one.

The mako, on the other hand, is another kettle of fish entirely. One of the strongest and most aggressive sharks found in Australia and a close relative of the dreaded white shark, the mako has a deserved reputation of being a worthy opponent at any size, often leaping clear of the water in giant 'cartwheels' and occasionally landing in boats—much to the horror of the crew. All makos deserve respect, whether they're 25 or 250 kilos, and can be relied on to provide plenty of excitement during the course of the fight. They're also extremely good on the plate, something that can't be said about the other shark species.

As the water temperature starts to top the 21°C mark around Christmas, big tiger sharks, many in excess of 250 kilos begin to turn up in berley trails right along the Sydney–Central Coast region. Tigers are actively sought by a lot of game fishermen and a heavy berley trail along the 190–240-metre line is the favoured technique for these deep-water leviathans.

Fifteen-kilo tackle is usually sufficient to knock over tigers even in excess of 450 kilos, and if there is any flaw in the makeup of these big sharks, it is their often fatal habit of coming to the surface to check out their tormentors. A bit of sharp boat driving, a maximum length wire trace and a 'deckie' with arms of indiarubber can often cut an hour or two off the fight. The deepest set bait is usually the first to go off, with striped tuna, big mullet, school yellowfin and silver trevally being the pick of the baits.

Whaler and hammerhead sharks respond to the same baits and techniques, although hammers can be extremely touchy around a boat, necessitating the use of extremely light wire (single strand is ideal) or, if things get really desperate, a heavy mono trace might produce a hook-up. On the other hand, hammers will crash a live stripy or a big slimy without a moment's hesitation so every fish has to be treated on its own merits.

The spring months also see the first marlin of the season hooked up, if not landed. Generally, 'the first marlin of the season' is a big striped, although in the past few years, a few big blues are starting to turn up as well. Stripes seem to be more tolerant of cold and dirty water, but will turn up in the hottest cobalt-blue water imaginable, so it pays to be flexible.

The mighty black marlin makes up the bulk of the marlin encountered along the stretch of coastline under examination, and can turn up anywhere from a few hundred metres offshore to way over the shelf. Anything from a small Christmas tree through to the biggest lure imaginable, can turn a black's head, but generally something between 20 and 35 centimetres is preferred. Bridle-rigged striped tuna are popular, particularly around some underwater feature such as a reef or sudden drop-off, but the trolling speed required to keep the bait alive and swimming happily, doesn't allow for much territory to be covered. The boat is often at mercy of wind and current, so dead baits and lures tend to be more popular.

Aussie anglers fishing known overseas lure-fishing locations such as Hawaii, have brought back a range of lures and techniques that have resulted in a veritable explosion of big blue marlin captures over the past season or two. Blue marlin were once considered fairly rare in New South Wales waters, but the growing interest in lure trolling and a drift away from 10-kilo tackle has seen a number of these big fish (nearly all of them are in excess of 100 kilos) hit the gantry, instead of being another entry in the 'one that got away' hall of fame.

Long, heavy mono leaders, big, straight-running 'pusher'-type lures rigged with two equally large hooks and rock-solid drag settings are important elements in the marlin equation, and needless to say 15-kilo tackle should be regarded as *light* tackle, with 24- or even 37-kilo being preferred.

Yellowfin tuna fall into two general categories along this stretch of coastline — the school fish up to 30 or 40 kilos that start to show up just before Christmas and the big blokes of 50 kilos or more that prefer the more temperate waters of autumn and early winter.

School fish respond well to Christmas trees, feather jigs, small to medium Konahead-style trolling lures, and grabbing yellowtail and slimy mackerel intended for their larger brothers.

Big yellowfin on the other hand, seem to have a studied aversion to lures, which is a little hard to understand when known overseas yellowfin hotspots produce these big fish on artificials as a matter of course. In Australia, live baits or strip baits in a berley trail produce the big fish and a lot of anglers specialise in using this technique. Live baits can take the form of yellowtail, slimy mackerel or nannygai and almost any fish flesh can be used as berley, although something with a high oil content is preferred.

The use of a berley pot has been popular in the past, but as anglers learn more about this fairly shy and wary fish, it is becoming apparent that the noise emanating from banging on the pot is more likely to scare the fish off than attract them. Consequently, cube trails of diced pilchards or fish flesh are finding favour with fish and angler alike. If the conditions are right it is possible to berley the yellowfin right up to the back of the boat — one of the most exciting sights a game fisher can experience.

Whole pilchards and cut baits can be floated back down the trail and this produces a lot of big fish, with the object of the exercise being to make the bait look like a part of the berley, so the yellowfin will inhale it with the rest of the cubes.

Once again, 24-kilo tackle is extremely popular, enabling smaller fish to be beaten quickly and tagged without suffering the stresses of a long fight, and still having the firepower to subdue a really big fish in deep water. Off Sydney, places like the *Marley* and *Garie* wrecks south of Port Hacking, Long Reef, The Peak and the continental shelf produce a lot of big fish. Anglers further north towards Port Stephens have a lot of success in the autumn months, working behind the trawlers as the net is hauled aboard. The yellowfin find the trash fish being thrown overboard easy pickings, and the amateur boats are quick to capitalise on these reckless feeding sprees.

Yellowtail kingfish abound along the New South Wales coast and can be found almost anywhere, from the rocky foreshores and bomboras, through to the deep reefs and fish traps offshore. Kings have a habit of schooling over the high peaks on a reef and a heavy metal jig or a live yellowtail (assisted to the bottom with a substantial lump of lead) will usually produce a result.

When the kings are up on the surface chasing bait, a deep-running minnow or a cup-faced surface popper will draw explosive strikes and it's also a good opportunity to pin a few big fish on light tackle while they're well away from their usual line-cutting haunts. A garfish, rigged either to swim below the surface with the aid of a 'chin' sinker, or to splash noisily across the surface, is particularly deadly on big fish, especially when they're chasing sauries.

Two exotic northern wanderers that turn up off the Sydney-Central Coast region from time to time are wahoo and dolphin fish. Wahoo are generally an incidental capture while trolling baits or lures for billfish or tuna, while dolphin fish usually can be found in residence under fish-trap floats or any piece of flotsam that affords them some degree of shelter and protection. Saltwater flies, Christmas trees, pink squids and medium-sized Konaheads all appeal to small to medium-sized dolphin fish, but a berley trail of cubed pilchards or a small live yellowtail is the best method of pulling the larger fish out of the school.

THE HAWKESBURY RIVER

Bruce Schumacher

What a magnificet river is the Hawkesbury. Situated just 40 kilometres north of the largest metropolis in Australia it can still maintain a reputation for the variety and quality of species that can be taken from its waters. It also offers some of the best river scenery to be seen along our coast, enticing fishers to pursue their sport in the most pleasant surroundings. The steep sandstone hills drop down to deep rocky foreshores and secluded sandy coves which provide protection from most winds. Unfortunately it is also this seclusion which limits access for shore-based anglers and the Hawkesbury is primarily a boat fisher's province.

The main river, from its entry to the sea at Broken Bay to the weir at Penrith, is traversable for 120 kilometres with a maximum tide influence in the main channel for peak run-out tides of 8 kilometres per hour. In the lower reaches, on the southern side, it has three major inlets, Pittwater, Cowan Creek and Berowra Creek.

Pittwater, a large bay near the mouth of the river, has a wide shallow entrance with deeper water as its southern end.

Cowan Creek, a deep-water inlet which in places exceeds 30 metres in depth, has many deep bays which shelve up steeply to tidal sandflats and are fed by small freshwater creeks. Besides the more common estuarine species, offshore species such as groper, cod, snapper and mackerel tuna are occasionally taken from the deep water and Cowan Creek is the traditional winter home of the hairtail which is discussed in more detail later. Boats can be hired at Bobbin Head, Akuna Bay and Cottage Point and launching ramps are situated at Akuna Bay and Apple Tree Bay at Bobbin Head.

Berowra Creek, further upstream, is similar in nature to Cowan Creek but shallower. Boat hire and a good public ramp can be found at Berowra Waters at the top end of the creek.

The excellent eating quality and its sporting ability make the black bream the most sought after species for most fishers. Although they can be found anywhere in the river on all types of bottom and in any depth, they are commonly fished for at night close in along the rocky foreshores. Drifting, or anchored a couple of boat lengths from shore and casting back to the rocks, is the established technique; but bream tend to be touchy under these conditions and you must fish as light as possible – 3-kilo line maximum and no sinker if possible, with plenty of free line to let the fish run before striking. A rising tide and no moon is the best time, with mullet gut, prawns and pudding the best baits.

Large numbers of bream are taken in the main river before and after they spawn at sea. As the fish move out in May and June and come back into the river during August and September, they tend to school in places such as Juno Point, the railway bridge and the road bridge, the Vines and Bar Point. Small tides and the last two hours of the run-out and the first hour of the run-in are definitely the best times, whether day or night. Rigs tend to be heavier due to the deeper water and moderately fast run of the tide; however, the fish are more aggressive and will take a bait hard and fast. Up to 7-kilo line is not uncommon with a running-ball sinker, which may be as large as a No 8 to get the bait down, but allow a long trace of 1 to 2 metres which lets the bait move around in the current. Preferred baits are nippers and large local prawns and, if the water is dirty, chook gut is a must. Berleying with wheat or laying pellets will definitely improve the catch.

Flathead are the lazy angler's fish, but what better way to spend a summer day than drifting around a sandflat with the chance of a flattie or two? Drifting is by far the best method to bait fish for flathead as it allows the angler to cover more territory and take the bait to the flathead as they lie buried in the sand and mud waiting for food to drift or swim past. The favoured rig is 4- to 8-kilo line with a running-ball sinker to a small swivel with a trace of the same line about 45 centimetres long to a 3-hook gang of No 2 to 1/0 hooks depending on the bait. Best baits are Western Australian pilchards, frogmouth pilchards and strip baits of mullet, tailor or yellowtail. Best times are dayligh hours on a run-out tide.

Some good drifting grounds worth trying are around the entrance between Juno Point and Lion Island, down the middle of the river between Brooklyn and Juno Point, the flats on the eastern side of Dangar Island and Milson Island and across the mouth of Mullet Creek. The bigger flathead tend to favour the deeper water along the edges of the shoals.

Live baiting and spinning also work well for flathead, but poddy mullet, the best live bait, are hard to find in the Hawkesbury; and lure fishing is confined to the upper reaches of Cowan Creek and Berowra Creek where the water is relatively clear.

Although not classed as one of our better sporting fish, be prepared to give flathead line when they approach the surface as it is at this point that they start their head shaking and will quickly saw through a tight line with their needle-sharp teeth. Take care when handling in the boat also, and watch out for those spines on either side of the head.

The big fish of the river, mulloway or jewfish, have been reported up to 50 kilos but one of 30 kilos is considered a trophy fish. The big jew hang around reefs and obstructions in the river, typical of which is Flint and Steel reef near the mouth and both the rail and road bridges and Bar Point. It is not uncommon, however, for them to be taken elsewhere in the deep channels as they move around the river. The rig for deep water is 20-kilo plus line, 100–200-gram barrel sinker with a short trace to a 6/0 to 10/0 hook. The rig is suspended below the boat about 2 metres off the bottom. Live bait such as yellowtail or tailor is preferred although fresh squid works well.

In shallower water the bait is left to free swim or float in the current and mullet and tailor fillets are worth a try. Best times are early morning and late evening particularly on the turn of the tide, with the top of the tide better.

Small school jewfish up to 2 kilos, commonly called 'soapies' because of their soapy smell, can be found just about anywhere in the river during the summer months. Rigs as used for bream and flathead and prawn bait are sure to catch a few.

Around about April hairtail, an eel-like fish, turn up in Cowan Creek to keep the hardy winter anglers happy until about July. Some of their recognised haunts such as Waratah Bay, Jerusalem Bay and Smiths Creek become crowded with boats just before dark as the anglers wait for the travelling schools to appear. The action is usually fast and furious when they do appear as they are an aggressive fish, not put off by noise or light, and they give a good fight even on heavy line. The common rig is handline of 15 kilos with a 6/0 hook or gang attached which can be free floated or weighted under the boat. Lines are set at different depths to find the fish and yo-yoing the bait will help to attract them. Hairtail will bite on any fish bait with live yellowtail, tuna or pilchards the best. Hit the fish

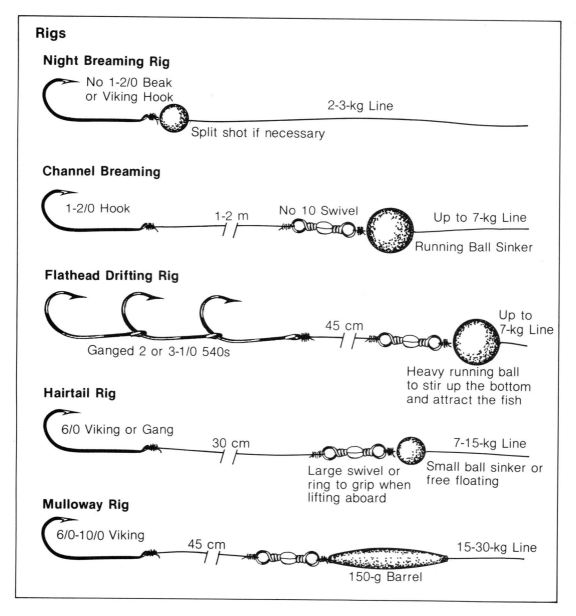

hard when they bite to set the hook as they have hard bony mouths with a frightening set of dentures highlighted by two needle-sharp, barbed fangs which can inflict a nasty wound. Although they may be caught at any time of the day or night the first couple of hours after dark on a moonless night are the best.

Other species also taken in the Hawkesbury include luderick, which are fished for along the rocky foreshores in Cowan Creek and the top end of Berowra Creek and in Pittwater around Church Point. Traditional blackfish gear is used with green weed for bait, but preferably Parramatta River weed. The local weed tends to be slimy.

Whiting are occasionally taken when fishing for other species in the sandflats particularly when using nippers for bait. Being a deep-water estuary the Hawkesbury is not recognised as good whiting territory.

From February to June schools of tailor work the entrance of the river and can be spun or bait-fished with pilchards around Lion Island, Barrenjoey and Flint and Steel. Bright moonlit nights are the best time but early morning and late evening will also produce fish.

Upriver, tributaries such as the Colo and McDonald rivers and Cattai and Webbs creeks have reasonable populations of bass during the summer. In the upper reaches eel-tail catfish can be caught and in the main river around Wisemans Ferry and Sackville estuary perch are plentiful. Carp, unfortunately, are now resident in the Hawkesbury; however, they have been caught up to 8 kilos and do offer good sport for light-line fishermen.

Above the weir at Penrith the local Nepean fishing-club members annually stock the river with trout and regular catches are taken, but only on bait.

Bait Gathering

There are no restrictions on the gathering of bait in the Hawkesbury river system other than in Cowan Creek and the waters above the road bridge at Windsor where the use of prawn drag nets, scoop nets and scissor nets is prohibited. Nippers and worms can be found on the flats in most of the bays and yellowtail, for live bait, can usually be found around the rocky foreshores in the bays, particularly where the deep water meets the sandflats.

Hazards, and Safety Measures

Saltwater catfish can appear in plague proportions in the Hawkesbury particularly on big tides and after heavy rain. They should be treated with respect as they can inflict a very painful wound from any of three spines around their head. Try not to handle them and simply cut them off and tie on a new hook.

The Hawkesbury is a busy waterway and should be negotiated carefully, particularly at night. The entrance can become very choppy with the combination of a run-out tide and a north-easterly wind, but would not be considered dangerous.

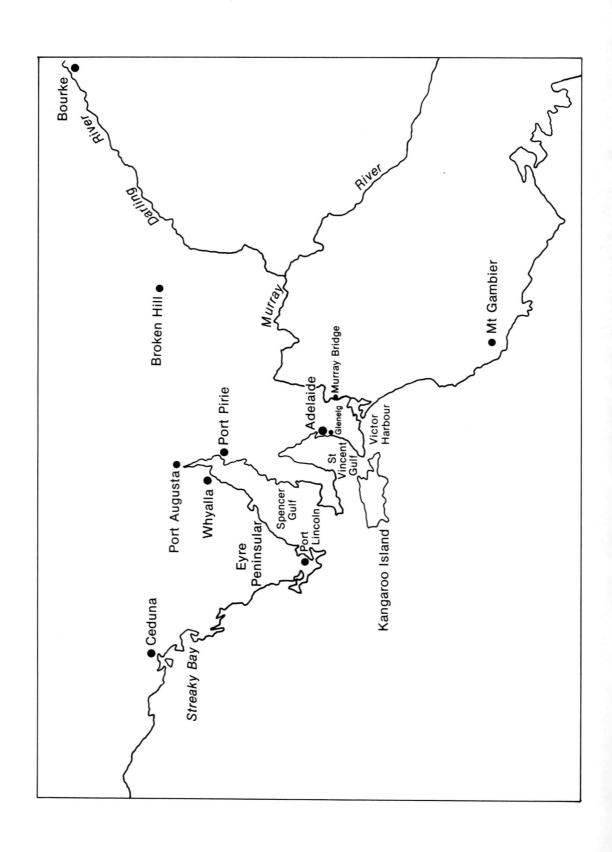

SECTION THREE

Western New South Wales, Victoria, and South Australia

VICTORIA AND THE RIVERINA-NATIVE SPECIES IN THE INLAND RIVERS

Fred Jobson

This area of Australia encompasses some of the biggest topographical differences possible, with everything from tiny alpine streams and lakes to the wide flat country and the majestic Murray River. The linking factor is that all these waters offer some of the best freshwater fishing in Australia as well as a wide variety of species.

The Murray cod, Australia's biggest freshwater species, is much sought in the Murray River downstream from the Hume Weir and in the many tributaries such as the Kiewa, Ovens, Goulburn, and Campaspe rivers that join the Murray in the Riverina district.

Despite some poor previous seasons, there has been a revival in the past years and there are now good numbers of Murray cod to be caught, ranging in size from small undersize cod, which should be returned unharmed, to 50-kilo trophy cod, and every size in between. Every week there are reports of 10- to 15-kilo Murray cod being caught by local and tourist anglers.

Three main conditions are needed when you select a location to fish for Murray cod, the first of which is plenty of current. The Murray cod dislikes the slow still holes and appears to prefer a fast current that can bring food to it. The still pools are largely inhabited only by carp.

Actually, even in the fast current area, the cod is in the sheltered water behind logs and only ventures out into the current to catch the food as it passes.

The second requirement for a Murray cod habitat is lots of snags. If you are not losing sinkers and hooks, the water is not snaggy enough. The cod is right in among the logs and this means that, getting a big one out when hooked is often impossible, even with very heavy line. I know of one clump of snags that has a 40-kilo cod in residence that has broken lines many times. The Murray cod seeks shelter and food in among the snags and submerged timber. The best depth varies but about 3 to 5 metres seems about right.

I also fish only where there is an undercut clay or rock river bottom, not on the sand. The clay banks are riddled with Murray crayfish and yabby holes, the inhabitants of which form a significant part of the cod's diet.

The best bait is without a doubt the big juicy, bardie grubs collected from under the limbs of the yellow box and red gums along the river banks. Collecting bardies is a laborious task best suited to the fit and experienced, and you can buy them from the many bait suppliers available.

Fresh Murray River shrimp are the next best bait and are relatively easy to catch using a trap in the shallow weed beds and around sunken timber. Shrimp cannot be purchased so you must catch your own. European carp makes a good bait for the trap.

Yabbies, worms, and small live fish will all catch fish and yabbies and live fish have the advantage of not being constantly attacked by carp. For best results, however, I consider that a big bardie grub is by far the best bait.

I prefer a running sinker rig but many local fishers use a snood above the sinker to try to avoid snags. The running-sinker rig offers less resistance to the fish despite its affinity to snags. Heavy line is used with many anglers using very robust tackle and lines up to 35-kilo breaking strain. A more sporting approach would be 10-kilo line and a stiff barra-type rod.

The best time of day varies as any weather changes or an impending storm can bring the native fish on the bite and should be taken advantage of. Usually from 4 pm to dark or later is best. During summer, when there are many speed boats during the day, early morning can

One of Australia's indigenous sports fish, the Macquarie perch. Once widespread throughout New South Wales and Victorian rivers, it now exists in limited locations. Lake Dartmouth in Victoria has one of its main populations. (Photo Fred Jobson)

avoid the maddening speed freaks.

Usually in about April-May and then October, the level of the water falls and clears, resulting in the best angling of the year, and the cod are ready to respond to trolling lures. Large Flatfish (particularly fluorescent-red), Flopys, Mudbugs, and minnow deep-divers are all good lures to try.

Murray cod have a very distinctive bite, much like the sharp rattle bite of a whiting. Observation of Murray cod in aquariums has shown that the first bite is when the fish grabs the bait, usually along with gravel and sand as well. If the cod is struck on this first bite the hook will often fail to penetrate the hard mouth parts. It is better to wait for the second bite when the cod has turned the bait around and is swallowing it.

Other species abounding in the Murray are silver perch, yellowbelly, redfin (English perch) and Murray crays, all being sought at different times of the year. One problem is that vast numbers of European carp are present and these take bait destined for more desirable species. The carp do give plenty of action and are sought by some ethnic sections of our diversified Australian community.

Silver perch of about 500 grams are in good quantities and very willing to bite during the day. Their bite is very much like the short savage bite of a Murray cod but there is no follow-up bite. Small hooks baited with worms, small pieces of bardie grubs or shrimps are good baits; and you should try to hook the silver perch as soon as they bite.

Yellowbelly (callop) are also present but not in very large numbers. Towards evening the down-current end of sandbanks along the beaches is a good location for both these species.

There is also a large number of redfin to be caught in the channels at times and in the lakes, such as the Hume Weir, Mulwala and Mokoan lakes, and Waranga Basin, which are in this area.

The Murray River at Cobram-Yarrawonga is one of the last bastions of trout cod. This endangered species has several identifying features to distinguish it from the similar Murray cod, one of which is an overhanging upper jaw. I would strongly recommend to all anglers that they join with the Victorian and New South Wales Fisheries staff who are trying to preserve this unique fish. Develop the practice of releasing any trout cod unharmed, irrespective of size.

The Riverina area of the Murray River offers excellent fishing, good launching and unlimited opportunities for all aquatic sports, great weather and blue skies, and friendly country people. Few parts of Australia are as well situated for a freshwater fishing holiday to suit all ages.

Lake Dartmouth, in the alpine country to the east-south-east of Albury/Wodonga offers the angler the chance to catch Macquarie perch, a species that is becoming increasingly rare elsewhere. These fine eating fish are up to 2 kilos in weight or even bigger although the average would be 700 grams.

Macquarie perch are usually found in schools which can take some time to locate as the lake is so large. Once a school is found, fast action can be expected. Bag limit at Lake Dartmouth is ten Macquarie perch per day and the legal length is 25 centimetres. There is a closed season from 8 November to 23 January although this can alter each year, depending on water conditions.

Worms are best bait but shrimp and small yabbies are also productive. The shallow water right in close to the shoreline, especially when the water is rising, provides the most fish. Over submerged tree tops in about 7 metres of water is also good.

A light trout spinning-rod outfit with 4-kilo breaking strain line is ideal for Macquarie perch. The usual rig is a small running sinker above 50 centimetres of trace and a No 4 or 6 hook.

A handful of sweet corn and chopped up earthworms at each spot you intend to fish will often help to concentrate the school of Macquaries in the area for you to catch when you return later in the day. Late afternoon into the night and early morning are by far the best times to fish and many good bags are made late at night.

In late October-early November, when the water in the streams warms up a little, the Macquarie perch assemble in the river arms preparatory to spawning. At these times the rocky outcrops can have large schools of Macquaries around them and bait fishing or spinning can give the biggest bags of the year. I would recommend to anglers that they release any Macquarie perch except a couple for a meal, as they are too precious a resource to be wasted by fish-hungry anglers.

The Macquarie perch's bite is very gentle and you must watch the tip of your rod at all times. Only a slight downward bob of your rod signals that a fish has your bait. When hooked, the fighting ability of the perch belies its cautious approach to the bait.

Dartmouth Dam also has perhaps the best brown trout fishery in Victoria as well as having many rainbow trout, but it is the Macquarie perch that will make this lake increasingly important to recreational anglers and fisheries researchers alike.

Hazards, and Safety Measures

Because of its altitude, Dartmouth Dam is subject to rapid deterioration of weather conditions. If the weather becomes bad, it is better to spend a miserable night safe on the nearest shore than to drown trying to make it back to the ramp.

Along the margins of the lake there are vast numbers of partially submerged trees that have become rotted and can come crashing down. Do not tie up to dead trees and fish under overhanging branches as there is a chance that limbs or the whole tree could fall into your boat.

OUT ON THE DARLING
Rod Harrison

For more years than most of us can remember, the Darling River has been a Mecca for the pilgrimages of inland anglers. This fishing pressure, to say nothing of the illegal and shady fishing practices we don't hear about, would seem to go beyond the capacity of a mere river to cope.

Yet, year in and year out, the Darling continues to produce. In so many places, kilometre upon kilometre of riverbank is lined with setline springers; sticks that take on the density of a picket fence, such are their numbers.

One must wonder how fish can live and travel through this minefield. But they do, and the fishers keep coming.

Some parties, and these include fishers who willingly travel from interstate to fish the Darling, return from their trip with vehicles laden to the axles with the weight of fish. Cricket-score catches are very much the name of their game.

They can often put their successes down to not so much sheer fishing skills, but catching the river on a rise. The fish are on a roll then.

Conversely, on a falling river one can give it one's best shots and go home fishless—convinced, in the majority of cases, that there are no fish there.

The level of ignorance amongst inland fishers exceeds the national average. By many times.

To fish the inland with consistent success, it is necessary to understand the biology of inland fish and how it links with the erratic nature of the inland climate—those years of drought that break the hearts of those people making a living off the land, droughts ended with rains that may swell rivers into uncontrollable floods.

Such extremes, which we tend to regard as natural disasters, characterise the Australian inland. It's the way it has always been, not the cruel intervention of nature that commentators use to describe the resultant human hardships.

Translated into fishtalk, this means that fish move when there's a rise afoot. Moving fish are hungry fish and therefore more inclined to feed.

In times of plenty, they accumulate considerable body fats which are often inadvertently left in dressed Murray cod and yellowbelly and lead to complaints about their eating quality. But don't tell that to an inlander. To them, there's no sweeter taste on the face of the earth.

Falling rivers tell the fish of hard times a'coming. Activity levels fall right off and if it is the beginnings of a big dry, the fish find a comfortable hole and sit it out, feeding only when necessary and absorbing body fats as a supplementary thing until the rains come again.

Fishers can keep tabs on river heights by tuning in on ABC rural broadcasts. Ideally, the best time to be fishing that Darling is during those times when an increasing run in the river is announcing the coming of a major rise.

Because of the black soil banks and the input of tributaries from the Queensland channel country, the Darling River—the stretch from Bourke to where it joins the Murray down in the borderlands—clears sufficiently for lures perhaps every five years.

The big dams on the upper reaches of many Darling tributaries take in much of the water that would otherwise flow into the sea via the Darling and Murray rivers. These impoundments bring about lower than normal river levels at times with a result that clear water is a greater possibility. A negative factor, however, is the presence of great numbers of European carp, which constantly stir the bottom with their feeding behaviour.

Inland prejudices die hard. Carp are still disdained by the majority of native born Australians. The hopeless situation that followed their takeover of the Darling and other inland rivers in countless droves, back in the early seventies, seems to have eased considerably. The Australian environment may have struck a blow in reducing carp numbers.

And contrary to much popular belief, cod and yellowbelly may have benefited in some ways from the ready and large food source they've made.

Fish like cod, yellowbelly, catfish and carp are catholic feeders. Cod and yellowbelly are highly predatory, taking live food, but they'll also scavenge, not hesitating about more inanimate things. Provided they're edible.

Catfish and carp are lower in the food chain—kind of vacuum cleaners in the river if you like.

The silver perch, or black bream as inlanders call the fish, has mixed habits which include feeding off the bottom and holding in the faster waters at the head of pools. It is a rather active fish, this being reflected in both an angling and table sense. Weight for weight as a sporting fish, it is on a par with the bass of the coastal streams. On the plate, it is somewhat tougher than either cod or yellowbelly.

Water quality seems to affect silver perch populations. There is reason to link their growing scarcity in the Darling with the pesticide and defoliant run-off from the cotton crops that are now leap-frogging down the Darling like agricultural dominoes.

Simple, unsophisticated bait-fishing techniques work fine in the Darling. The most productive and trouble-free rig of all is simply a ball sinker mounted directly atop a Mustad No 540 hook; the one they call the French pattern.

Think live bait—small fish, crayfish and shrimps if you're looking for cod and yellowbelly. In any case, provide movement to the bait with the rod tip. Fish sense those twitches and will come to investigate.

Soft baits like wood grubs and worms and crushed crayfish (peeled tail) send out an odour, which will be picked up by the sensory systems of a fish. Some fish are so highly sensitive in that department that they can detect smells in concentrations as small as one in a million. The copious juices that ooze from a wood grub will bring a cod running.

When using baits which rely on their 'smell' value, think about positioning them so that you're getting some advantage from where the current may take the scent.

Fishing the Darling is much more than throwing a line into the deepest part of the river and hoping.

St Vincent and Spencer Gulfs- Small-Boat Fishing

Shane Mensforth

While South Australia may lack many of the true sport and game fish available along the continent's north, east and west coasts, it does provide the small-boat operator with a feast of top-class table species. St Vincent and Spencer gulfs are relatively shallow waterways and, as such, are perfect habitats for whiting, garfish, snapper, snook and small to medium-sized salmon. These species are all quite plentiful and within range of the owners of boats of 5 metres and under.

The King George whiting is South Australia's most important commercial and recreational fish. Its habitat ranges from shallow inshore reefs in less than 10 metres of water, to offshore grounds in depths of up to 30 metres. Although the St Vincent Gulf whiting fishery is still quite productive, Spencer Gulf seems to yield the best catches and the largest fish. This stems from the smaller degree of angling pressure placed on Spencer Gulf, which is well away from Adelaide and other large centres of population.

Many thousands of South Australian recreational fishers specialise in whiting exclusively. It's a fun fish to catch and without peer on the plate, so there is little wonder that it is the number one target species. Largely because of the whiting's enormous popularity with the small-boat brigade, it enjoys one of the best managed and maintained fisheries in the country. The local Department of Fisheries monitors whiting stocks very closely through well established tagging programs, and fairly tight bag limits (30 fish per person per day) ensure that the amateur effort doesn't make too large a dent in overall numbers.

Catching the King George whiting isn't all that difficult for the small-boat angler. Most inshore reefs around both gulfs hold reasonable numbers of fish, particularly in the winter months, and with the use of a good-quality echo sounder, it becomes simply a matter of probing the reefs until a school is located. Berley is also important, and crushed cockles (pipis) or squid will bring whiting to the baits in short order. Again pipis and squid are good baits, but marine worms, mussels and razor fish are almost equally effective.

Out in the deep-water areas, where the average size of King George whiting is far larger, techniques vary slightly. Heavier sinkers must be used and distributing berley effectively is a little more difficult. Specially designed 'berley bombs' are brought into play on the deep-water grounds and these get the berley down near the bottom before it's released, so that it can be concentrated in a given area and hold the fish close to the boat.

Some of the better locations around the gulfs for the whiting fisher include Port Hughes, Foul Bay, Port Victoria, Hardwicke Bay, Ardrossan and Port Broughton. Off metropolitan Adelaide, the large volume of boat traffic ensures that the fishing won't be as good as in the lighter-fished country areas, but there is still some good whiting action to be had around the capital for the angler prepared to put up with a bit of competition and stick at the task.

Big snapper are the fish for which South Australia has earned a boasting-sized reputation via the national angling media. And indeed there can be no question that there are more monster reds in the two gulfs than can be found in any other location in the country. It is also true, however, that only relatively few South Australian small-boat fishermen catch good snapper all of the time. Snapper fishing down this way is very much an activity which has to be worked at constantly to achieve a high level of success. Once again, both gulfs hold substantial snapper populations, but Spencer Gulf is the more reliable producer.

The snapper inhabit offshore reefs but, like the whiting, are often found inshore and even well up inside the estuaries. They have a particular affinity for the shipping channels which lead into the various ports and harbours. The channels at Whyalla, Wallaroo, Port Pirie and metropolitan Outer Harbour are all top locations for 10-kilo plus reds.

As most of the snapper are fished for in water shallower than 20 metres, light line and small sinkers can be used in the majority of locations. The standard snapper outfit used by the small-boat fisherman consists of a fast-action jig-stick style rod, with either a baitcaster or threadline reel. Ten-kilo line is the norm, with many snapper chasers now going a little lighter in response to the sportfishing boom. Western Australian pilchards are one of the most popular baits, but any fish fillets, squid or crustacea will normally bring results. As most of the snapper fishos seek only big fish exclusively, 6/0 hooks (usually Mustad suicides) are the popular size and these are tied on a metre or so of 22-kilo nylon. A running sinker rig is generally preferred.

Snook are another of the South Australian boaters' favoured species. These are very closely related to the toothy barracuda of tropical climes, and are a great table variety. Trolling small metal lures or strip baits presented on ganged hooks produces the best bags of snook, and shallow water over weed beds appears to be the optimum situation in which to locate them.

Paravanes are popular trolling aids in the area, and these are commonly connected to a hand spool holding a hundred metres or so of thick nylon. The secret when snooking seems to be getting the lure or bait down as close to the weed beds as possible, and the locally produced Blue Line paravane does that job admirably. Once a patch of snook is located, they are trolled in anti-clockwise direction and it's not uncommon to pull two to three dozen fish in a short session.

Surface feeders, like garfish and tommy ruffs, are also plentiful in both gulfs. These two varieties are commonly found together and are easy to berley up in good numbers. Light tackle and a floating rig are the way to go for a feed of tommies and gar, and gentles (blowfly maggots) are by far the best bait. Garfish can also be nabbed at night time with the aid of a powerful spotlight, and this is a very popular occupation in shallow water on still summer evenings.

Since the boom in popularity of squid as table fare, thousands of South Australians have recently armed themselves with jags and spend many hours probing the inshore weed beds of both gulfs. Yo-zuri-style squid jags, although horrendously expensive, are clearly the most effective tools for gulf squidding.

A real shot in the arm for small-boat fishers has been the initiation of a program by the Department of Fisheries to install a large number of fish aggregating devices (FADs) in both gulfs. Artificial reefs have been part of the South Australian scene for some time, but this new program has increased the number of FADs dramatically. Tetrahedral-shaped bundles of tyres, ballasted with concrete, have been put down in their hundreds offshore from such centres as Whyalla, Port Augusta and Port Pirie, and these are particularly effective aggregators of whiting and snapper. Sunken derelict barges in deep-water areas are also very productive artificial 'reefs' and these occur offshore from Yorke Peninsula and metropolitan Glenelg.

Although gulf waters are immune from the swells of the Southern Ocean, they act like giant funnels with winds from the south or south-west.

A nasty short chop builds up in double quick time when the wind gets up, which makes for extremely uncomfortable fishing conditions. During the summer months, the afternoon sea breeze may reach 25 to 30 knots – something akin to the West's Fremantle Doctor – and this makes life a real hassle for the operators of small boats.

Gulf tides are also a bit of a problem on occasions. The 'dodge' tide phenomenon is unique to just a handful of locations worldwide, and South Australia is part of the élite group to be burdened with it. During each fortnightly tide cycle, the amount of movement between high and low water gradually diminishes until there is little, if any, water exchange at all. The dodge situation lasts for about 24 hours, until the water begins to move again and the tides slowly build toward the middle of the cycle. When the dodge prevails, most school fish like snapper and whiting become lethargic and less inclined to feed, so it is generally regarded as a poor time to go fishing.

Launch and retrieve facilities around both gulfs generally leave quite a bit to be desired. Most of the larger centres aren't all that badly off, but once you get to some of the small, yet very productive resorts like Port Hughes, Port Clinton and Marion Bay, putting a boat in becomes a definite problem, and one which must be rectified by the appropriate authorities as soon as possible.

St Vincent and Spencer gulfs are unique

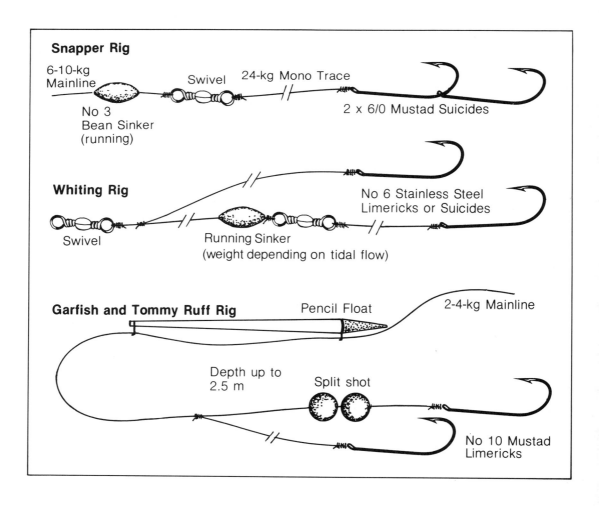

waterways, which can prove extremely productive for small-boat fishers. They appear to be coping with much increased angling pressure very well and, if managed and maintained at current levels, should continue to provide excellent catches for years to come.

FISHING ALONG THE BIGHT

Shane Mensforth

The seashores along the Great Australian Bight are among the continent's most spectacular expanses of coastline. Countless unspoiled surf beaches and rocky headlands, spread over almost 2000 kilometres, provide a smorgasbord of angling locations which cater for scores of local and visiting fishers each year.

The list of species available along the Bight for the shore-based angler is a lengthy one, although salmon and mulloway are undoubtedly the two most popular targets. The owners of four-wheel-drives will have a definite advantage as far as beach fishing is concerned, particularly in the areas west of Ceduna. Several productive beaches are accessible to conventional vehicles, but the general trend is that the more remote and unfished an area is, the better the chances will be of scoring an outstanding catch.

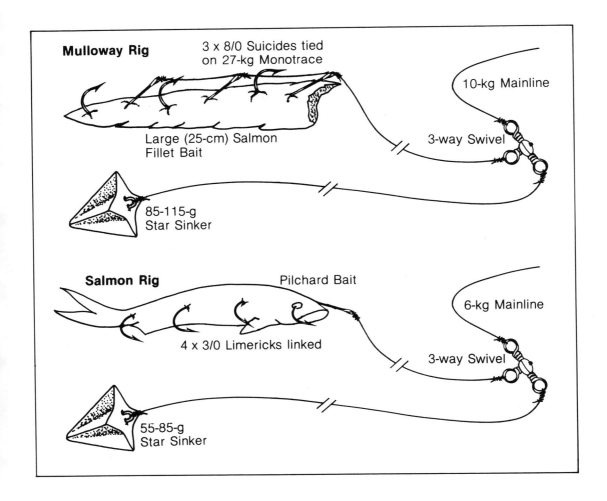

Salmon are present on virtually all beaches from Port Lincoln to the Western Australian border, and while they can sometimes be a nuisance to the serious mulloway specialist, they are almost invariably big and great sport in the surf. Convention Beach, Lock's Well, Sheringa, Scotts Bay and Talia are just a few of the renowned producers of salmon of up to and beyond 5 kilos. Both bait and lure fishing from the beaches will yield plenty of fine salmon, as well as the odd outsized tailor.

Mulloway fishing appears to be at its best from Streaky Bay westward, with the beaches beyond Ceduna by far the most consistent producers of big jew. Whaler sharks are also ever present along these beaches, and many a mulloway specialist has cursed the toothed villain which has mutilated his prize jew in the last line of breakers. Standard surf fishing equipment — usually a sidecast or overhead outfit — is well suited to Bight mulloway fishing, and large salmon fillets appear to be the number one bait.

Snapper, blue groper and assorted rock species are to be found around most of the headlands separating major beaches. Fowlers Headland, at the eastern end of Scotts Bay, is a top producer of reds and there are often yellowtail kings in the area as well. All of these rocky headlands are exposed to the swells of the Bight, however, and should only be fished in calm conditions. Rock fishing commonsense is definitely a high priority when tackling the west coast.

For those perhaps a little less ambitious than the surf and rock specialists, there are several productive jetties situated within sheltered bays, and these are well worth investigating. Tommy ruffs, snook, garfish and squid make up the bulk of the jetty catch, and the piers at Elliston, Streaky Bay, Thevenard, Ceduna and Fowlers Bay are perhaps the pick of the bunch.

As is the case with many other South Australian angling locations, fishing the Bight is extremely dependent upon weather conditions. Most of the beaches and headlands are directly exposed to the wrath of the Southern Ocean and wipe out in no uncertain manner during a blow from the south or west. Summer sea 'breezes' often make fishing difficult in the afternoons and early evenings, and winter gales have predictable effects. The weather begins to stabilize somewhat in March and April, however, and this is probably the optimum time to head for the Great Australian Bight.

ADELAIDE TO VICTORIAN BORDER- ROCK AND BEACH
Shane Mensforth

South Australia's south and south-east coasts comprise turbulent surf beaches, spectacular cliffs and headlands, and quiet sheltered bays. Although most of these areas are heavily fished, they continue to yield worthwhile catches for persistent anglers.

From Adelaide to Cape Jervis, at the tip of Fleurieu Peninsula, the coast is protected from Southern Ocean swells and the beaches are shallow and calm. Mullet, yellowfin whiting and the odd mulloway are the main catch here. The rock platforms between Myponga and Rapid Bay all produce a variety of species, including silver drummer, squid, snook, tommy ruffs, garfish, leatherjackets and the occasional salmon. While the fishing on the near-south coast may not be spectacular, it will usually produce a good mixed bag of table species.

From Cape Jervis eastward, the influence of the Southern Ocean is evident in coastal terrain. A series of sheer cliffs, deeply eroded by wind and wave, prevents access for several kilometres. Nearer to Victor Harbour, these cliffs are broken by Parsons and Waitpinga beaches — two of the best-known and widely fished surf beaches in the State.

Both Parsons and Waitpinga are usually well endowed with inshore gutters. Salmon, mullet, tailor and mulloway are taken from both beaches, but increased fishing pressure has caused them to be a little less predictable in recent times. Lure fishing is extremely popular here and most of the occasional large tailor caught in the area fall to metal spinners. There are nearly always some salmon to be found on either beach, but the average size is nowhere near what it used to be. Back in the seventies, 3- and 4-kilo salmon were common at Waitpinga, but specimens of 1 kilo or less appear to be the norm these days.

Mulloway of mixed sizes are taken spasmodically by salmon fishers, but some really big fellows (30 kilos and upwards) are caught by those prepared to put in long sessions after dark. Squid heads and large slabs of salmon are the baits which account for most of Waitpinga's XOS jew.

The massive headland which divides Parsons and Waitpinga beaches is also a great spot to try when the swell is down. Caution should be exercised when fishing the rocks here, however, as several anglers have been swept to their deaths while bobby-corking from the exposed platforms.

East of Victor Harbour, the coastal terrain flattens out in a series of long, well-formed beaches. The Murray River ends its lengthy journey seaward near Goolwa, and the area adjacent to the river mouth is one of the most famous mulloway hotspots in Australia. Some truly massive jew have been pulled from the surf directly outside the Murray mouth, and most of these are taken on lures after dark. Top lures for this location include the Gardie, Juro Shiner, Stingsilda and the large rubber tails such as Mr Twisters and Scroungers.

The expanse of surf beach which runs southeast from the mouth of the Murray is a four-wheel-driver's paradise. Access to this beach can be gained via several tracks which cross the Coorong. The Forty-two Mile, Tea Tree and the Granites are three of the more popular entrance routes. Once again, salmon and mulloway are the major target species here, with mullet and gummy sharks an added bonus.

Restrictions apply to beach driving in this area and overnight campers must obtain a permit from the Department of Parks and Wildlife before contemplating an extended stay. But the rewards for persistence along this stretch of beach can be tremendous. The roadhouse at Salt Creek, near the Forty-two Mile Crossing, has a display of pictures, which record all of the best jew captured in the general area. If venturing near Salt Creek, it's worth while calling in at this roadhouse for some inspiration!

Low rock and more surf beach continue southeastward around the shores of Lacepede Bay. The cliffs between Robe and Beachport aren't easily fished, and are exposed to some of the south-east coast's most unpredictable weather. Salmon, sweep and various rock varieties are common catches in this area, but caution is a top priority when tackling the rocks here.

Just over the Victorian border, the Glenelg River empties into the Southern Ocean and the river mouth and adjacent estuary provide excellent fishing. Bream, mulloway, salmon trout and mullet are the most commonly caught species around the Glenelg, and this is an extremely popular holiday venue with South Australians and Victorians alike.

As beach and rock fishing predominate along the State's south and south-east coasts, long rods and robust reels are the favoured outfits. Sidecasts, threadlines or overheads mounted on 4-metre surf sticks will do the job admirably, and 10-kilo line is a sensible proposition for most situations. As previously mentioned, a four-wheel-drive vehicle will put the angler within reach of most of the productive locations, but it's possible to walk into some beaches and headlands and still pull good fish.

Western Australian pilchards are the mainstay of the south-east's beach fishers, and salmon, school jew and gummy sharks will respond to these rigged on ganged hooks and placed thoughtfully in deep gutters. If chasing larger

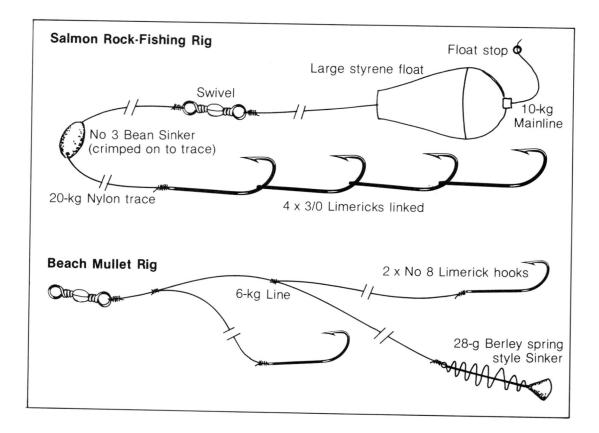

mulloway, whole mullet, salmon fillets, or hefty slabs of fresh squid will keep the pickers at bay. All beaches in this area are home to black stingrays of unnerving proportions, and these can become a real nuisance during an all-night vigil chasing jew.

The weather is a major factor in determining the outcome of a beach- or rock-fishing sortie to the south-east. The Southern Ocean shows no respect whatever for visiting anglers, and it's not uncommon to lose a substantial portion of a fishing excursion in this area because of high winds and rough seas. South Australians are hardened to weather-induced disappointments, which are part and parcel of wetting a line in their State.

TROUT FISHING IN SOUTH AUSTRALIA

Shane Mensforth

Although South Australia is renowned for being the driest State in the world's driest continent, there is some excellent freshwater fishing to be had by those persistent enough to put in the hours and do the necessary research. Both brown and rainbow trout can be found in the streams north and south of Adelaide, as well as some bulky redfin, but you have to be prepared to travel to outlying areas to sample the best fishing.

There is no government-initiated stream-stocking program in operation in South Australia, but there is an enthusiastic bunch of fellows attached to the Fly Fishing Association who regularly seed the rivers. The Fly Fishing Association receives only a minor financial grant to assist its stocking efforts, and without the dedication shown by its members, trout fishing would be non-existent there.

Some of South Australia's very best freshwater angling comes from the area well north of the capital, where the climate suggests that trout fishing shouldn't really be on. The Light, Wakefield and Broughton rivers all run through the State's mid north—a region which experiences hot, dry summers and a relatively low winter rainfall. Both trout varieties seem to thrive here, however, and the three streams mentioned above yield more than their share of the State's top fish each year.

Fishing methods employed on the inland waterways vary from place to place, but spin and bait fishing appear to be the most popular. It seems an anomaly that the fly-fishers put the trout into the rivers, but probably don't take as many out as the lure and yabbie brigade. Popular artificials with the spin anglers include the old favourites, such as Celtas, ABU sonnettes and spoons, but there is a current boom in the usage of small minnow lures. Rapala Mini Fat Raps, CD5s and CD7s are enormously popular, as is the Rebel Crawdad in the smallest size.

For the fly-fisher, the red and black Matuka and the hare's ear nymph stand alone as the most commonly used artificials. Dry-fly fishing is not widely practised, as substantial insect hatches occur infrequently.

Yabbies are far and away the most effective bait for the trout, as they make up the bulk of the diet for all freshwater species. Tiger worms, shrimps and mudeyes are also common offerings and these are generally fished below a quill or bubble float around the snags and weed beds. Bait fishing appears to account for a large percentage of the bigger trout taken each year.

Unlike many of the trout streams popular with anglers in the eastern States, most South Australian inland waters are deep and slow flowing. Stealth and patience are prerequisites for success, but the rewards are often far greater than visiting anglers from interstate may anticipate.

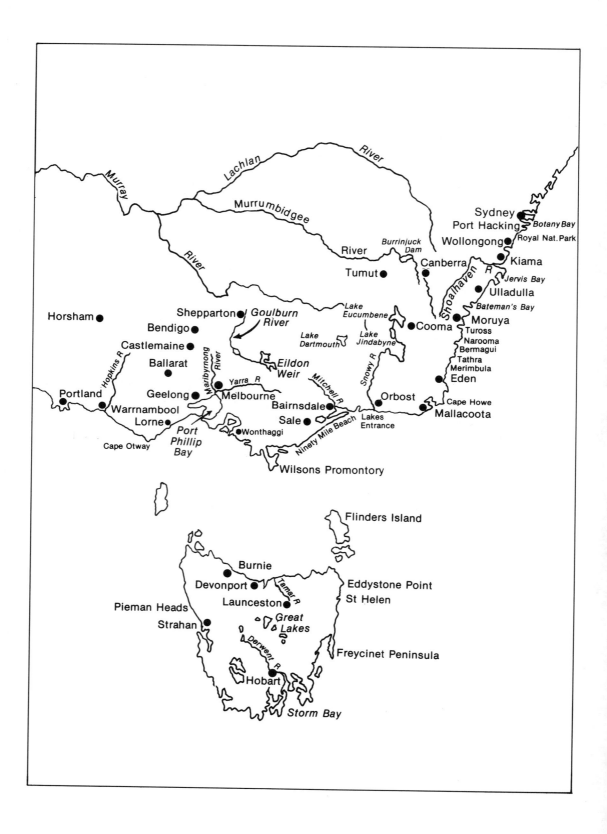

SECTION FOUR

South-Eastern Australia

SYDNEY HARBOUR
David Lockwood

There is no disputing the fact that Sydney Harbour is the birthplace of recreational fishing in Australia. Even now, two centuries since the pioneers first shot a line in its waters, it continues to hold a formidable reputation.

If nothing else, this alone stands as a triumphant reminder that the harbour has endured the ravages of progress and, more importantly, increased fishing pressure from both amateur and professional alike.

All-up, Sydney Harbour is a huge body of water and within it over 50 species of fish are regularly taken by amateur anglers.

Surface fish like tailor, salmon and even small tuna are often taken by lure fishers around the more seaward end; bottom dwellers like flathead, whiting and red bream are a common capture by 'bait soakers'. Bream and luderick are a year-round proposition from along the shorelines, and bigger predators like jewfish and kingfish still make regular showings.

The harbour of Australia's largest city is also the nation's most popular and widely used recreational fishery. Any sunny summer weekend will reveal evidence of this — thousands of hopeful anglers scattered along the shorelines and flotillas of fishing craft scooting about the place.

But even though the harbour has defied the odds to come out still and sustain this recreational fishery, in an opposing sense it also has the uncanny ability to defy many anglers' efforts at catching fish! There are several causes for this, and the necessary 'ground rules' of correct location, bait choice, fishing times and techniques all warrant special attention if you are to be a successful harbour angler.

One thing is certain, no matter what the outcome, Sydney Harbour is the most stunning natural waterway in the world. Just stretching out on a shoreline rock in one of the many hidden bays and watching the day come to a close, is sure to have you coming back for more.

Locations

Choosing the 'right' fishing location is a crucial prerequisite for successful fishing anywhere. In Sydney Harbour, this is doubly so! There are literally hundreds of productive fishing spots in the harbour and to single out a few is almost insulting.

What you'll find common to all 'Sydney's top fishing spots' is that they contain some form of fish-attracting feature. If you're a shore-based angler, then the key words here are habitat and water depth.

Under the banner 'habitat' consider such pointers as available food. Feeding grounds include the more wave-stricken and washy areas around the entrance to the harbour, the more tide-influenced rocky shoreline points running up to both the Spit and Harbour bridges, and many of the protruding points and oyster-lined bays in the upper reaches. Fish-attracting features such as wharfs, piers, rock walls, marinas, and even boat ramps all provide a habitat for fish to feed and seek shelter as well.

Fish such as whiting, flathead and bream which fancy all manner of harbour environments often forage and feed along the sandbanks out from most small beaches and coves found downstream from the bridges, particularly around high tide.

Water depth is also a consideration when eyeing-out a prospective fishing location and is closely related to the time of day you are fishing.

First up, any spot that has deep water close to the shore is favoured, not only because all fish will move to deep water as the day progresses, allowing more productive fishing time, but also these spots are more influenced by tide, making good feeding grounds.

Secondly, deep water close to shore will result in the fish being closer at hand, so lighter tackle can be used and it is also easier to hold the fish in that area (by using berley).

Thus, both boat and shore-based anglers should seek a spot with prominent fish-holding features and relatively deep water close by.

Prime Fishing Times

Things are pretty 'black and white' when it comes to the best, most productive time of the day to fish Sydney Harbour—*when it's at its quietest*.

The twilight zone around dawn or dusk and a couple of hours either side of it are the most active feeding times for all manner of fish in the harbour. This isn't to say you can't strike good fishing through the day though, mid-week especially, but generally you'll find harbour fishing tough going around noon.

The only exception to the rule is during days of really foul weather, when the skies are overcast and pelting down rain. If you can battle the elements, you'll often strike good continuous fishing, even more so when the harbour water is well discoloured from recent heavy rains—an often frenzied feeding time for fish!

Fishing Techniques

Fishing techniques always vary from one angler to the next—it's obvious at any popular Sydney Harbour fishing spot. What many hopefuls don't realise though is that only a small percentage of these anglers are catching quality and quantities of fish.

Invariably, this is a direct result of either 'using' or 'not using' the correct tackle, rigs and bait. There are hundreds of rigs and items of tackle to choose from—thankfully only a handful of these are needed to catch most fish species in Sydney Harbour.

As far as tackle is concerned, a medium-weight rod between 2 and 3 metres in length, coupled with either a medium-sized threadline or Alvey reel capable of holding at least 200 metres of 4- or 5-kilo line is quite adequate. Or if you prefer the simplicity, cheapness and direct feel of a handline, a cork with a couple of hundred metres

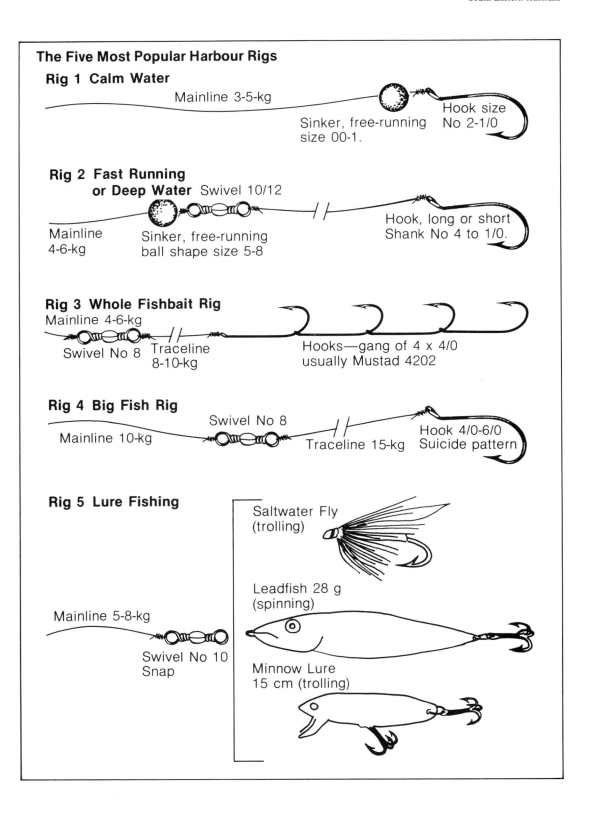

Sydney Harbour Fish Guide

Species	Season	Rig	Bait	Best time of Day
Blackfish	year-round, peak in autumn	Specialist rig consisting of float and 3-metre drop to hook	Green weed either string or cabbage	Daytime, run-in or run-out tide
Bream (silver)	year-round, best in autumn	Rig 1 or 2	bloodworms, prawns, nippers, pilchard, pudding, cheese, etc	dawn or dusk
Crabs (blue swimmer & mud)	summer	Crab traps	whole fish or frames, lamb bone	daytime, high tide and night for mud crabs
Flathead	summer	Rig 2	worms, prawns, fish fillets or Mr Twister lures	falling tide preferably in morning or afternoon
Flounder	"	"	"	"
Garfish	"	Rig 1 with a float and No 10 hook	worm, prawns, or bread	daytime
Hairtail	winter (June/July)	Rig 3 or 4	live fish or whole pilchard	moonlit nights
Jewfish	summer	Rig 2 or 4	worms, prawn, whole live or dead fish	night and evening/early morning
John Dory	winter	Rig 4	small live fish (yellowtail, tailor, etc)	daytime
Kingfish	year-round	Rig 3, 4, or 5	live small fish, whole pilchards or lures	daytime. Best in early morning/afternoon
Leatherjacket	year-round	Rig 1 or 2 with small No 8 hook	prawn, worms or mussels	daytime
Mullet	year-round	Rig 1 with small No 10 hook	bread, prawn or worm	daytime
Prawns	summer (Christmas)	Prawn nets and gas lights	N/A	night, no moon, run-out tide
Rays	summer	Rig 2 with No 3/0 hook	prawn, whole or chunks of fish	day and night. High tide
Red Bream	summer	Rig 2	worms, prawn, tuna, pilchards, or nippers	early morning best
Salmon	winter	Rig 3 or 5	lures or whole pilchards slow spun	daytime early morning or evening
Shark	summer (Christmas)	Rig 4 with wire tip	whole live mullet, tailor or yellowtail	early morning or night at high tide

Sydney Harbour Fish Guide

Species	Season	Rig	Bait	Best time of Day
Tailor	year-round (Easter and Christmas)	Rig 3, 4, or 5	lures, live fish or whole fish bait, eg, pilchards	early morning, afternoon into night
Trevally	winter	Rig 1, 2 or 3	fish bait, worms, nippers & prawn	early morning, night
Tuna	summer	Rig 5	lures either spun or trolled	early morning best
Whiting	summer	Rig 1 or 2 with No 8 hook	worms, pipis, nippers or prawn	Rising tide, night or day.

of similar breaking-strain line will very pleasantly suffice.

A secondary outfit, either rod'n'reel or handline fitted with heavier line, say around 10 to 15 kilos, can also be useful for tossing out a live fish, or big slab of fish, for jewfish, tailor, kingfish, big flathead and other predators.

In all cases, make sure you use a supple line from a reputable stable — one that is not likely to tangle.

For terminal tackle all you really need is a small tackle box containing about four different hook sizes and styles, a similar selection of sinkers and a few packets of brass swivels — a cost-effective outlay of around five dollars.

Your range of hooks should include some small size 10s for catching bait and other small-mouthed fish, some size 6s for whiting, blackfish, leatherjackets, etc, some 1/0s for bream, flathead, trevally and the like, and some larger 4/0 to 6/0s if you intend to use heavy gear.

Sinkers should be used only when necessary. If you are fishing a quiet bay or harbour spot and can cast the required 12 metres or so, you'll catch far more fickle harbour fish than by using a big chunk of lead.

But this isn't always possible due to wind or strong tidal flow, so purchase a few size 0 ball sinkers, a few No 2s, a few No 4s and a couple of 28- to 40-gram bean sinkers to cover most conditions. Swivels should be kept as small as possible — sizes 10 or 12 are fine. A few floats if you intend chasing blackfish, a knife, a torch, a rainjacket, a keeper net or other device to keep your catch fresh, a landing net, and adequate food and drink in the ubiquitous esky will have you well set up to fish Sydney Harbour and its environs.

Bait Choice

Another important prerequisite to successful harbour angling — and one which sets many good anglers apart from the 'hopefuls' — is the use of good bait.

It is hard to surpass the live varieties for most applications or at least the very freshest bait you can purchase. Live bloodworms, pink nippers, beachworms and fresh harbour prawns are undoubtedly the best baits. They are available from most good tackle stores or bait suppliers in the metropolitan area.

The only exception here is after a big fresh when the harbour estuary is discoloured; it is then that the use of other baits can mean better catches. Baits of strip steak, mullet gut, chicken livers and gut, pudding (a mixture of flour, cheese and strong-smelling sausage) and even cubes of cheese all produce good results, especially on the prolific harbour bream.

Alternatives to these baits include pilchards, whitebait, crabs, tuna cubes, mullet strips and plain old bread, but these are second rate compared to the live varieties. And as a closing note, it is also beneficial to use healthy supplies of berley, not only to attract the fish, but also to keep them in the one area, allowing longer productive fishing time.

Hazards, and Safety Measures

Even though Sydney Harbour is regarded as one of the nation's safest fishing frontiers, there is danger for the inexperienced 'boatie' and to a lesser degree, for the shore-based angler.

Boat-going anglers should exercise particular caution around the shipping channels throughout Port Jackson which are clearly marked by buoys and are also prohibited anchoring zones; anywhere along the ferry and hydrofoil routes; near the Sow and Pigs Reef situated in the main channel between Watson's Bay and Obelisk Beach (marked by buoys); and anywhere around the seaward end of the harbour during a decent ground swell.

Shore-based anglers really only need exercise commonsense in regards to correct footwear. Good fitting sandshoes are recommended when fishing the upper reaches of the harbour, an area often plagued by oyster-encrusted rocks. Sandshoes or rock plates are best if fishing the more exposed rock spots near the Heads. All anglers should be extra cautious during heavy seas and swell as many of the fishing spots in the lower reaches are surprisingly exposed, potential death traps for the unwary.

BOTANY BAY
Dick Lewers

Covering an area of more than 100 square kilometres, Botany Bay, New South Wales, lies approximately 10 kilometres to the south of Sydney. An important recreational fishing ground for thousands of amateur anglers, its waters also support a commercial fishery of some 134 licensed fishers, about a third of whom actively fish at any one time. Two rivers, Georges River and Cooks River, feed into the bay, the larger—Georges—being more important in terms of recreational fishing.

Popular fish species to be found include bream, flathead, tailor, kingfish, sand whiting, mulloway, flounder, luderick, sea mullet, trevally, leatherjacket, and garfish. Snapper, Australian salmon, bonito, rock blackfish, and blue groper, can be caught from the ocean rocks to the north and south of the entrance. Blue swimmer crabs, the occasional mud crab, and prawns, can also be taken within the bay's confines.

While most fishing is carried out from a boat, there are plenty of breakwalls and beaches around the bay's perimeter to satisfy the land-based angler. Breakwalls should be approached with caution, however, for their construction is rugged and a fall could incapacitate and make rescue difficult.

Tackle for the boat fisher should consist of either (or both) a 10-kilo handline, or a 2-metre hollowglass or graphite-composite spinning rod and a threadline reel with a spool capacity of at least 200 metres of 7-kilo nylon line. Small to medium sidecast reels are also popular.

Hook sizes depend on the species angled for: bream, No 1; flathead, No 3/0-5/0; flounder, No 6; Garfish, No 12; Kingfish, No 3/0-5/0; leatherjacket, No 10-12 long shank; luderick, No 8-12; mullet, No 12; mulloway, No 5/0-7/0; tailor, No 3/0 (ganged 4/0 or 5/0); trevally, No 2; and whiting, No 4-6.

Wire traces are needed for tailor, but are not necessary when using ganged hooks. Sinker sizes are best kept as small as will allow the bait to hold the bottom in the different tidal currents. In areas where the tidal or river current is minimal, no sinker is preferred, especially when fishing for bream. A landing net with a generous mouth, eg 45-centimetre diameter, and a gaff with a metre-long handle, are other important accessories.

The best baits for the above species are:

Bream: live saltwater yabbies, bloodworms, fresh prawns (Sydney Harbour prawns are best if available), fillets of mullet, mullet gut

Flathead: fresh prawns, yabbies, whitebait, blue pilchards, poddy mullet

Mulloway: squid, king prawns, blue pilchards, fillets of mullet, bloodworms, octopus tentacle

Tailor: ganged hooks with blue pilchard or garfish

Trevally: prawns, yabbies

Leatherjacket: prawns, squid flesh

Whiting and flounder: bloodworms, sandworms, yabbies

Luderick: green weed

Kingfish: fresh squid, blue pilchards, yellowtail

Mullet: dough, pieces of fresh prawn

Garfish: pieces of prawn, fish and squid flesh

Generally, the best time of the year to fish the bay is from October through until June, though there can be excellent fishing for tailor, bream, and flathead during the winter months. Mulloway favour October through to February, and kingfish are best sought during November and December. Flathead produce best from November to May.

Boat fishers will find that drifting is to be preferred for flathead and flounder. Tailor can be taken during a drift, but are best fished for using blue pilchards on ganged hooks trolled slowly behind a boat or cast to a feeding school. Bream are common near breakwalls and over reefs, eg, Watts Reef, and along the groynes that reach out into the bay along the Kurnell side. They are best fished for at night.

Watts Reef which is a shallow reefy area lying about 800 metres to a kilometre east of the oil wharf at Kurnell, is an excellent bream area that must be fished at night on a rising tide for best results. It can only be reached by boat.

Land-based fishers can successfully fish Lady Robinsons Beach for flathead, whiting and tailor, and the Cooks River breakwall for bream and trevally. School mulloway are also taken from this wall, especially during October to January following heavy rain. The breakwall on the northern side of the airport runway is a good spot for luderick, and chopper tailor often school in the area.

On the north side of the bay in the Port Botany area, the breakwalls fish well for luderick, bream, school mulloway, tailor, and trevally. Further to the east, Bare Island is a popular land-based spot for luderick, and the capture of snapper, trevally, and teraglin is not uncommon. On the other side of the bay, along the southern shore at Sutherland Point, luderick can be taken from the rocks.

Spinning from any of the beaches for flathead and tailor is not a waste of time. Lures such as the Wonder Wobbler, ABU Toby, Flopy, Mr Twister, and Vibrotail are proven takers of these species, while the Flopy can attract bream as well. Slow trolling these lures behind a boat is a popular method of fishing for tailor.

Crabbing and Prawning

At certain times of the year, Botany Bay abounds in blue swimmer crabs, prawns and, to a much lesser extent, mud crabs. The best months in which to catch blue swimmer crabs are from October to April, and the most popular method used is the setting of a hoop net in the shape of a witch's hat. Up to five nets are allowed per person, and the user's name and address must be prominently displayed on a tag attached to the net.

The taking of prawns is subject to certain regulations governing the type and size of nets used. Full details can be obtained from the Division of Fisheries, PO Box K220, Haymarket, New South Wales 2000.

Because laws can change from time to time, it is advisable to check, with the local Fisheries

Inspector, the location of any waters closed to prawning and crabbing.

Caution

Boat fishers should be aware of the bombora which is located some 400 metres south of Bare Island. In calm conditions it can be safely fished, but rising seas can render it extremely dangerous. It should be identified from your marine chart before venturing into the area, and approached with caution at all times.

SYDNEY ROCK AND BEACH

David Harrigan

Sydney anglers flock to the many headlands and beaches in the metropolitan area between Barrenjoey and the Royal National Park. And in spite of the population pressure, serious anglers still enjoy some good sport there.

Sydney is noted more for its rock fishing than its beach fishing. Much of its coastline is dominated by headlands with fishable platforms, but its beaches are short and steep. Nevertheless they too can produce fish for the skilled angler.

The Headlands

Sydney rock-fishing areas fall into two broad patterns:
1. Tall, sheer cliffs with no fishing platforms below them, for example, the cliffs of the eastern suburbs around Dover Heights and parts of the Kurnell Peninsula. Fishing in such places is done from the very tops of the cliffs.
2. Wave-washed platforms, above the water-line but frequently washed by swells, creating washes and drifts. Wave-washed platforms are found on all major headlands; Whale Beach, North Head, Bondi, the Malabar-Cape Banks stretch and many parts of the Royal National Park are well known. This type of platform typifies Sydney rock fishing.

Sydney Rock Species

The wave-washed platforms support good numbers of luderick (blackfish) feeding on the lush growth of green weed and sea cabbage. Probably the most popular Sydney rock fish, the luderick is caught year round, reaching a peak from April to September.

A fine sporting fish, the Sydney rock luderick averages between a half a kilo and one and a half kilos. It is a specialist's fish; hundreds fish for nothing else. They fish the washes and drifts using long, soft rods, centrepin reels and line in the 3- to 4-kilo class, with a bait of green weed or cabbage suspended under a float (see diagram of luderick rig).

Luderick can be caught throughout the day, especially when the water is vigorous, but mid-afternoon onwards, when the sun goes behind the cliffs, is the best time.

The same platforms also harbour the rock blackfish, alias black drummer or 'pig'. Sydney has many famous drummer grounds and the largest officially recorded, 9 kilos, was taken at Jibbon.

Largely vegetarian, but also feeding on shellfish and crustaceans, drummer up to 4 kilos are still common. They seldom stray far from weed growths and cunjevoi beds. The prime drummer season is from about April to October.

Drummer specialists seek this immensely powerful fish with heavy fibreglass rods and large sidecast reels loaded with line from 9 to 15 kilos and strong hooks in sizes 1/0 to 2/0. Baits include cunjevoi, prawns, crabs, bread and clumps of sea cabbage. Floating or lightly weighted baits are favoured (see diagram of drummer rig) and berleying with bread enhances results.

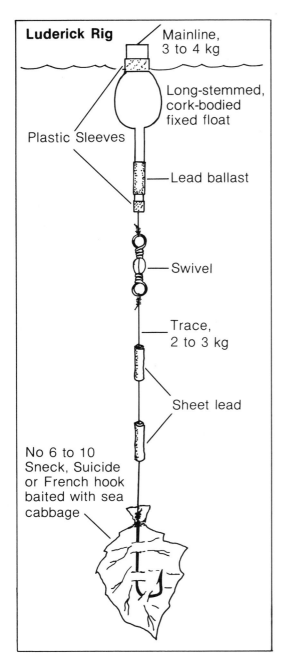

A typical Sydney luderick rig. Floats vary greatly in size and buoyancy depending on water conditions. The float is fixed at depths from 1 to 3.5 metres, depending on depth of water fished, to put the bait just above the bottom or at mid-water. The lighter trace is used to facilitate break-offs in the event of snagging.

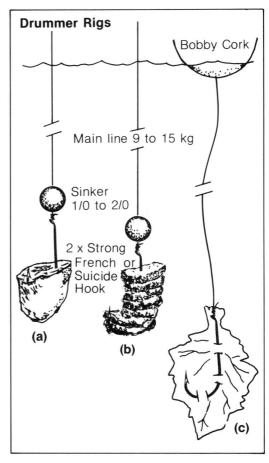

Typical drummer rigs. As bait, cunjevoi is used in (a) and bread crusts in (b) and small ball or bug sinker rests on the hook; just enough weight to allow the bait to sink slowly. Anchoring baits on the bottom is much less successful. Rig (c) shows a large clump of sea cabbage suspended under a bobby cork, another proven drummer taker.

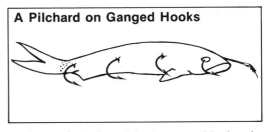

A Western Australian pilchard on ganged hooks takes tailor and salmon and many other species off the rocks and beaches of Sydney.

Blue groper have returned to Sydney in good numbers, with fish to 10 kilos a possibility. Groper are found in close to the platforms, searching for red crabs — by far the best groper bait. There are groper on almost all Sydney headlands with the northern suburbs rocks and the Royal National Park noted producers.

Heavy tackle is required to stop these powerhouse fish, with specialists using line of 10 kilos to 30 kilos or more. A bag limit of two groper per angler per day applies in New South Wales and taking groper by spear is prohibited.

Most Sydney headlands produce bream, which seek out crabs, shellfish, mussels and small baitfish around the ledges, cunjevoi beds and washes.

Sydney bream fishermen use floating or lightly weighted baits in the close washes, or throw out wide onto the sand. Standard bream baits such as prawns, bloodworms and yabbies are successful, but red crabs and Western Australian pilchards are most favoured.

Bream are a year-round fish, but late summer and autumn are probably the best seasons. Fishing is best at dawn or dusk and some big catches are taken through the night.

From April to September, anglers casting pilchards on ganged hooks or artificial lures, seek tailor off the rocks at dawn and dusk. Most headlands have recognised tailor spots, with Barrenjoey, Whale Beach and the Malabar-Cape Banks stretch being noted producers of tailor in the 1-2-kilo class. The same tactics can produce Australian salmon of good size.

Trevally invade the headlands in big numbers from April to September and any platform fronting reasonably deep water can produce them, especially if berleyed. They take many

Baiting with red crab, as practised by bream and groper anglers.

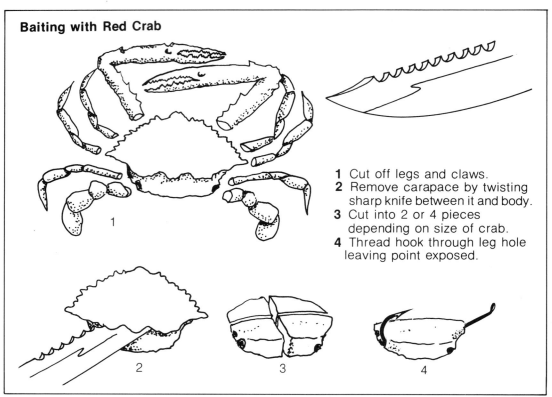

Baiting with Red Crab

1. Cut off legs and claws.
2. Remove carapace by twisting sharp knife between it and body.
3. Cut into 2 or 4 pieces depending on size of crab.
4. Thread hook through leg hole leaving point exposed.

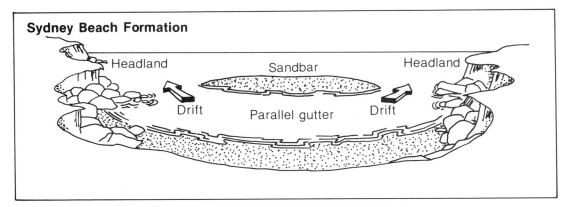

A typical short Sydney beach formation. The small parallel gutter is a tailor indicator, and the gutters next to the headland are worth trying for bream.

baits with prawns, yabbies and bloodworms the best. Sydney trevally usually run in the half- to 2-kilo range, but they provide exciting sport and will often take small lures.

A few Sydney headlands display exceptionally deep water in close, where land-based gamefishing is practised. Specialists spin or live bait for pelagics such as longtail, yellowfin and mackerel tuna, bonito and kingfish. It was at Whale Beach that this branch of the sport took off in the 1960s. Other spots which occasionally produce pelagics include Ben Buckler and Curracurang in the Royal National Park.

The Beaches

The shortness and steepness of Sydney's beaches, and consequent infertility, limit their fishing potential. The longer ones, the Narrabeen-Collaroy stretch, and Wanda-Cronulla, are the most consistent for surf fishing. On the shorter beaches, the almost permanent gutters at each end, where the beach meets the headland, are the most likely spots.

Sydney Beach Species

In summer, all beaches have some whiting, but Narrabeen and Wanda are the most consistent. They will take beachworms, pipis, yabbies and prawns, but bloodworms are the best by far. Sydney whiting are shy, and light tackle should be used. Beach crowds make dawn and dusk fishing almost mandatory.

Tailor run on Sydney's beaches from about March to September, taking whole pilchards cast into the surf at dawn or dusk. The best formation for tailor is a gutter running parallel to the shore with a good covering of white water from the outer sandbank. Flathead, Australian salmon and bream are often taken the same way.

Mulloway can be caught after dark during summer and autumn, but it is a waiting game. The northern beaches offer better prospects than those south of the harbour, and those near lagoon entrances, such as Narrabeen and Long Reef are most favoured. Most mulloway are school size, but the occasional big fish falls to live baits and fresh slabs of tailor cast into the deeper holes.

Tides, Wind and Weather

The prevailing summer wind in Sydney is the north-easterly which can reach 25 knots or more in the afternoons, and produce very bumpy, sloppy surface conditions. Few Sydney rock-fishing spots are protected from it and it can create difficult sideways drift on the beaches. Summer also produces strong southerly busters, usually of short duration, and occasional big ground swells from distant cyclones.

In winter, the westerly wind prevails, initially creating smooth, clear conditions in close. But after a couple of days it produces a condition known as 'rollback', with a violent swell. Winter also produces many strong southerly storms, the swell from which can wipe out rock fishing.

Rock and beach fishers dislike the calm, gin-clear water conditions common in winter, preferring a swell sufficient to create some movement. In dead flat conditions, it is especially important to fish when the light is off the water.

Generally, rock fishers prefer the rising tide in shallow areas and the falling tide in the deeper spots, but there is no hard and fast rule. Every spot has its own conventions. Beach anglers prefer the last half of the rising tide.

Hazards

Rock fishing has claimed many lives in the Sydney area, mostly through anglers being washed in by big swells. Sydney's wave-washed platforms are highly susceptible to such occurrences, and demand strict adherence to the rules of safe rock fishing.

Some spots such as Bluefish Point and Yellow Rock at Malabar have appalling records, but any platform holds danger for the unwary. The danger of the rollback is again emphasised.

Some spots require climbs down vertical cliffs and anglers are advised to avoid these areas unless they are competent climbers and are with someone who has done it before. They should be wary of ropes, pegs and ladders others have put there. Many are old and rotten.

The best insurance for the new-chum Sydney rock fisher is to join one of the many Sydney fishing clubs which have experienced rock-hoppers in their ranks, before venturing onto the rocks.

THE ILLAWARRA TO THE VICTORIAN BORDER

Richard Allan

This hop, skip and jump guide to a majestic stretch of Australia's eastern seaboard begins in New South Wales, at Bald Hill on the southern boundary of the Royal National Park, the beginning of the Illawarra escarpment, and ends at Disaster Bay almost at the Victorian border.

Bald Hill is historically famous for the experiments conducted there with engines and box kites by Lawrence Hargreaves whose pioneering work played a vital part in the development of the aeroplane. It is appropriate that Bald Hill is now one of the best-known and widely used jumping-off points for dare-devil hang-gliders who soar over spectacular ocean and bush scenery.

Within this approximate 600 kilometres there are numerous locations which offer great fishing, areas which remain almost as untouched as they were when the continent was formed, and scenery to enjoy if the fish are not cooperative.

There are countless beaches and headlands and rock platforms. In contrast to those of the north coast, the beaches, with one or two exceptions, are smaller and deeper (some just tiny patches of sand cuddled by headlands and cliffs). The rock areas range from flat platforms to sloping faces that dip into deep water and ledges on cliffs, many of which are reached by ropes or difficult tracks.

Within the environs of Wollongong, the third largest city in New South Wales, there are beaches from Stanwell Park in the north to Windang in the south; and between the many beaches are rock fishing areas to cater for novice or competent fishers. At Belambi, Wollongong Harbour and Port Kembla Harbour there are breakwaters and wharves.

From Wollongong the Princes Highway passes through renowned fishing towns: Kiama, Ulladulla, Bateman's Bay, Moruya, Narooma, Merimbula-Pambula and Eden are well known. Others, equally famous, such as Shellharbour, Gerroa, Gerringong, Greenwell Point, Huskisson, Jervis Bay, Sussex Inlet, Bermagui, Tathra, Boydtown and Womboyn are a few kilometres' diversion from the highway.

With the help of a map—most of those prepared for specific regional areas are excellent—it is easy to find Bass Point, Culburra, Currarong, Cape St George, Berrara, Mollymook, Tabourie Point, Bawley Point, Pretty Beach, Durras Lake, Long Beach, Malua Bay, Broulee, Moruya Heads, Congo, Tuross Heads, Potato Point, Cuttagee, Bournda Beach, Tura Beach, Jews Head and Green Cape, and as many others.

All are easily reached and most of them offer both beach and rock fishing, if not adjacent, then within reasonable distances. Very often, and especially during the holiday periods, many of these places usually are less crowded than the main towns.

For the visitor to the Illawarra—South Coast, the most difficult decision is not which fish to seek but which spot to fish. Another decision, which requires more willpower, is to control the sudden impetuosness and enthusiasm to get a line in the water off some enticing rock platform. It must be emphasised that no rock location should be fished until at least a quarter of an hour has been spent watching the wave action, ensuring there is a safe approach and an escape route. If you are alone—or without the right footwear and gear—it is wiser to not fish.

However, the corner of many beaches near such platforms or headlands can be as productive as the water out the front of them.

A distinct advantage of this coastline is that if the wind or bumpy seas create uncomfortable or hazardous fishing conditions, there are estuaries or lakes within short distances where it might be possible to fish—and often successfully—without enduring the discomforts of a wind-whipped beach or being soaked by spray from breaking seas.

In many of the centres there are also piers and wharves and breakwaters where the less energetic can fish, or youngsters can be introduced to the joy of the recreation, with the chance of catching a worthy saltwater species.

The Fish and the Most Likely Times

Whatever is said about fish, predicting their exact behaviour is the most difficult—whether it is when they should bite, or the preferred bait. Because of this unpredictable factor, anglers should not be surprised if they catch a fish which usually bites during the day at night, or one which takes a bait in a period regarded as out of season for that species.

Along the last third of the coast (and occasionally further north), fishers from Victoria and Tasmania and even South Australia might catch fish with which they are familiar; and fishers from the north may land a fish they believe is normally caught only in those States. There is an overlap with southern bream, King George whiting, sea sweep, barracouta (although this fish appears off the Sydney coastline in some years), Tasmanian trumpeter and snook often encountered.

Bream, both yellowfish and southern, are present all year round, but the best time is autumn through winter. They are catholic in their food intake, but pipis, sandworms, yabbies, squirt worms, prawns, pilchards, fish fillets, baby octopus, crabs, cunjevoi are all eaten. Mullet gut is a particular favourite of mine. Have two or three of the suggested baits and fish light (without a sinker) and use plenty of berley.

Basically a herbivore, the luderick prefer weed or cabbage and good growths of this on pylons of wharves and on rocks will indicate a likely spot. However, growths of cabbage or lettuce on rock platforms also show that water frequently sweeps the area and caution may be required to fish for them safely. The luderick is also partial to squirt worms. They are present all year round but are more prolific in the late summer to winter months. They require special floating rigs which are described in the previous chapter. Black rockfish, also affectionately called pigs and mistakenly drummer, are an autumn-winter proposition. They prefer plenty of action on the water with white foamy surfaces. Growths of cabbage and cunjevoi are usually present on the rocks where the pigs are consistently caught. A weed-eater, they often bust-off luderick anglers' gear, but they are caught on cunjevoi, abalone gut and bread. A steady stream of soaked bread is a good berley. Heavier gear than that used for luderick is necessary.

The silver drummer, which can be more brutish to anglers than even rock blackfish, occupy the same locations. They are not as good to eat as the luderick or rock blackfish.

The Australian salmon is present on the far south coast all the year, but schools migrate north reaching the Illawarra towards summer, returning south in the autumn. This fish is exciting to catch on lures from both the rocks and beaches. They bite freely on whitebait, pilchards, garfish, yellowtail, fish strips and squid, either cast and retrieved or suspended under a bobby cork.

Sadly, there appears to be a decline in the number of tailor and research is being done to help establish the possible reasons for this. 'Chopper' or immature tailor are present throughout the year in most areas. The large fish gather around Gabo Island about January, moving north to reach the Illawarra about March. They respond to the same lures and baits as salmon. Early morning and into the dark are prime times but on overcast days they are often caught.

It is every angler's ambition to catch a granddad of a snapper, one with a big bump on its forehead. Each year such fish are taken by rock-hoppers, but it is the smaller (red bream or squire) specimen that is most likely to be caught. The deeper water with gravelly or broken rock

Probably the most popular rock species caught off Sydney, the luderick is a daytime proposition. It is widespread right along the New South Wales coast. (Photo Richard Allan)

bottoms are good locations but a drop-off into really deep water (often requiring long-distance casts) is a prime spot for this fish. A bait unweighted or with a minimum of lead allowed to wash around the edge of white water often is successful. It can appear at any time, especially in sheltered bays after particularly rough seas, but from spring through summer is the season and dawn and early morning (before the sun brightens the water) and from dusk into the evening are the best times. I caught my largest south-coast snapper in April off a beach on a garfish intended for tailor. It was 8 kilos.

Pilchards, garfish, yellowtail, mullet fillets, salted tuna or trevally, octopus, squid, salmon fillets, large prawns are all good baits. If available, cubes of sweep or long fillets of freshwater eel are well worth trying.

Whiting are a summer fish, both sand and King George members of the family mixing freely in the southern part of region. Sandworms, bloodworms, squirt worms and pipis and occasionally peeled prawns are the preferred baits. Often a receding tide in the morning is a productive time and the use of light gear and keeping the bait moving the best method.

On the most southern of the beaches some large sand flathead are caught through summer and into autumn. To the north the size diminishes but some good dusky flathead are caught, specially near lake outlets and river entrances. Flathead respond well to many spoon-type lures and the plastic twisters. Garfish, pilchards, small fish and slabs of fresh fish fillets on ganged hooks moved slowly along the bottom will catch the fish. A rising tide in the mid to late afternoon is a good time to seek flathead on most beaches, but they are also caught at all hours of the day and even into the night.

The other fish most want to catch is a big mulloway (jewfish). A guide to this fish's arrival is usually the summer phenomenon when small river or 'bully' mullet move from one river to another. Then they are present until the autumn exodus of the large mature mullet on their northerly spawning migration concludes. Seeking food—sheltering mullet, yellowtail, luderick, pike, tailor, prawns and crab, etc—they visit the beaches and inlets mainly in the evening.

Live yellowtail, tailor and slimy mackerel (under a bobby cork off the rocks) are excellent baits but sizeable fillets of tailor, salmon, luderick, squid, sandworms and octopus will be taken.

At many rock locations right along the coast there are resident kingfish. Regular fishers usually know of some; a few of us in the Wollongong area have had some unsuccessful confrontations with these, conservatively estimated to exceed 25 kilos, who must be wearing an array of hooks and lures. A live bait such as yellowtail under a bobby cork or partly inflated balloon is one method, but they often attack fish-like lures and plastics. In general, the kingfish are around from November but the tackle busters are more likely to be met towards April.

Apart from the fish mentioned, others caught by fishing with bait along the stretch of rocks include trevally, sergeant baker, cowanyoung (horse mackerel), slimy mackerel, yellowfin seapike, occasional short-fin pike (snook), gurnards, sea sweep and trumpeter (the last two mostly in the most southern section). Barracouta

From late autumn through winter the John Dory visits many harbours and inlets. Fishing with a live bait around moored boats and alongside wharves is an effective method for this fish. (Photo Richard Allan)

are more numerous in this area.

The cowanyoung, pikes and barracouta readily hit lures so spinning is one way to save bait.

There are groper and a red crab is the top bait. A limit of two per day only can be taken and heavy gear is a 'must'. Fish down the front of rock faces and use plenty of crab pieces and sea urchins as berley.

Fishing a live yellowtail from the wharves, piers and among moored boats in such places as Port Kembla, Kiama, Ulladulla, Bateman's Bay, Bermagui, Tathra and Eden, will often produce that prince of table fish, the John Dory. It's a daytime fish and the autumn and winter months are the time.

In the summer to mid autumn, striped tuna, mackerel tuna and bonito can be taken on high to medium retrieve-speed spinners from many headlands.

Much of the bait mentioned is readily available throughout the area. There should be no trouble in catching yellowtail and garfish for bait and sandworms or beachworms are plentiful on many of the beaches as are pipis, although these have disappeared from many of the beaches of the Illawarra region. In many of the estuaries yabbies can be pumped. Cunjevoi is available along the rocks but care and calm conditions are necessary when harvesting this and also crabs. Prawns can be scoop-netted in season in most estuaries.

For those without the inclination to collect their own bait, there are shops or garages with supplies of frozen pilchards, garfish, mullet gut, yellowtail, whitebait, etc. In centres where professional fishers operate there is usually fresh fish available.

Equipment

From the piers and wharves and some breakwaters line on a cork or caster is basic but efficient. In the popular holiday periods it may be more convenient and less troublesome to use from piers and wharves than a rod and reel as the bait can be dropped directly down in front. From many beaches a handline is fine, for distance is frequently not the secret of catching fish from these. One about 4- to 6-kilo breaking strain will suffice.

A medium-fast action rod about 3.5 to 4 metres long, suited to the reel to be used (sidecast, threadline or overhead) will allow fishing for the majority of species from both the beach and rocks. For bream, tailor, salmon, flathead, whiting, trevally, pike, barracouta, snapper, etc, a line about 5-kilo breaking strain is ample. A spare spool filled with about 8-kilo breaking-strain line will handle kingfish, mulloway, large snapper, rock blackfish and most others (even though there may be occasions when a line twice as thick would not stop some large specimens).

If the budget allows, a lighter rod about 3 metres with 3-kilo breaking-strain line is more practical for whiting, bream and baitfish (and can be quite successful for luderick).

A selection of sinkers would include the smallest snapper lead (about 28 grams), which is excellent for rock fishing, as well as light and medium-weight spoons. Light and medium-weight helmets for the beach and medium and heavyweight barrels for live baiting (under bobby corks) should also be included, along with balls (from 00 to about size 4), plus an assortment of split shots.

The use of a heavy sinker is one reason for fewer fish. Large sinkers are not necessary for good casting distance, which results from the correct matching of rod and reel and line and casting technique. There are fishers using a sidecast who can toss an unweighted pilchard the same distance as others using sophisticated reels and weights. When a sinker is necessary it should be the lightest to suit water conditions and the gear being used. And it should be running.

The following hooks in sizes to suit the baits being used and the fish being sought will cause no problems: Kendall Kirby, in sizes 10 to 12 long shank for catching bait and sizes 4 to 8 for whiting; Viking in sizes 2 to 8/0 for bream, trevally, snapper, mulloway, etc, and in sizes 1 and 1/0 extra strong for rock blackfish; the same

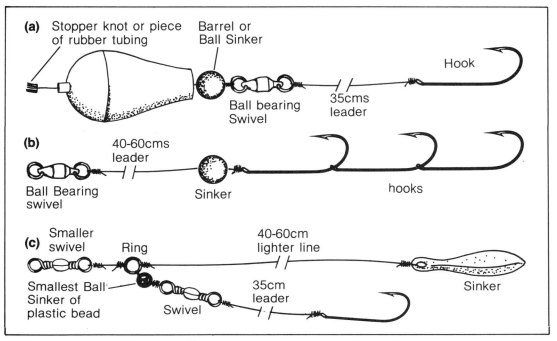

(a) Bobbycork float rig suitable for rock or ocean fishing for most species. (b) For use spinning with live bait or lures. (c) Popular running rig for rock fishing.

hook or Sproat in sizes 8 to 12 for luderick; and sizes 3/0, 4/0 and 5/0 in Mustad 4202 for ganging.

Slightly more expensive, box or ball-bearing swivels are more efficient in reducing line twist. A guide to the correct size is that the thickness of the wire loop should not exceed the thickness of the diameter of the line.

Other items are some brass rings and a spool of line about 50 per cent stronger than the line on the reels. This is for leaders. I am not an advocate of wire traces unless sharks are the specific target. Ganged or linked hooks prevent toothy fish such as barracouta and tailor biting the line. A 50-metre spool of line lighter than the main line is recommended as a dropper for sinkers.

To complete the gear the tackle box should include a sharp knife, a small file or abrasive stone for sharpening hooks; a pair of pliers; pencil, quill and stemmed floats; weighted tapered and unweighted torpedo-shaped bobby corks; and some basic first aid items such as antiseptic and sticking plaster.

The Illawarra and South Coast beaches and rocks offer a variety of fish to be caught. To enjoy catching them from many scenic and convenient locations requires only an exploratory spirit. There are hazardous areas and even safe areas can become dangerous – so commonsense and no risk-taking will make sure you enjoy the area more.

SMALL-BOAT AND LIGHT GAME

Steve Starling

Australia boasts the highest per capita ownership of trailerable power boats in the world. This is hardly surprising considering the combination of mild weather, accessibility to the coast, expendable income and leisure time enjoyed by so many of our citizens, particularly those living along the populous south-eastern seaboard between Sydney and Adelaide.

The primary recreational use for these tens of thousands of power boats is amateur fishing in its many forms. Offshore reef fishing, sport and light-game angling account for the lion's share of this trailer-boat effort.

Boat anglers heading offshore from our south-eastern coast pursue a wide variety of target species. These range from bottom dwellers and reef fish such as flathead, morwong, snapper and nannygai through middleweight battlers like kingfish and mulloway (jewfish), to the true 'game' species: tuna, wahoo, sharks and marlin.

The motivation for chasing these diverse fish ranges from the purely pragmatic desire to provide fresh meals of seafood, right through to the esoteric pursuit of challenge and sport. More often than not, however, offshore anglers are sparked by a combination of these forces; enjoying equally the thrill of the hunt *and* the chance to feed family and friends. Indeed, the distinction between so-called 'meat' anglers and their 'sporting' friends becomes less distinct each season as traditional eating fish such as snapper are targeted on lightweight fun tackle whilst species like the big tunas—once regarded as inferior table fare—enjoy an increasing gourmet status. Modern offshore fishing truly does allow anglers to have their cake *and* eat it!

The largest percentage of trailer-boat fishermen working off the south-east coast still fish primarily for the 'big three' of bottom fish—snapper, flathead and morwong. To this short list may be added a vast number of incidental captures, including the small but tasty nannygai, leatherjackets of various types, trevally, rock cod, sergeant baker, school sharks and others too numerous to mention. In colder southern waters these are joined by the likes of warehou, snook (short-finned pike), lingcod and trumpeter.

The time-honoured methods for catching these fish centre on the use of heavy lead sinkers which carry the baited hooks rapidly to the sea floor and hold them there. These mini-anchors are normally coupled with stout lines—usually handlines—to facilitate rapid recovery of hooked fish and to alleviate cut fingers. This traditional style of bottom bouncing may be practised from either a drifting or an anchored boat, though most devotees prefer the variety and lottery-like chance of the drift.

Refinements to this standard bottom-fishing approach emerged as anglers realised that thinner lines and lighter sinkers generally produced better bags, particularly in hard-fished areas close to cities and popular holiday ports.

Angling evolution has taken a further step with the advent and widespread acceptance of the 'floater' system; a combination of lightly weighted or unweighted baits fished on fine lines with the help of a berley trail to attract and hold fish. This form of fishing is most often performed from an anchored vessel.

It would not be an exaggeration to say that this floater technique has revolutionised bread and butter fishing inshore of about the 60-metre line, particularly where snapper are involved. However, the system proves equally effective on trevally, kingfish, morwong and many other species.

Another adaptation of the floater system involves casting baits, and sometimes lures, into the broken white water or 'wash' around rocky headlands, offshore islands and submerged bomboras. Although more widely practised in northern New South Wales and southern Queensland, boat-based wash fishing enjoys a growing popularity in the south-east as well.

Floater fishing and wash casting both allow a great deal of flexibility in the choice of tackle, though 6- to 8-kilo breaking-strain handlines or medium-weight threadline (spincast) outfits are universally popular and well suited to the task.

Today, boat anglers involved in bottom bouncing, floater fishing or inshore wash casting regularly broaden their horizons by also fishing live or rigged dead baits aimed at such highly desirable species as kingfish, mulloway and tuna. Mostly, these baits are suspended in mid water

The mulloway ('jewie') is present around most of Australia. It is not just the boat angler who catches this fish. Beach, rock and estuary fishers take many large specimens. (Photo Steve Starling)

under a float and are deployed off a medium-weight outfit built around a 4/0 to 6/0 size overhead reel and 1.7 to 2 metre jig-style rod.

A further refinement of the floater system has led in recent years to the advent of strip baiting or 'cubing' – perhaps the ultimate weapon for regularly taking the big yellowfin tuna which frequent south-eastern waters between Sydney and Mallacoota in late summer and autumn. This style of angling, with its ever-present possibilities of connecting with gamefish weighing 80 kilos and more, demands the very best in equipment, and is usually undertaken with heavy gear and lines of 15- to 37-kilo breaking strain.

The same tackle used in strip baiting for big tuna is also employed in the presentation of live or dead baits and the trolling of lures for large gamefish like marlin, sharks, wahoo and dolphinfish (mahi mahi). Once the sole province of big, well-equipped cruisers, gamefishing is today done from surprisingly diminutive craft.

The south-east has its share of famous gamefishing ports, with the rustic New South Wales township of Bermagui clearly leading the pack. It was here that American cowboy novelist and grandfather of gamefishing, Zane Grey, pioneered the sport back in the early 1930s, and it is here that so many national and world records are still broken each season. However, the advent of trailer boats has added many other names to gamefishing's list of ports in the south-east. These include Port Hacking, Wollongong, Greenwell Point, Currarong, Ulladulla, Narooma, Merimbula, Eden and Mallacoota, while further west Warrnambool, Port Fairy, Portland and Port MacDonell have carved themselves niches as gamefishing centres, as have the sometimes prolific bluefin tuna and albacore grounds of eastern Tasmania.

For those lacking the equipment, the funds or the desire to mix it with the real heavyweights, our south-east also offers exceptional light and medium tackle sportfishing for tailor, Australian salmon, bonito, kingfish, trevally, barracouta, pike and the smaller tunas.

A very popular and successful method of taking these pocket gamesters is to troll lures or baits behind a slowly moving boat, especially close to headlands, over reef complexes and near baitfish concentrations. Minnows, spoons, leadheads, flies and rubber or plastic squids all have their days as top producers in this angling style which, to many, offers just the right combination of thrilling sport and fine table fare.

Of course, offshore lure fishing is not limited to trolling. Artificials may also be cast and retrieved or spooled to the seabed and jigged or cranked back to the surface. This is a particularly productive way of taking kingfish and trevally, though all sorts of other surprises turn up, especially when soft-plastic tailed jigs or smallish bucktails are used in conjunction with a little berley. The next good catch of snapper taken this way will certainly not be the first.

All in all, offshore trailer-boat fishing from the south-eastern corner of our continent has plenty to offer, whether you seek the surge of adrenalin that comes with hooking a big, active fish on light gear, or the mouth-watering delight of tucking into a meal of fresh seafood.

The Bar Bogey

Many of the harbours, rivers and inlets in south-eastern Australia offering ocean access to trailer-boat anglers feature shallow, potentially dangerous entrances into the open sea. These silted barriers, which may break heavily in storm seas or certain states of the tide, are commonly referred to as 'bars'.

Bar crossing in small boats is an acquired skill best learnt through careful observation, instruction by more experienced operators and cautious experience on 'safer' crossings. Always remember that discretion is the better part of valour. Any skipper in doubt should refrain from tackling a 'working' bar rather than take any risks with his own life, those of his crew, and the rescuers who may be compelled to come to his aid should the worst occur.

A few of the 'rules' of bar crossing include the insistence that everyone aboard don a lifejacket during the crossing, that the fuel tanks be safely full and the motor(s) running smoothly, and that the situation has been thoroughly assessed by the skipper.

In the final instance, the skipper must have enough confidence in his own ability and the seaworthiness of his craft to carry on through once committed. Remember, more bar accidents occur through faint-heartedness and a panic-induced turning back in mid-crossing than through the bold determination to carry on.

THE NEW SOUTH WALES SOUTH COAST- RIVERS AND ESTUARIES

John Turnbull

Between Nowra on the New South Wales coast and Mallacoota Inlet on the Victorian border lies some of the prettiest coastline and best fishing anywhere. All along this magnificent shoreline, a continuous series of rocky points lance out into the sea, alternating with long stretches of golden sands interspersed with a great number and variety of estuaries and inlets.

Much of this lovely coastline is accessible by road, but much can only be reached on foot, and there is something for everyone. Families looking for easy picnicking and a place to casually wet a line will find plenty to satisfy them, while more serious anglers seeking escape from the madding crowd have only to explore the less accessible inlets, estuaries and rivers to find almost every imaginable form of sportfishing, both saltwater and freshwater. Take the Clyde River, for example.

The entire length of the Clyde and its tributaries form a famous fishery in its own right.

The long estuary, most of it mangrove-lined or timbered, provides year-round opportunities for catching bream, luderick, flathead, whiting and prawns, and its annual run of mulloway attracts anglers from near and far.

Upstream, in the freshwater section, lies some of the most beautiful scenery in the world, though only small sections are easy to reach, so that adventure-minded anglers must be prepared to bushwalk or canoe. The lower reaches, where the river runs wide and deep, is best savoured by small boat or canoe, and most of the fishing is done with standard estuary rigs for bream or flathead, though many also spin for tailor and for bass.

The uppermost reaches are dominated by the towering pinnacle of the Pigeon House, a spectacular mountain which stands out in solitary splendour when viewed from any point of the compass. It was named by Captain Cook during his first voyage of discovery because of its distinctive shape. A road from Ulladulla gives access to a well-marked walking track which leads to the top of the Pigeon House, and the superb views it provides of the mountains to the west, the ocean to the east, and the lovely coastline spreading to the northern and southern horizons, make it well worth the effort of climbing there.

Only a canoe can navigate the rapids and shallows of the top end of the Clyde beyond Pigeon House, only canoeists and bushwalkers enjoy the superb scenery where this waterway has carved canyons down through the ancient sandstone plateau, creating great craggy cliffs, 'castles' and other amazing landforms. Only the most enthusiastic bass fishers ever cast plugs into the deep pools lying close beneath the huge, protective gumtrees, and few places in today's world provide better opportunities to enjoy the wilderness experience.

But the Clyde's freshwater section and its many tributaries—some of them excellent fisheries in their own right—hold more than bass and mullet. Here is one of the last bastions of that small but superb fly-fishing species, the now-rare Australian grayling, and a few of its creeks have been stocked with trout.

Trout anglers know that Australia's coastal rivers are too warm for trout, but along this region of the Great Dividing Range are several streams which originate high above sea level and are shaded from the afternoon sun by the range's bulk, and so remain almost as cold as the alpine streams of the Snowy Mountains.

Unfortunately, the lack of sufficient quantities of brown trout (best suited to coastal streams because they 'stay' put and don't migrate to sea as rainbows do, and also grow larger because of their much longer life span), has caused the streams to be mainly stocked with less-suitable brook trout and rainbows, which have failed to produce stable, self-reproducing populations. Surprising numbers of brown trout, some quite large, do survive in the higher sections of several creeks, however, to surprise and delight adventurous anglers who may stumble on them. One which I caught, in a headwater of the Shoalhaven River when plugcasting for bass, weighed a healthy 1.46 kilos.

The Shoalhaven, Clyde and Moruya rivers were once Holy Grails for bass anglers from as far afield as Sydney, but their bass populations have now declined. The reason is two-fold—commercial fishing pressure in the estuaries which has disrupted their spawning, and environmental degradation. The first is due to estuary netters unintentionally destroying large concentrations of spawning bass (which reproduce in the brackish water at the upper limits of estuaries), while the latter is the result of deforestation.

It may seem strange that timber-cutting should affect fish in rivers, but the evidence is obvious in the middle reaches of the Clyde River, and even more dramatically so in the once-superb bass fisheries whose surrounding forests are being clearfelled for woodchips near Eden. Timber-cutting exposes large areas of soil to erosion, by depriving it of the protective forest canopy above, allowing rain droplets to pound directly onto the bare soils, washing them down slopes into the streams and rivers. The fine topsoils are often carried far out to sea as mud—abalone divers at Mallacoota have complained that once-productive reefs up to 10 kilometres offshore have suffered siltation following clearcutting, but the coarser sands are deposited in river pools, choking them.

This devastates the natural food chains, rendering formerly productive pools too shallow for the many species which require deep water, and making whole rivers no longer navigable, even by canoe. It thus destroys their value to the nation for recreation, river transport and water supply. The Wallagaraugh River, one of two main tributaries of Mallacoota Inlet, has suffered almost total loss of its bass, freshwater mullet (a main food for bass), platypus and duck populations following clearcutting in its catchment—a tragedy for Australian angling, since this was the only great, undisturbed bass river still left on the south-eastern corner of the continent.

In most of this region's rivers, the siltation caused by deforestation has so degraded the middle sections of waterways, by shallowing once-deep pools and reaches, and disturbing the aquatic food chain, that bass no longer inhabit them in large numbers year-round as they once did. Consequently the best bass concentrations are now found in the estuaries during their spring spawning, and in the upper sections of the remoter tributaries during summer. Anyone wanting good bass fishing in summer, when most bass angling is done, should explore the smaller tributaries, looking for streams which still have natural, weedy bottoms with deep pockets, rather than the shallow sandy bottoms typical of streams subjected to siltation from timber-cutting or land-clearing for agriculture and grazing.

The same is true of the estuaries. Estuaries which have featureless, sandy bottoms are unproductive, compared to those with fertile expanses of weedy areas. Among the weeds are the baitfish which attract predators such as tailor, flathead and mulloway, and it is along the channels and drop-offs among such weed beds that casting and baitfishing bring the best results. Wading weedy shallows and casting for flathead and tailor, or drifting in a small boat or canoe, can provide exciting sport in such places.

An unusual feature of the estuaries and inlets along the southern part of the South Coast are the estuary or southern bream. These are a distinctly different species from the bream found further north (which also inhabit these same waters), and they are not only good eating fish which grow to a reasonable size (about 2 kilos), but they will often take lures as savagely as a bass or mangrove jack.

As their name suggests, they are fish of the southern estuaries, and are not found in large numbers north of Eden, but from Bega southwards, their numbers increase, until they become the most common estuary fish in Gippsland. Being such good lure-takers, they provide exciting angling for anyone fishing with spinners, bass plugs or trout flies. Since the same waters also hold estuary perch and bass, it can be impossible to know what kind of fish has taken one's lure until it has been landed.

On one plugcasting expedition in Mallacoota Inlet, I landed a bass, a silver bream and a southern bream on three consecutive casts, and also caught a flathead and a tailor from the same spot, while several curious luderick also followed the lure, and the commotion made by a goodly sized jewfish could be sporadically seen as it chomped a baitfish out beyond casting range.

Many of the smaller estuaries between Bega and the Victorian border are rarely fished because of their lack of habitation and distance from big cities – the area is about equally distant from both Sydney and Melbourne – so anglers who desire to get away from it all should be able to find exactly what they want here. The best way to explore it is to buy maps of the region, and scan them for those sections of rivers, estuaries, lakes and inlets which have little or no vehicle access. A small boat or canoe is invaluable for exploring, and provides access to many areas larger craft cannot penetrate.

An examination of the region's maps also shows many rocky points and estuary mouths not accessible by road, some of which provide excellent fishing. One such which I discovered always yields superb fishing on outgoing tides, when baitfish are swept out of a small estuary into the mouths of the salmon, tailor and occasionally kingfish which wait in ambush. Such fishing can be truly hectic – on one occasion I landed 32 fish in 60 minutes!

The region has much to offer anglers, for as well as inland fishing, the fertile offshore waters provide excellent bluewater angling during the seasonal migrations of gamefish such as tuna, marlin and kingfish.

Hazards, and Safety Measures

The South Coast of New South Wales is situated at latitudes which are subject to easterlies which roar in across the Pacific, and cold fronts which move up from Bass Strait. These cold fronts sometimes form 'northerly outbreaks' which dump snow on the southern end of the Great Dividing Range almost down to sea level, blocking inland access routes such as the Brown Mountain Road from Cooma, and making them extremely hazardous.

Such weather occurs mostly in winter and spring, however, and poses little danger to anglers fishing the rivers and estuaries, provided they take normal care during floods and storms. Severe easterlies do, however, bring almost unbelievably rough seas rolling in across the Pacific Ocean to smash against headlands, beaches and estuary mouths, so that anglers fishing estuaries from boats should keep well clear of the mouths in such conditions. They should also be aware that even in the best weather, Pacific swells can make the bars guarding estuarine and inlet mouths extremely dangerous.

Always seek local advice when contemplating outside fishing, and be aware that bar conditions can change while fishing outside, so that it may not be possible to get back inside safely again.

ACT AND ENVIRONS
Bryan Pratt

The Australian Capital Territory and surrounding areas of New South Wales contain numerous small streams and a number of larger rivers and lakes, mostly above 600 metres altitude, which drain eastward to the Pacific Ocean or westward to the Murrumbidgee and Murray rivers.

The region consists of a mixture of mountain and lowland habitats which broadly encompass the upper and lower altitude range of trout and other introduced fish species and the upper limit of many native species, with considerable overlap where both types of fish occur.

The smaller streams represent a somewhat ephemeral habitat for fish and are characterised by heavy flows in winter and declining flows in summer. The larger streams typically are deeper, warmer and more sluggish and provide a more permanent and greater variety of habitats than the smaller streams.

Together they drain a diverse group of catchments ranging from largely undisturbed, cold, high-mountain eucalypt forests and woodland through extensive pine plantations, lower-altitude land cleared for cropping and grazing and areas heavily modified for city and urban development.

With a regional population approaching 500 000 and a strong orientation towards outdoor recreation, it is predictable that lakes and streams in the area are subjected to strong fishing pressure.

All these streams are characterised by strong, cold winter flows, with lower flows and elevated temperatures during summer. Many are subject to intense drought stress at intervals of at least four to five years. Reduced oxygen levels in summer are a dominant feature of the environment and a significant factor in determining the capacity of streams to carry trout, native fish or both. Excess water turbidity or muddiness associated with run-off from disturbed rural and urban areas is a major problem.

Most of the significant lakes in the region, including Wyangala, Googong, Pejar and Burrinjuck in rural areas and Burley Griffin and Ginninderra in urban Canberra, are man-made. The exception is Lake George, a large, natural body of water which currently does not carry fish of angling significance. Three other lakes, the Cotter, Bendora and Corin reservoirs in the ACT, carry large stocks of fish but are used for domestic water storage and are not open to angling.

Lakes are important in that they commonly carry large and diverse fish stocks; provide an expanded habitat for local fish stocks; often provide new habitats which enable new species of fish to survive in the area; and serve as a refuge for fish which might otherwise be at risk during periods of intense drought stress.

On the less-desirable side, lakes by necessity act as a barrier to essential upstream and downstream migration of fish and require the release of cold water to downstream areas, rendering them less suitable to native fish.

Brown and rainbow trout can be found in most streams in the region, notably in Paddys, Cotter, Shoalhaven, Queanbeyan, Sherlock, Ballinafad, Strike-a-Light, Bredbo, Numeralla, Molonglo, Lees, Condor, Gudgenby, Orroral, Naas, Swamp, Boorowa, Abercrombie, Crookwell, Lachlan, Tumut, Goobarragandra, Yass and Murrumbidgee rivers and creeks. Populations are sustained by natural breeding where suitable spawning facilities exist, or by stockings with fingerlings from private and government hatcheries, or both. Repeated attempts to establish populations of brook trout and Atlantic salmon in the streams have not been successful.

Brown and rainbow trout are found also in most of the major lakes in the region. In addition to trout, other introduced fish in the region include European carp, goldfish, and mosquito fish with a small population of weather loach and an expanding population of redfin perch.

The streams and lakes contain variable populations of native fish, including the small forage or food species galaxias, Western carp gudgeon, smelt, and the now rare or endangered river blackfish and Macquarie perch. Eels are found in all streams flowing eastward to the sea and occasionally in the Murrumbidgee River. The endangered trout cod is thought to still survive in one small section of the Murrumbidgee River. Catfish are common in the Lachlan River system and Wyangala Reservoir but not elsewhere.

Significant populations of golden perch, silver perch, and Murray cod occur naturally throughout much of the region and in recent years have been established, re-established or distributed more widely by stocking with fingerlings from private and government hatcheries. The most important angling stocks are found in Wyangala, Burrinjuck, Burley Griffin, Ginninderra and Googong, and in the larger streams such as the Murrumbidgee and Lachlan rivers and the lower reaches of some of the smaller streams.

Angling in the region is highly seasonal and is dictated partly by the habits of individual fish species, partly by climatic factors, and partly by legal restrictions.

Most trout streams are open during October to May inclusive, but closed during June to September to enable the fish to spawn undisturbed. Non-trout streams and lakes are open to fishing all year round. Stream trout fishing commonly is at its best during spring and autumn when water flows and oxygen levels are highest and water temperatures lowest.

Lake fishing follows a roughly similar pattern but is more variable because it is more dependent on the activity of insect and other food items. Spring and autumn fishing usually is good; winter fishing declines as temperatures drop to their lowest point. During summer the best fishing is usually in the early morning and late afternoon and evening when the fish move into the upper layers of water and closer to shore in search of food.

The position is largely reversed with native fish, which are most active during summer and least active during winter. This reflects the differing backgrounds of trout, which evolved in the colder waters of the northern hemisphere, and native fish which evolved in the warmer waters of Australia.

Both native and introduced fish show strong migratory tendencies and anglers can take advantage of this knowledge by fishing in the most appropriate locations along the annual migratory routes. Trout migrate from the lakes and lower reaches of rivers to spawn in the upper reaches of small streams in autumn and winter. Browns migrate first, usually during March-June, followed by the rainbows in May-September. After spawning the fish return to their major feeding areas.

Murray cod, golden perch and silver perch tend to over-winter in the lower reaches of the larger streams and in lakes, then move back upstream during October-December. They then disperse along the rivers during summer, often penetrating for a considerable distance upstream before returning to the winter habitats during March-May.

Fishing techniques vary according to fish type, time of the year, stream and lake conditions and personal preference.

Bait fishing for trout is popular throughout the year and the most commonly used baits are worms, mudeyes, shrimps and yabbies, fished with a small sinker on the bottom or with a bubble float. Fly-fishing is popular and highly effective, especially during early morning, late

Golden perch range throughout the Murray-Darling river systems. This one is from the Murrumbidgee River near Canberra. Bait or lure fishers will catch this Australian native fish. (Photo Bryan Pratt)

afternoon and evening feeding periods. Popular fly patterns include:

Wet: Phantom, Black and Red Matuka, Craig's Nighttime, Mrs Simpson, Hamills Killer, brown nymph, green nymph, Mudeye, Fuzzy Wuzzy, Bloody Mary, Smarts Hopper, Muddler Minnow, Coachman, Greenwell's Glory and stick caddis.

Dry: Coachman, Hairwing Coachman, Glen Innes Grasshopper, Hackle Hooper, Black Ant, Black Gnat, Tups Indispensable, Coch-y-Bondhu, March Brown, White Moth, Iron Blue Dun and Muddler Minnow.

Lure fishing is universally popular and both lure casting and trolling are effective. Popular lures include Celta, Imp spoon, Wonder spoon, Wonder Minnow, Wonder Wobbler, Abu Droppen, Mepps Black Fury, Jensen Insects, Pegron Minnow, Baltic Minnow, Tasmanian Devil, Tiny Tad, Flatfish and Kwikfish.

Bait fishing for native fish also is popular right through the year and essential in waters too turbid for lure and fly fishing. Best baits include worms, shrimps, mudeyes and small yabbies for silver and golden perch and shrimps, wood grubs, live fish and yabbies of any size for Murray cod.

Fly-fishing is not especially effective for native fish usually because it is too difficult to get the fly down to the levels at which native fish are stationed. When they can be reached, however, golden and silver perch will readily take large flies such as Mrs Simpson, Hamills Killer and Taihape Tickler, and particularly flies with orange and yellow patterns such as Dog Nobbler.

Lure fishing for native fish is popular and effective, but restricted mostly to the summer months. Deep diving lures, imitation yabbies and frogs and large spoons are preferred, although many fish are taken each year on so-called 'trout' lures. Best lures for silver and golden perch include Tiny Tad, Deeper Dan, Hellbender, Helldiver, Abu Hi-Lo, Rapala Fat Rap, Flopy, Bennett-McGrath Minnow, Wee Wart, Wonder spoon and Hot 'n 'Tot. Larger versions of these lures, together with Big Pike Getum and large flatfish are more favoured for Murray cod.

Open-face spinning reels are almost always used for bait fishing and for light lures when fishing for trout and native fish. Baitcaster tackle is more commonly used with heavier lures and when fishing for native fish. Lead-core trolling line to enable deeper waters to be fished more effectively is coming into increasing use.

Fishing rules and regulations in the ACT and New South Wales are broadly similar except that no licence is required in the ACT. Special regulations apply to some waters such as Pejar Reservoir where power boating is not permitted and Googong Reservoir where power boating is limited to electric motors. In addition, because Googong is a terminal domestic water storage and the subject of a long-term experiment in public usage, angler access is strictly controlled and no night fishing, camping or water contact sport is allowed.

Information on angling in the region can be obtained from offices of the Department of Agriculture in New South Wales at Goulburn, Yass, Jindabyne, and Cooma, and in the ACT from the ACT Administration in Canberra and at Googong Dam and local tackle shops.

THE SNOWY MOUNTAINS AND THE MONARO REGION

John Turnbull

The Snowy Mountains and Monaro region of southern New South Wales is the largest and best trout-fishing area on the Australian mainland. It contains a great diversity of trout-fishing waters, ranging from streams and rivers at only some 600 metres elevation (below which summer temperatures are too high for trout populations to thrive), to the uppermost streams of the Snowy Mountains at nearly 2000 metres elevation. Within this area is a vast maze of small brooks, creeks, rivers, natural lakes, and the huge impoundments of the Snowy Mountains hydro-electric scheme.

The higher streams are under snow for months each winter, while the lower ones receive snow rarely. During droughts, these lower streams often cease flowing and can dry up entirely, losing their entire trout populations. A local body of anglers, the Monaro Acclimatisation Society, stocks depleted streams with fry or fingerlings raised in the Gaden Trout Hatchery at Jindabyne.

Visitors to this area are often confused by the term Monaro, sometimes mistakenly applied to the entire region. The Aborigines who once inhabited this land referred to the rolling, largely treeless (because of winter frosts so severe that few seedlings can grow) foothill country north and east of the Snowy Mountains as the 'Manneroo', which became Anglicised into 'Monaro'. For trout fishers, 'Monaro' refers principally to the district around Cooma, Nimmitabel and Bombala, through which flow some of the richest trout streams in the world.

The adjoining Snowy Mountains district contains all the continent's mountains higher than 2000 metres elevation, as well as the mainland's most extensive snowfields, which feed a vast maze of streams and rivers, many of them visually very attractive.

This mountainous area is the source of three great rivers, the Murray, Murrumbidgee and Snowy rivers, all of which are well stocked with trout in their upper reaches, and also contain native species such as Murray cod, Macquarie perch, silver perch and golden perch in their lower reaches. The Snowy River was once one of Australia's two greatest bass rivers – the Hawkesbury was the other – but since its flow was reduced to a trickle by the Snowy Mountains hydro-electric scheme, these superb sportfish have ceased migrating upstream to the foothills of the Snowy Mountains near Dalgety.

In general there are only trout in the cooler highlands above about 1000 metres elevation, and only native species where the rivers warm as they leave the mountains a few hundred metres elevation lower down. In between there exists a mixed population of trout and warm-water species such as perch and cod.

The Snowy Mountains form one of the most popular areas for outdoor recreation on the continent, and the National Parks and Wildlife Service, which administers Kosciusko National Park, estimates some three million visitors enter it each year, mainly anglers, skiers, bushwalkers and tourists.

The region can be broadly divided into four types of water – hydro-electric dams, natural lakes, eroding streams and silting streams. The dams are most popular with tourists who are only casual anglers, for the tourist centres on them (particularly Lake Eucumbene and Lake Jindabyne) provide facilities such as accommodation, boat hire, tackle sales and guiding services. The natural lakes are on private property and so are mainly inaccessible, but most of the streams are available to the public.

The higher, faster-flowing rock-bottomed, *eroding* streams of the mountains proper, produce mainly smaller trout rarely exceeding half a kilogram, but the slower, weedy, richer, *depositing* streams of the foothills grow much larger fish. Trout of eroding streams are hungrier and thus usually easier to catch, while the well-fed fish of the silting streams are much fatter, warier and more difficult.

Most of the silting streams are called 'eastern streams' by local anglers, because they flow more or less eastwards towards the Snowy River. Among the better known are the Mowamba River, the Maclaughlin River, the Bombala River, the Delegate River, and all their tributaries. Some, however, are tributaries of the Umeralla and other rivers which flow into the Murrumbidgee on the northern side of the Monaro.

A not uncommon occurrence when fishing the 'high country' of South-Eastern Australia—playing a brown trout in a stream. (Photo John Turnbull)

The entire region is very rich in aquatic life, especially insects such as the mayflies and caddisflies which are the principal food of trout. On the Monaro they sometimes form mating swarms so dense that they look like mist rising off the water. During such swarms, or when the insects are hatching, the trout feed enthusiastically and conspicuously, providing an ideal opportunity for anglers to match wits and tackle with huge trout.

The region is well stocked with both brown and rainbow trout, but despite efforts to introduce brook trout to the streams and Atlantic salmon to some of the dams, these two exotic species have not become established.

Most of the higher, eroding streams hold mainly rainbow trout, while the richer lowland streams hold mainly brown trout which are more tolerant of the higher temperatures, and so more drought resistant. Brown trout have been present for about a century, and natural selection appears to have produced a heat-tolerant strain which is much better suited to Australian waters than other trout.

Fishing Methods

Fishing methods can be broadly divided into two categories — fly-fishing in the streams, and spinning, baitfishing or trolling in the lakes and dams. There are, however, many skilled fly-fishers who fish the dams, and some spinner and bait anglers who fish the streams. (Trout may only be fished for with a single rod held in the hand.)

Fly-fishing is the art of casting imitations of the tiny insects which trout eat, in such a way that the trout are unaware of the angler's presence, and accept the mimic fly as a natural one. Generally reckoned by experts around the world as the most delightful and challenging of all angling methods, fly-fishing is at its best in fertile streams such as those of the Monaro, which have such large populations of aquatic insects that the trout spend much of their time sipping them down off the surface. Trout 'rising' this way can be spotted from a considerable distance, making it possible for skilled anglers to stalk and cast to individual fish. This kind of fishing is similar to hunting, involving the skills of streamcraft and stalking as well as casting, playing and landing.

Since the brown trout which predominate in most Monaro streams are extremely wary and have superb eyesight, it is necessary to use very fine lines or 'leaders' to prevent them realising that the artificial flies are not real flies. (Real ones are too delicate to cast.) This makes them very difficult to land, adding another challenging dimension to an already difficult sport. Such fishing is very exciting and rewarding, however, and few who try it long enough to become reasonably skilled at it, ever abandon it.

Dam fishing is very different to stream fishing. Designed to capture the vast amounts of water released by the spring thaw from the alpine snowfields, the water levels of these Snowy Mountains dams vary greatly each season. The consequent lack of a stable littoral zone prevents the establishment of weed beds and the vast populations of aquatic insects on which good fly-fishing depends. These dams do have periods of excellent fly-fishing, however, particularly during early summer when their waters are rising and inundating new areas of shoreline, causing their fish to concentrate around the edges where they are most accessible to anglers.

For much of the year the fish are found away from shore in the depths, however, so trolling, baitfishing and spinning are then more productive. Worms and mudeyes (dragonfly nymphs), are the most popular baits, usually fished on spinning tackle under a 'bubble' float, and flatfish, Celtas, Tasmanian Devils and Baltic Minnows are the most popular lures.

Trolling with wet (sinking) flies can also be productive, and special techniques have been developed of trolling with baits (usually worms), behind various attractors or lures. The theory is that the fish are made curious by the large lures and come to investigate, and then take the small bait being towed behind.

Spring and early summer, when the water is warming and dam levels are rising, are the best fishing times. This is also the time when the largest hatches of aquatic insects occur, creating regular surface feeding sprees by the trout. Mid-summer fishing is usually poor, except at night or very early in the day, but can be enlivened if grasshoppers are blown onto the water. Trout are passionately fond of hoppers, and will gorge on them whenever possible, even when water temperatures are above their comfort zone.

The dams are open for fishing all year round, but the streams are closed during winter to allow the trout to spawn without disturbance. Opening and closing dates vary from year to year, and some streams are subject to different closed seasons than others, so visitors should check with local authorities before fishing. A freshwater angling licence is required, and can be obtained from sports stores, police stations and fishery inspectors.

THE VICTORIAN COAST-SURF AND ROCK FISHING

Fay Zeuschner

Victoria's coastline, with its beautiful open surf beaches, dangerously rugged rocks, and the promise of good catches, entices anglers to travel long distances in pursuit of many different species at various top fishing spots.

Salmon are the most sought-after species with anglers, after parking their cars, often walking long distances carrying on array of fishing equipment. Mullet, snapper, gummy sharks, flathead, trevally and tailor are also available to the surf angler.

Off the rocks, sweep, luderick, flathead, snapper, salmon, leatherjackets, tailor and gummy sharks provide excellent sport. Parrot fish, considered an inferior table fish by serious anglers, are popular with holiday anglers, adults and children, as they readily take baits and abound in large numbers.

Fishing Tackle and Techniques

Over the last few years, surf and rock gear has improved considerably with new technology. Graphite-composite rods are now lighter as well as stronger and lighten the load of the searching angler. It is not essential for anglers to use heavy gear. Although 4-metre rods are popular in the surf, 3-metre rods are also ideal, particularly for women and children who find this length easier to handle and cast. The fish are often close inshore, and it is not necessary to cast far especially with a berley trail encouraging them to feed in closer.

The most popular reels are large threadlines filled with 6- to 10-kilo line. Overhead reels are also popular but are recommended only for the more experienced caster. A surf bag is essential to enable easy carrying of equipment, as well as a surf gimbal to ease the strain of holding onto the rod for long periods.

A rod with a soft tip is best, enabling the angler to see the bites easily, and if the angler is serious about catching a good bag of fish it is advisable to hold the rod with a firm line at all times.

Rigs should be kept as simple as possible with sinkers just heavy enough to cast out and hold bottom. Remember generally to use small ganged hooks in No 2 or No 3 as you can always catch large fish on small hooks but not small fish on large hooks. The Mustad pattern 7766 is an excellent hook for surf fishing. Every area requires a different approach, with baits and rigs, and anglers should find out the local techniques used and where the fish are biting.

Rock fishing can be dangerous, so be careful and alert at all times. Three-metre rods are ideal coupled with a good quality spinning reel filled with 4-kilo line. Small ganged hooks are preferred with either a ball or bomb sinker. In both rock and surf fishing a moving bait will often attract the fish.

A rod holder is an ideal piece of equipment to assist in keeping the reel off the sand as well as giving the angler a rest. Small bait buckets attached to the angler's belt save time when the fish are biting quickly and consistently.

It is important to remember that to catch fish, you must practise fishing where the fish are, and you must use the right bait. The fish will not come to you—the reverse applies.

Bait, Lures and Berley

Pipis are one of the more productive baits in Victorian waters with whitebait, bluebait, pilchards and squid proving successful as well. Cunjevoi and locally pumped sandworms and saltwater yabbies are also exceptional baits.

Lures such as the Pegron Alligator, which is an outstanding lure for large flathead, as well as shiners, sliced irons, pilchards, wobblers and Toby lures are essential for increasing opportunities to catch fish both off the rocks and in the surf. Blue and white saltwater flies have also been successful in Victorian waters in producing fine bags of salmon, particularly off the rocks.

Berley is needed to keep schools of fish in the area and can easily be prepared at home by filling an onion bag with a mixture of chopped pilchard or whitebait in tuna oil, staking it in the water and fishing in the berley trail as it's washed out with the pounding waves.

Time and Tides

Surf and rock angling is a year-round sport, and though many anglers fish during the finer months of the year, autumn and winter are often the most productive seasons. At these times it is necessary for anglers to wear clothes that will keep them warm and dry—full length waders, wet-weather jacket and warm hat are necessary. The migratory run of salmon into Victorian waters usually occurs in late March and runs through until August. Mullet are also in large numbers in the surf and smaller size 6 to 8 hooks are essential to hook these small-mouthed fish.

Tides are important when fishing surf and rocks and usually the two hours before top of the tide provide the waters necessary to encourage fish to feed in close over new grounds in deeper water, putting them within easy casting distance of the patient angler.

It is advantageous to approach both surf and rock beaches at low tide to check where deep holes and gutters are. Many anglers prefer to fish away from other anglers; however, when a group of anglers fishes close together in the one hole, the fish are often kept on the bite or in the area longer with multiple baits in the water. Up until the top of the tide and until the ebb provide superb sport with fish often eagerly taking baits and resulting in double hook-ups.

Best Fishing Areas

Thousands of holidaymakers and keen anglers fish Victoria's well-endowed surf beaches intermingled with craggy outcrops and a licence is not required to fish the coastline.

Bemm River surf beach in a wilderness area produces some of the State's best salmon up to 4 kilos each. Large ganged 3/0 or 4/0 hooks with whole pilchards may be used here to advantage. Although smaller hooks and baits catch fish here, it has been consistently proven that the larger baits account for bigger fish.

The surf beaches are enormously long with the Ninety Mile Beach in Gippsland well known for its productive night-time angling for gummy sharks. Golden Beach and Paradise Beach are two of the more popular areas along here with a variety of fish consistently caught. Mixed bags are not uncommon and whole pilchards on 3/0 or smaller hooks are successful. There are many large crabs in this area and it is recommended not to leave baits idle for too long as they disappear quickly to these greedy creatures. Using large ganged hooks enables easier hooking of these delicate-tasting but interfering crabs. Schools of salmon often average around 2.5 kilos with surface-feeding tailor also providing excellent sport on lures and moving baits.

Walkerville South provides excellent catches of winter whiting, flathead, barracouta, leatherjackets and salmon for the rock-fishing enthusiast. Surf beaches at Cape Patterson and Inverloch often provide great sport with schools of small salmon and mullet.

Kilcunda provides excellent surf and rock fishing and the locals produce good catches of various fish, including flathead, leatherjackets, sweep and salmon, using 'cunjie' cut off the rocks with a sharp firm knife.

To the east of San Remo is the Punchbowl which is a brilliant spot for rock fishing, consistently producing superb catches of large salmon and snapper. Whiting may also be caught here and squid, whitebait, pipis and pilchards are all baits likely to catch fish. Woolamai on Phillip Island is the most popular surf beach on this island and is frequented by many holiday-makers during the summer months. Salmon and mullet are the most prolific species caught on pipis, pilchards and whitebait.

Flinders, Cape Schanck, Phillip Island, as well as the Punchbowl, provide the best rock angling closest to Melbourne.

The back beaches of the Mornington Peninsula include Gunnamatta, St Andrews, Rye and Portsea and provide excellent surf fishing with many schools of salmon and mullet moving through these waters. Pipis, whitebait, small bluebait and cut pilchards are top baits. These beaches are popular and provide easy access for Melbourne's metropolitan anglers.

At Ocean Grove on the Bellarine Peninsula, surf fishing is often inconsistent although anglers fishing just before the top of the incoming tide may land snapper and the odd gummy shark. Further south there is a sewage outlet, and if your sense of smell is not offended by the odours here, good catches of snapper, a fish which loves to eat rubbish, are available. At Torquay with its beautiful wide sweeping beaches, surf and rock fishing are productive during autumn and winter.

Along the majestic Great Ocean Road from Anglesea through Lorne and onwards, anglers can catch fish surrounded by some of Victoria's most breathtaking scenery. Often low duck-grey clouds hover close to the earth, releasing a mist of rain which mixes with the wild spray of a perpetually moving ocean and encompasses the angler.

Apollo Bay, a cool and beautiful seaside town, is situated in some of Victoria's most rugged landscape and provides excellent angling in the surf and off the rocks. Marengo Beach at Apollo Bay is one of the most famous and productive surf beaches in Victoria with trevally, salmon and mullet being caught here in consistently large numbers. Pipis are a top bait, and whitebait, bluebait and cut pilchards also take fish.

Johanna, south of the rugged Otway Ranges, is a gem of pure escapism from the worries of the world, where salmon create happy problems by attempting to throw the hook in the sometimes thunderous and dangerous surf.

Further west are the picturesque surf beaches of Peterborough and Warrnambool, where anglers will find excellent accommodation.

Approximately 25 kilometres past Warrnambool, the beautiful and sheltered beach of Killarney is pure pleasure to fish, and is an ideal spot for young families. Rocks to the right also produce well. Whiting is the most sought-after species here during the summer and autumn months with locally pumped worms and saltwater yabbies the top baits. Snapper and flathead are also caught. The quaint fishing town of Port Fairy further west offers a serene environment, with mullet, gummy shark and salmon often caught.

Portland, and further west Bridgewater, also provide anglers with excellent catches of fish at

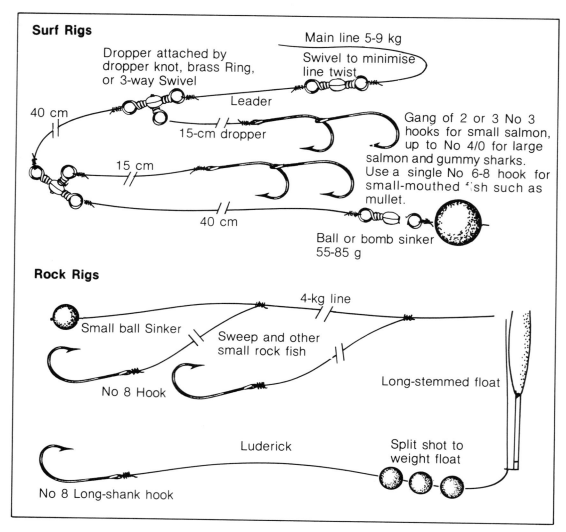

times with salmon being the most sought-after species, and occasionally snapper.

Angling is a sport which may be enjoyed by the whole family in a relaxing and healthy environment, with the rewards waiting to be gathered. It is an exciting moment when a young angler lands his or her first fish, and angling trips become memorable experiences.

Hazards, and Safety Measures

1. *Always* keep an eye on the sea. Never turn your back on it and be very cautious when there is a moderate to heavy swell.
2. Never fish alone.
3. Blue-ringed octopus inhabit Victorian waters. Always check rock pools for these before allowing children to play in them — a bite from a blue-ringed octopus can be fatal.
4. Wear sneakers or cleated footwear on rocks to prevent injury or slipping.
5. Do not go far into the surf to cast as there are many strong and dangerous undertows in Victorian waters.
6. Keep gear well above the high-tide mark.
7. Familiarise yourself with legal minimum fish lengths.
8. Take all rubbish home.

Victorian Coastal Rivers and Estuaries

Rex Hunt

Victorian anglers have many estuarine waters available to them, most within easy reach of the main cities along the coast.

In the east there is Mallacoota Inlet which comprises two lakes linked by a deep narrow-bodied water called the Narrows. Mallacoota Lakes are fed by the Genoa and Wallagara rivers which at times can produce magnificent bream fishing, especially in dry weather and then again in spawning time which occurs in September and October each year.

Best baits for the bream are sandworms and locally pumped bass yabbies known as nippers. Other baits that have been successful are shrimps, cut pilchards and crabs.

The inlets and rivers also hold other species like flathead, yellow-eye mullet, luderick and at times good runs of tailor.

Towards Lakes Entrance there are two estuaries that offer the serious angler great fishing—Tamboon Inlet, fed by the Cann River, and Sydenham Inlet fed by the Bemm River, have for years been the mecca of bream anglers. They have survived so-called progress and remain among the most productive estuaries. While the main species are bream, good hauls of yellow-eye mullet and trevally can be taken. There are also populations of estuary perch, sometimes wrongly called bass, in these waters. The best times for both these waters is the spring when the rivers are subsiding after winter rains.

Around Lakes Entrance and Bairnsdale there are some of Australia's premier estuary waters where you can catch many species of fish. A boat is not essential and the Gippsland Lakes would have to be one of the most accessible waters in the land.

Tourism is big in the district and there are several full-time bait collectors who supply the anglers with their needs. For the bait gatherer the area offers large supplies of sandworms, which can be obtained from the sandbars at low water, and prawns, shrimps, cockles, crabs and garfish.

The most prolific fish is the southern bream. It keeps coming back for more despite the hundreds of thousands of fish that are taken from the system each year. Added to this, there are more than a dozen full-time professional netters who work the lakes' system.

The main fishing areas in the lakes themselves are at Kalimna where there is good deepwater fishing for snapper, flathead, salmon, trevally, luderick and big bream along the walls. Flathead, bream and mulloway are taken at Metung and in the warmer months the King George whiting is very prolific among the weed beds.

The stretch of water that joins Lake King to Lake Wellington is called Hollands Landing or McLellands Straits. Despite the strong tide these waters hold some of the best bream in the system.

Three rivers feed the system. They are the Mitchell River which flows through the township of Bairnsdale, the Tambo which rises in the highlands above Bruthen, and the Nicholson which is a relatively short stream not affected by the flooding of the Mitchell or the Tambo.

Great hauls are made in all these rivers with the lower reaches of the Mitchell from the 'Cut' up to the area known as Two Bells being very prolific as are the upper reaches of the Tambo to the cliffs.

Best times for the bream in the rivers are late winter and early spring. The best bait is sandworms but at times the fish will bite freely on prawns, bass yabbies, shrimps and cut garfish.

The Gippsland Lakes compare favourably with many of Australia's estuarine systems and the fishing is very good indeed. Near the tiny South Gippsland coastal town of Inverloch is

Andersons Inlet. A very fast tidal body of water it offers some excellent fishing. The main species caught are salmon, King George whiting and yellow-eye mullet. Best time of the year is summer with some excellent salmon fishing in late autumn and early summer. Best baits are local pipis taken from Venus Bay, with silver lures used for the salmon. Into the system flows the Tarwin River which is famous for its good runs of mullet, bream and estuary perch. At times there have been some nice gummy sharks caught at the mouth of the Tarwin.

The Powellet River enters Bass Strait between Wonthaggi and Kilcunda. Subjected to heavy flooding and weed growth it offers reasonable fishing especially when the entrance is open to the sea. Bream, mullet and perch are all to be caught on locally netted shrimps. Big eels are also in the river and the best baits are bullock's liver and earthworms.

The next main estuary is at Barwon Heads where the Barwon River meets the sea. This is a very tidal estuary, which holds a host of fish, including trevally, bream, mullet, small snapper known as pinkies, salmon and the much-sought-after mulloway. Big mulloway are taken here mainly on live bait of small mullet and salmon. Best times for the mulloway are in November and March and most fish are caught in the dark of the night by anglers slowly rowing in a small boat. There are, at times, good mulloway taken at anchor with fillets of salmon and mullet. It is also then that anglers can catch good bream on local sandworms and bass yabbies in the fast water. I have found it best to fish well downstream of the boat as the fish seem to work their way into the tide.

Port Phillip and Westernport bays have been covered elsewhere in this book. However, there are three very important estuaries that run into Port Phillip Bay that do produce good quantities of mullet and bream.

The Patterson River at Carrum has been changed from what was once called an 'open sewer' into a glorious waterway which offers fantastic boating. It is a haven for the bream and mullet which feed on the hordes of shrimps in the coral and weedbeds. Sandworms are very prolific at Carrum and can be pumped at low water. Best time for the bream is early morning in the autumn and winter and the mullet appear to be there all year round. Berley of bread, tuna oil and bran is ideal to attract the mullet. Other baits besides shrimps and worms are dough made of flour and water, peeled shrimps, and boiled mutton flap with a lacing of curry, which is deadly on mullet.

The Yarra River at Melbourne is on the receiving end of jokes from interstate about its running upside down, but both the Yarra, and Maribyrnong, which enters the system at Newport, have a good stock of southern bream which take all recognised baits including fresh chicken. They are caught mainly around pylons of wharfs. Mullet are also very plentiful and can be caught well up the tidal reaches of both rivers.

Best time for the Yarra and Maribyrnong is in the spring when the fish enter the system from Port Phillip Bay. In years of dry weather other species have been caught as far up as Essendon, which is near the fresh water of the Deep Creek System. Small snapper, mulloway, and trevally, as well as sea-run brown trout, have all been caught in the summer months. One of the best baits for the Maribyrnong in summer is cut Western Australian pilchards.

The Werribee River runs into the bay on the western side near Werribee South. It has some five kilometres of fishable shores and boat and bank angling are rewarding. Best time to fish for the bream and mullet is in October and November. The fish seem to make their way to the top of the river during this time and the best baits are sandworms, squirters (bivalve molluscs), shrimps and bass yabbies. For the mullet I prefer sandworms exclusively.

At times in the winter small salmon known as bay trout enter the lower reaches of this river and provide good sport on light tackle.

The Hopkins River at Warrnambool is a

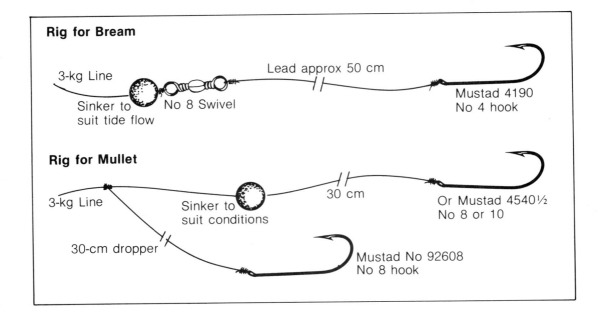

majestic river that is without doubt one of the top producing estuaries in Victoria. For years there was a problem with local bait. In 1979 the Australian Anglers Association held its biennial convention there and sandworms were freighted from East Gippsland. The results were amazing as some of the best bags of bream and mullet ever to come from the river were presented to the weighmaster. Since then good stocks of sandworms, locally known as pod worms, have been discovered and the bream fishing continues to be wonderful. Best times are October and November and then again in March and April. Mulloway enter the river in spring and provide good sport on light gear right through until early winter.

Victoria has some magnificent estuarine waterways containing some of the best fighting fish. The main thing is to have the right gear, long light rods with light line, the right baits, locally and freshly collected, and local knowledge. For this the locals are most helpful. The main species of fish is the southern bream. It is prolific so if you place enough baits in enough places you will succeed.

WESTERN PORT
Geoff Wilson

Unlike Port Phillip Bay, which is a lagoon with its deepest area virtually in the centre, Western Port is an intricate system of channels branching like the veins and capillaries of a giant circulatory system. There are great expanses of shallow water where the mud and sand are exposed when the tide is out so take care when navigating this water. The main navigational routes are marked with International Association of Lighthouse Authorities cardinal marks and beacons.

Western Port has two entrances to Bass Strait: the major channel used by shipping is on the western side of Phillip Island, the lesser channel running between San Remo and Newhaven runs around the eastern side of Phillip Island.

Principal species sought in Western Port are whiting and snapper, but this water offers a greater variety of edible fish than does Port Phillip Bay as anglers' bags tend to demonstrate.

The deeper waters of the main and lesser channels all produce snapper throughout the warmer months of the year, and the sandbanks produce whiting. At the bottom of the tide, virtually all species are confined to the channels because much of the shallow ground dries. The tides run strongly in Western Port because of the considerable rise and fall compared with Port Phillip. This tidal effect is increased further by the channel system which becomes visually apparent as the tide goes out.

Separated from Flinders and Balnarring by the treacherous Middle Bank, access to the main shipping channel in the lower reaches of Western Port is from Cowes on Phillip Island and Stony Point on the mainland. The south or bottom end of the main channel is a favoured snapper mark, particularly early in the season when boats anchor up along the line-up of beacons 9, 11 and 13 which are out from, but on the opposite side of the channel to, Grossard Point on Phillip Island. Anglers fishing along the channel banks must carry a range of snapper leads so that lead can be increased or decreased as the flow of the tide speeds up or slows down.

The continuation of the main shipping channel into Western Port is up through the North Arm past a fairly narrow passage between Sandy Point on the mainland and Tortoise Head on French Island. Before this point is reached though, mariners and anglers have a choice of proceeding up the North Arm to Hastings, Tooradin or Warneet, or branching to the east up the East Arm to Cowes and Corinella, or taking the lesser, but more sheltered Gardners Channel around the south end of French Island.

All channels produce snapper, but the most productive big snapper area in Western Port is the head of the North Arm from Lysaght jetty to Bagge Harbour where Eagle and Crawfish Rocks are noted features among snapper anglers.

Famous for its excellent catches of whiting, the Middle Spit is an elongated sand bar running parallel with the main channel right up the west

Sometimes a surprising variety of fish is taken during a fishing outing on Western Port as this catch shows. (Photo Geoff Wilson)

side of French Island, but separated from it by a narrow passage of deep water running close in to shore. This channel also produces good catches of snapper.

Access to the Quail Bank, an excellent whiting ground, is from Warneet where there is a good boat ramp and facilities in Rutherford Inlet. Here, bags of King George whiting sometimes rival those taken in the better areas of Port Phillip Bay.

From Bagge Harbour east into the head of Western Port, cardinal marks must be closely observed to avoid numerous hazards and shallow water because this area is a maze of shallow sand bars and fairly narrow channels. The township of Tooradin is at the head of the Tooradin Channel in Sawtells Inlet. Facilities here include a double boat ramp with car park and washing facilities. There are excellent whiting grounds in the head of the Westernpoint Bay including the 'Post Office' and the waters around Joe's Island and the Outer Bank.

The deeper areas of the Tooradin Channel produce snapper, as do the Bourchier and Bolton channels which are not fished much because of their lack of navigation marks.

In the top end of Western Port snapper and whiting rigs become more conventional because the tide flow is much reduced in this area, so running sinker rigs are frequently used for

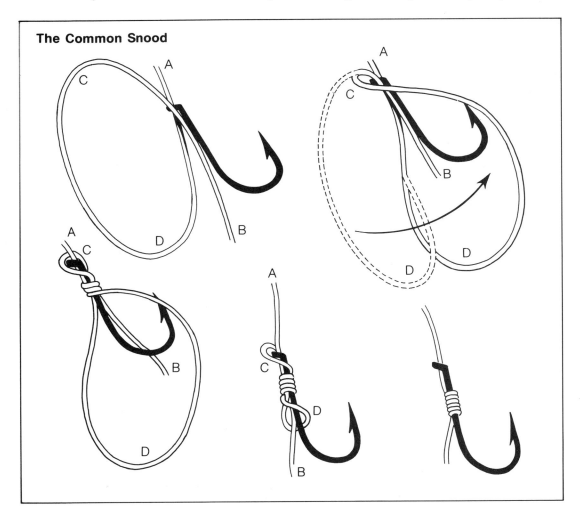

The Common Snood

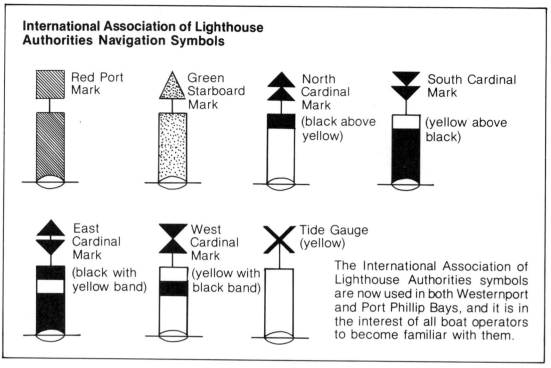

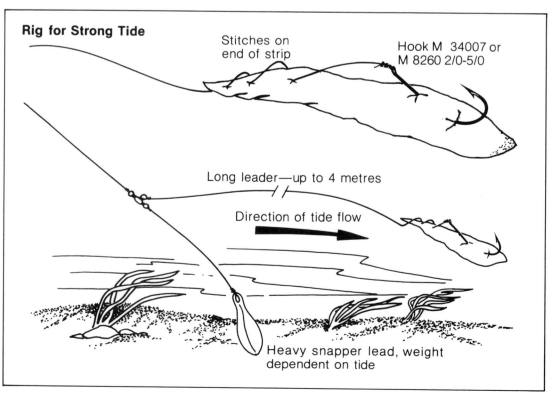

snapper as they are in Port Phillip Bay.

The junction of the Tooradin Channel with the Upper Tooradin, Charing Cross and Irish Jack channels is known as Charing Cross. These waters produce good catches of whiting, as do the adjacent waters of Blind Bight (Gentle Anne), Cockayne and Lyalls channels.

South of French Island, the East Arm runs past Cowes through to Corinella and Grantville where there are good ramps and caravan parks on the mainland. The deeper waters produce snapper, particularly around Snapper Rock, which is centrally located in the channel off Corinella. The shallower waters of Guys and Tenby channels produce a wide variety of fish including whiting. So too does the French Island Bank on the other side of the channel from Corinella.

The second channel entering Western Port comes in from San Remo. It is narrow, deep, and very fast flowing. Few anglers fish this water because heavy blankets of weed coming down the channel make fishing almost impossible on the ebb tide. However, at the turn of the tide, it does produce about an hour of fairly easy fishing when a variety of fish including snapper can be taken in comfort.

There are boat ramps at Flinders, Balnarring, Stony Point, Cowes, Corinella, Grantville, Hastings, Warneet, Tooradin and Blind Bight.

Land-based fishing locations can be found at Stony Point Jetty, Flinders Jetty, Cowes Jetty, Phillip Island Rocks (use caution) and Red Rock (east side of Cape Woolamai and 40 minutes' walk from Newhaven). You can fish the deep channel at San Remo, too, but the restricted time of slack water means you must time your trips to coincide with the tide.

Hazards, and Safety Measures

Navigation All hazards adjacent to approaches to population centres and boat ramps are marked with IALA cardinal marks. It pays to be familiar with these.

Stranding The large rise and fall in the tide, and the fact that large areas of ground are uncovered as the tide falls, make stranding a real hazard. It is not serious when compared with other hazards, but it is most uncomfortable to be immobile on a vast expanse of mud, particularly at night and for hours at a time.

The Middle Bank The most life-threatening hazard is the Middle Bank between Flinders and the western side of Phillip Island. Boats navigating this water must exercise extreme caution because the dangerous Middle Bank has claimed over-confident mariners and anglers over the years and probably will claim more.

Phillip Island The rocks on Phillip Island facing Bass Strait sometimes provide good fishing, but unexpected swells have claimed lives here in the past. If you fish from any of these ledges, keep a watchful eye on the sea.

PORT PHILLIP BAY
Geoff Wilson

Port Phillip Bay is a 2000-square-kilometre lagoon which serves as a combined estuary for the ten separate rivers and creeks flowing into it. The main body of water is a shallow basin averaging about 10 metres deep with a maximum depth in the centre of about 24 metres.

A shallow bank averaging about three metres deep runs around the perimeter of the bay. It also extends across the bay just inside the entrance where it is heavily striated with tidal scouring and channels used by shipping.

The entrance to Port Phillip Heads is only 3000 metres across and this constriction not only causes the tidal current to run very fast, but delays the time of slack water for approximately three hours until after both the high- and low-tide extremes. This is the time the level outside the bay takes to equalise with the level inside, and *vice versa*. The bay entrance is called 'The Rip'.

Fishing is restricted both by the strong tides and by proclaimed anchoring restrictions in the vicinity of the Heads. However, inshore from the shipping lanes, excellent fishing for a wide variety including pike, salmon, whiting, silver trevally, garfish and squid can be enjoyed.

At Point Lonsdale and Queenscliff, on the western side of Port Phillip Heads, there are jetties open to the public, and there is a good boat ramp at Queenscliff. At low tide there are exposed rock platforms under both the Point Lonsdale and Queenscliff lighthouses which produce a good variety of fish and some squid.

Nepean Bay on the eastern side of Port Phillip Heads is off limits to land-based anglers, but with a boat you can troll for salmon or anchor up and catch big King George whiting. Squid is an excellent bait for these. Yellowtail kingfish are regularly caught in summer and autumn 600 metres or so offshore from the power lines at the start of the rock wall at the base of the dune face in Nepean Bay. The ebb tide produces most fish.

Commercial fishermen use heavy leaded handlines to catch them, but angling enthusiasts prefer to anchor here in about 12 metres of water and fish with lures running back in the tide behind the boat, or cast to rising fish with lures like the Cotton Cordell popper.

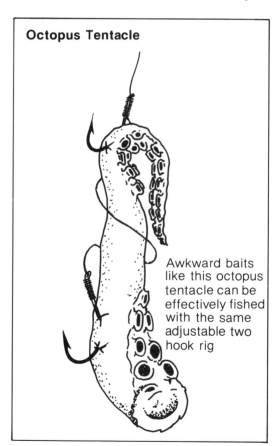

The adjustable two-hook rig used for baiting up with the live garfish is also a good rig to use with a piece of 'occy' tentacle.

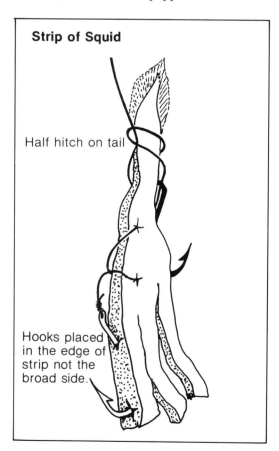

Baiting with a strip of squid for snapper using a two-hook rig: one sliding on the trace, the other tied to the end of the trace. Hook size depends on the size of the bait and the fish being sought but 2/0 to 5/0 are common sizes.

However, if you do anchor too far out, you could face a heavy fine for encroaching on the liberally defined shipping lanes, so take some care and preferably obtain a copy of the boating restrictions from the Ports and Harbours Authority.

Swan Bay is the shallow lagoon between Queenscliff and St Leonards. Its southern entrance is the Queenscliff boat harbour where you may fish provided you do not obstruct the harbour entrance. Silver trevally bite well in here on the rising tide between September and Christmas.

The northern entrance to Swan Bay produces gummy sharks using cut baits on slack water, particularly on the bottom of the tide, and excellent catches of big bank flathead are made on the shallow banks in January and December.

Dividing Port Phillip from Western Port, the Mornington Peninsula is serviced by the Nepean Highway and has good boat-launching facilities at all major population centres. The best of all is probably the Patterson River complex near Carrum. Patterson River is also a good spot to fish for bream and mullet so you have an alternative fishing spot if the weather is too rough to go out.

Snapper entering Port Phillip Bay appear in their greatest numbers early in the season along the Peninsula with anglers taking good catches from boats from the end of September until mid-December.

King George whiting are taken in good numbers from the inshore grounds but their average size would be less than 250 grams. Flathead are abundant but small. The only fishers who seem to get big flatties on a consistent basis are those spearing flounder at night, particularly near Rosebud and Rye.

Land-based anglers have a number of options including the rock platforms at Mount Martha and the Mornington pier, both of which produce snapper during, and immediately after, a strong onshore blow.

From Williamstown to Elwood could be called the head or top of the bay. It includes the combined estuary of the Maribyrnong and Yarra rivers and the Port of Melbourne so there are restrictions on small craft. If your intention is to fish the Port of Melbourne area, obtain the handbook of regulations from the Ports and Harbours Authority.

Despite heavy shipping and occasional pollution incidents, this area of the bay fishes well. There are launching facilities at Williamstown and at the St Kilda marina, and numerous piers and jetties for land-based anglers to fish from.

The Maribyrnong runs into the Yarra just above Newport and the two run to sea as one.

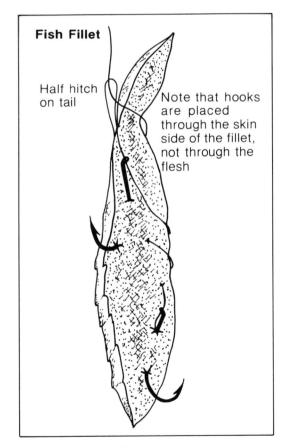

Baiting with a fish fillet for snapper.

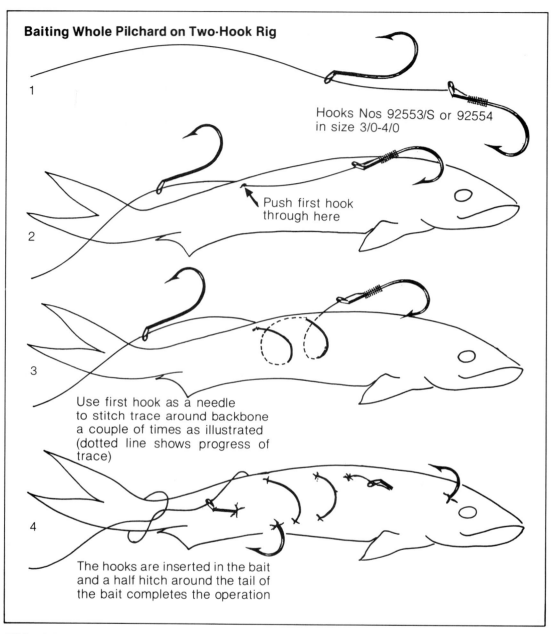

Pilchards have become the most popular snapper bait in Port Phillip Bay because they are readily available in good condition and the fish take them well. Here is an effective way to rig a pilchard on a two-hook rig, one sliding, one fixed.

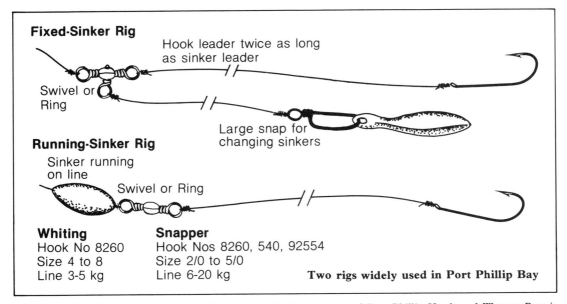

Two rigs widely used in Port Phillip Bay

Fixed Sinker Rig Used mainly for whiting, but in the faster waters of Port Phillip Heads and Western Port it is used with heavier line and larger hooks for snapper. When using this rig in a strong tide, it is important to be able to change sinker weights as the rate of flow increases or decreases. For this reason, a snap-lock is used at the end of the line. With heavier lines just a loop in the end of the line is more satisfactory.

Running Sinker Rig This is a widely used rig for snapper in Port Phillip Bay. The whole idea is that the fish can take line through the sinker before feeling any pressure.

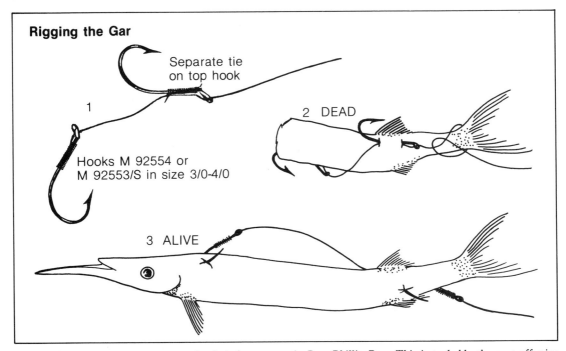

Live garfish have become a very popular bait for snapper in Port Phillip Bay. This is probably the most effective way to rig a live garfish.

Bream are the most eagerly sought species here, and some good bags are taken. One favourite spot is the water-cooling canal which runs from the Newport Power Station into the Yarra. Here bream, tailor and mulloway are often caught in good numbers. Another good spot is under Westgate bridge where, as well as the species already mentioned, you are likely to get a good-size snapper as well. Around the end of March seems to be a good time to fish here.

Williamstown, Altona, Point Cook, Werribee South, Little River and Kirk's Point all have good offshore fishing but restricted beach access because of government installations like the RAAF base at Point Cook and the Melbourne Metropolitan Board of Works sewage farm at Little River. There are good boat ramps at Altona and Werribee, and a rather exposed ramp at Kirk's Point.

The Werribee River itself offers good bream fishing and access is unrestricted from Werribee South. If you wish to enter from Little River you need a MMBW permit to use their roads.

Werribee South and Kirk's Point are noted areas for King George whiting and the anglers who fish these waters regularly will take fish when other anglers are not getting a bite. A good knowledge of marks and laying on the mark is essential on these grounds.

The whiting grounds also produce good catches of squid. These can be caught by anglers at anchor or on the drift using baited jigs or the Yo-zuri jig.

The Bellarine Peninsula is serviced by both the Portarlington and Queenscliff roads from Geelong. There are boat ramps at Point Richards, Portarlington, Indented Head and St Leonards.

The dominant feature of the peninsula for anglers is the Prince George Bank, which is an extension of the bank which runs almost all of the way around Port Phillip Bay. The bank itself produces excellent catches of whiting, squid and flathead, and some areas also produce good catches of small snapper. Gars are also abundant.

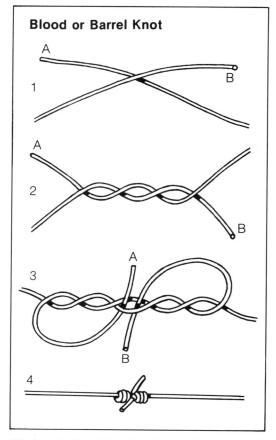

The blood or barrel knot is widely used for joining lines of the same or similar diameters.

Out beyond the bank, small flathead are in plague proportions, but on the change of tide they seem to go off the bite; this is the best time to try for a big snapper out here.

The jetties are Portarlington and St Leonards are both popular with anglers, but the St Leonards jetty is my choice for snapper, particularly during and after a northerly blow.

Corio Bay is the Geelong arm of Port Phillip Bay. It is divided into the inner and outer harbours. A sand bar running between Avalon and Point Henry physically divides the bay, but a dredged channel allows the passage of shipping to the Port of Geelong.

In the inner harbour, or Port of Geelong, there are boat ramps at St Helens and at Limeburners Point. The outer harbour has three ramps:

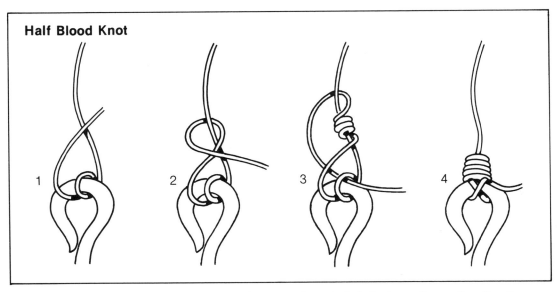

The half blood is one of the best knots for tying nylon to metal, particularly in the small to medium-line diameters. Widely used by snapper fishermen in Port Phillip Bay.

Avalon and Kirk's Point on the north side, and Clifton Springs on the south. All these ramps are shallow and exposed, suitable for only small craft in good conditions.

A unique feature of the outer harbour is the extensive mud oyster bank and spit (known as the Wilson Spit) which extends right out past the shipping channel from the northern side at Point Wilson. Though devastating on tackle, the bank and spit provide some of the most prolific ground in the whole of the Port Phillip–Corio Bay complex for big snapper and whiting.

The inner harbour is a fairly featureless, muddy basin which produces few fish for most of the year. However, it does produce a disproportionately large number of snapper over 7 kilos compared with most other areas, particularly in the so-called off season or winter.

Whiting grounds in the inner harbour are limited to Avalon and Stingaree Bay, because the shallow banks providing feed are very narrow at other spots.

The Geelong wharves produce good catches of sea bream and warehou, silver trevally and mullet, while a line on the bottom will sometimes pick up a snapper. The jetties around Corio Bay are good producers of garfish and small whiting, particularly in the late summer and autumn.

Hazards, and Safety Measures

Port Phillip Bay is a safe, sheltered water with few hazards. The most common trap is sprung when calm conditions—particularly in the early morning—lure small-boat operators too far out onto the bay where they can be caught off guard when a stiff breeze whips up later in the day.

Navigation hazards are few. There are some bad inshore shoals between Beaumaris and Sandringham on the eastern side of Port Phillip, and close inshore on the northern side of Corio Bay in the Avalon–Point Wilson area. All of these hazards are accurately charted in *Creeks and Harbours of Port Phillip* by Richard Hawkins, a most helpful book for mariners on Port Phillip Bay.

Port Phillip Heads is the most dangerous piece of water most mariners and fishers are likely to come across. The main problem is that there are so many wind and tide combinations that have

Snapper of this size are regularly taken from both Western Port and Port Phillip Bay. (Photo Geoff Wilson)

to be known. However, the most dangerous situation exists on an ebb tide, particularly when there is a strong southerly wind, or a southerly swell.

The safest time to enter or leave Port Phillip Heads is when the current is running in. For more detailed information I would refer the boat user or angler once again to Richard Hawkins' work already mentioned.

Inside Port Phillip Heads is the Great Sand, or the Port Phillip Sands. The main channels through the sand are well marked, but problems can arise with various tide and wind sets here. The sands are little more than a potential stranding hazard.

The greatest insurance a boat angler can have in Port Phillip Bay against mishap is a seaworthy craft with a well-serviced motor. Two-way radios are an additional safety aid and the law provides for certain items like life jackets, oars, flares, fire extinguisher, bucket and torch in case of unforseen difficulties. However, it should be stressed these are mainly for emergency use.

TROUT IN VICTORIA
Rex Hunt

There are two species of trout in Victorian waterways, the brown and rainbow. Both have been successfully liberated into streams and lakes although it is generally accepted that browns do better in streams and the rainbows are more at home in the lakes. There are only a couple of instances where the marriage of the two species has been successful.

The Goulburn River runs from Eildon Weir right down to the Murray River. The stretch of river between Eildon and Seymour is the most heavily fished in Victoria and one of the best producing. Here both brown and rainbow trout live happily together. The rainbows prefer the faster-running stretches of the river and the browns obviously like the slower-moving sections.

The Goulburn like all other waters in the State receives liberations of trout from the Snobs Creek Hatchery near Thornton. Each year over a million trout are liberated into lakes and streams in Victoria.

Another water with both browns and rainbows is the Dartmouth Dam which was formed by the damming of the Mitta Mitta River in the north-east high plains. Hundreds of thousands of rainbow trout have been released into Dartmouth, but at the time of writing there has never been a release of brown trout into this lake. Despite this, the fact is that the brown is the most dominating species in the catches. It is felt that the streams feeding 'the Dart' are almost perfect for trout breeding and, therefore, the brown trout fishery is in good order.

Victorian waters are presently under review. There have been suggestions that a number of waters will no longer be stocked in the State because of poor returns and lack of suitable food. This is a good move, as surely fifteen top producing waters are better than 115 poor fishing waters. In the past there have been trout released into waters where later surveys revealed no trace of the liberated trout. At about one dollar each fish it becomes very expensive if the trout do not survive.

In Victoria most lakes and streams are within an easy day's drive from Melbourne. Lake fishing for trout in Victoria can be very rewarding and, despite the interest in fly-fishing, there really is not a lake that consistently produces good hauls of trout to the artificial fly man.

Best catches are taken in lakes by using natural baits, such as worms and mudeyes fished about a metre under a bubble float. Lures are also very good value and the method using a Ford-Fender attractor a metre up the line from the lure or bait has been very successful. Also around the lakes are some very good spots for shore-based lure casting and the specialist lure tosser can fish many waters that would be unable to be fished with bait.

Rivers and streams in Victoria are dominated by the amount of flow that comes down. The main stream is the Goulburn River and during the hotter weather most of the water is used for irrigation. This ensures a very good flow of water during the period when most other streams are running low.

Bottom fishing with worms and saltwater mussels is the most productive when the streams are in flood in the spring.

The flooding of rivers brings untold food into the streams and, if there is an extra fall of late snow in the highlands, the muddy water can last almost till December. When the streams subside the trout have to go in search of food. They rely on grasshoppers and crickets joining other sub-aquatic life in the water. It is then that the lure or fly anglers come into their own.

One of the most heavily fished waters is Eildon Dam. It is fed by feeder streams like the Goulburn, Jamieson, Howqua and Delatite rivers. It is also fed by the Big River which forms a very productive arm of the Eildon Dam.

By far the most prolific of the trout in Eildon is the brown. Most trout are taken either by trolling lures slowly behind a boat or by fishing with mudeyes, worms and yabbies among the huge amount of dead trees in the lake. Despite the presence of thousands of juvenile redfin the lake still holds some of the State's best trout, which can be taken by most methods of angling.

Lake Dartmouth is gradually filling and the fishing can only get better. Well-known Victorian RACV fishing writer Fred Jobson was responsible for introducing the latest 'hot fish' producer to the lake. The combination of trolled cow bell or Ford-Fender attractors with a lure like a Tasmanian Devil or Wonder Super Duper will generally take fish. An interesting variation is the use of bait instead of a lure behind the attractor. A bunch of worms, a single scrubworm and a mudeye have all taken excellent catches in the past few years. With Dartmouth it seems that some conventional methods have been replaced by the try-anything style of the modern-day thinking angler.

There is excellent accommodation in the township of Dartmouth and the launching ramp can take boats up to 6 metres. Lake Toolondo near Horsham is gaining a reputation as the State's top brown-trout fishery. Located near the Rocklands Dam on the Glenelg River, Toolondo was once known as Bartons Swamp. It was decided to divert water from Rocklands in the 1970s. In 1983 Victoria suffered a huge drought. The trout at Snobs Creek Hatchery would have died if they were not released into a suitable water. As this lake was cold and the only fish in it were good size redfin, it was decided to release some 100 000 brown trout. The release proved successful and now each year more than 40 000 browns are released.

Best method here is the mudeye fished under a bubble or a quill float among the dead timber which covers most of the lake. Toolondo is alive with suitable trout food like yabbies, mudeyes, gudgeon and smelt (a small whitebait-like fish). The winter is best and a little chop on the water helps. Trolling with lures is also very successful with the Tasmanian Devil the most productive.

Near the Victorian town of Castlemaine is the Cairn Curran Reservoir. A medium-size water that dams the Loddon River, it offers some excellent brown trout during the spring and late autumn. Best baits are worms and mudeyes and the best lures Wonder Wobblers and Tasmanian Devils cast or trolled. It is during the spring that the wet-fly fisher can have some good sport around the drop-offs from the grassy banks.

Best flies are Craig's Nighttime and Muddler Minnow. A slowly retrieved longtail like the red and black Matuka can be deadly.

Other productive lakes in Victoria that hold sufficient stocks of trout for worthwhile fishing are Lake Purrumbete near Camperdown, Lake Modewarre near Geelong, Blue Rock Dam near Trafalgar and Hepburn Lagoon near Daylesford.

Mudeyes are the top bait in all these waters.

The main stream is the Goulburn River and despite the everchanging height and temperature of the water there are still good hauls of fish coming from it.

Many fishers still use garden worms with a great deal of success. Saltwater mussels are excellent when the river is discoloured after rain. The new synthetic bait called CATCHIT is also very productive and recently produced many fish in the AAA trout competition.

I prefer to fish lures in the Goulburn because I can cover much more water than the bait or fly fisher can. My preferred lure is the old-style Tiger devon and the ever popular Celta; Spinwell Tylo and Silver Wobblers have all taken fish.

Fly anglers prefer to fish the late summer or autumn when the trout feed on grasshoppers or beetles. I have done well on flies like the Red Tag, Greenwell's Glory, Coch-y-Bondhu and Cinnamon Sedge.

Other rivers in Victoria that hold good populations of fish include the Mitta Mitta River in the north-east high plains, Ovens River at Bright, Yarra River between Warburton and Yarra Glen, Mount Emu Creek and the upper reaches of the Hopkins River.

Wherever you go after trout remember that by presenting your bait or lure in a natural manner you will have success eventually.

VICTORIA AND TASMANIA – GAME FISHING

Bill Classon

Victoria

Serious gamefishing in Victorian waters has really only taken off in the last decade. This has been without doubt due to an increasing interest of anglers in the scene, rather than an outright lack of fish.

Although Victoria boasts one of the oldest and most respected game clubs in Australia (and the world!) – The Swordfish and Tunny Club – it was not until a sportfishing club – Penninsula – showed interest in sportfishing and gamefishing in the early seventies that its popularity grew.

By the late seventies gamefishing was well established in Victoria, with the thriving Gamefishing Association of Victoria boasting many new clubs and a strong growth. Some keen sportfishing clubs played a part in this, especially in exploring the areas off Barwon Heads, Apollo Bay, Warrnambool and Marlo.

Gamefishing off the Victorian coastline is currently a fairly healthy scene, with two exceptions: one has been the absence of southern bluefin tuna from Victorian waters for four years now, and the other is the apparent lack of interest many local gamefishers have in their own waters. However, solving the first problem could solve the second. On the subject of the southern bluefin tuna, there are some encouraging signs. Some reasonable stocks have reappeared off the east coast of Tasmania (1986–87), and there has been some local feedback at Barwon Heads, and at the southern end of Wilson's Promontory (1986). I firmly believe the bluefin will re-establish well enough for a sportfishery, but arguing with government to limit bluefin to a sportfishery in inshore waters will be difficult!

Of the other species of tuna to visit Victorian waters the albacore is by far the most prominent. Many gamefishers are unaware of their presence as they inhabit the deeper waters well out to sea. I have encountered these zealots on a number of occasions, but always in at least 60 metres of water or deeper, three to 30 kilometres seaward. Though their schools are vast, their size is small. Mostly they are immature fish in the 1–5-kilo range which puts many anglers off fishing for them; however, their table qualities and fine light tackle performance should offer all the attraction needed.

This black marlin was taken off Greenwell Point on the south coast of New South Wales. Its southern range stops about Bermagui but game and small-boat fishers from Tasmania and Victoria have the opportunity to tangle with striped marlin and other game fish. (Photo Steve Starling)

There is, of course, one other factor that the thinking, top-class gamefishers see in these schools of albacore. This is that they are an ideal bait size for large predators, and although Victoria is not yet credited with a viable cold-water marlin, broadbill, big-eye fishery, these vast schools of 'bait'-size albacore should hold the key.

Jim Allen, one of Victoria's best gamefishers, gives these vast schools of albacore as the reason for the presence of good marlin in Bass Strait. Over the past three seasons he has fished the waters off Flinders Island in late February when the albacore are about. Using live albacore he has managed to hook three striped marlin, the biggest of which was easily an 'All Tackle' World Record. Unfortunately all were lost, the large fish mainly because it was 'under-gunned' on 24-kilo tackle.

As to the other specific areas around the coast, Mallacoota is certainly the ground to produce gamefish of the style of Bermagui. Tackle, techniques, the fish and fishery are all similar. Unfortunately the 'notorious' bar and the fact that Bermagui itself is only two hours up the road, cause many people to bypass the State's most eastern gamefishery.

Marlo and Lakes Entrance both offer heaps of potential with southern bluefin and yellowtail kingfish at the right time of the year. The pick of this vast area is undoubtedly Cape Conran and the grounds seaward and including 'Beware Reef'. There does seem to be some semi-permanent population of big kingfish at Beware, and there has been considerable speculation of big tuna in the area (January–May). The launching ramp at Cape Conran is semi-open to the ocean swell and suited for boats of 5 metres and under.

Further west we have the vast grounds off ports Welshpool and Albert, encompassing Wilson's Promontory and extending out and around Flinders Island some 80 kilometres plus to the south. Professionals say that amateur anglers know nothing of the potential of the area. Striped marlin and broadbill are present, as are big-eye, triple-figure southern bluefin and world record yellowtail kingfish. Bait for these big pelagics is ultra plentiful – albacore, barracoota, squid, trevally, and cowanyoung schools are here by the hectare.

These grounds may never be opened up, however, unless thinking changes. Eighteen- to 30-metre charter boats are needed for these waters, complete with an experienced skipper.

Port Phillip Heads, 'The Rip', and the waters seaward are very sadly overlooked by Melbournian gamefishers. This area is a lot more productive than many people imagine. This again is big-boat water (8–15 metres), and it is puzzling to see so many big gamecruisers moored in the pens around the bay and yet so few ever out on Victoria's No 1 gamefishing ground. The Heads are mainly fished by people in 5-7-metre craft that often run into difficulty in the area due to the small size of their boats.

Southern bluefin over 100 kilos have been hooked and lost over the years in the Port Phillip Heads area. The Rip is also famous for its huge, hard-fighting kingfish as is Barwon Heads for its light-tackle blue and mako sharks.

Further afield around Seal Rocks, there are at times big white pointers as testified by Terry Tichener's capture of a 500-kilo plus specimen in 1985. Further out (3–6 kilometres) off the Heads, and west, to roughly off Bells Beach, there are good grounds producing big sharks – hammerheads, makos, blues, grey nurses and possibly whites. The best capture to date has been a 220-kilo mako by Daryl Mawson of Geelong in 1987 off Bells Beach.

Another light-tackle ground for sharks has been developed off Apollo Bay. Here the best time is January through to June, and the main species blue, mako and hammerhead to 100 kilos. There is also a resident stock of huge yellowtail kingfish at Cape Otway. Apollo Bay offers a very safe and reliable port to launch and retrieve all size craft. Further west lies Warrnambool which also is well known for its light tackle sharkfishery over the summer months. So much so that the Warrnambool Offshore and Gamefishing Club runs a very successful tournament between Christmas and New Year. There have also been several thresher sharks caught in the area over the last few years.

On the western extremities of the State are two ports, Fairy and Portland, both well known for southern bluefin tuna until their numbers declined through overfishing by trawlers a few years ago. At that time a number of successful gamefishing tournaments were held in the area over May-July, and concentrated on the bluefin. Now the scene is also mainly small sharks. There are, of course, the huge whites of Lady Julia Percy Island and possible broadbills in the canyons off Portland, but both prospects seem to be largely ignored by the gamefishers.

Certainly the state of gamefishing in Victoria is not as bad as generally painted. The scene, however, must move away from essentially trailer boats to much bigger and more capable boats that can reach the grounds where the really big fish are.

Tasmania

Victorians could take a leaf out of the Tasmanian book in that a lot of the gamefishing in Tasmania is done out of large charter boats (10-20 metres), due to rough conditions.

The main gamefishing region of Tasmania is the east coast with Eaglehawk Neck the base. Here the southern bluefin is king with fish in excess of 150 kilos possible. Nearly all bluefin are taken by trolling, although use of live small albacore will produce big bluefin and marlin.

This east coast of Tasmania is the only place in Australia where one can reliably expect to take a bluefin in excess of 50 kilos. The run normally starts in February with smaller fish between 10 and 25 kilos and, on good days, boats can hook and land anything up to twenty tuna. April, May and June are the top months for the bigger fish. Each year the locals are pegging the scene with increasing efficiency with the result that black and striped marlin are being hooked and landed at times. Tasmania has the advantage of deep water very close to shore as well as a huge supply of food for big pelagics—albacore, squid, mackerel, cowanyoung and many other schooling species not well known to mainlanders.

This east coast of Tasmania offers a big challenge to locals and to visiting gamefishers. The area is nowhere near fully explored, and is by far the best place to chase a big broadbill. In years to come this fish-rich water off Tasmania is really going to open the eyes of many mainland gamefishers.

TASMANIA-RIVERS, BAYS AND ESTUARIES
Alex Schaap

Tasmania has an abundance of sheltered bays and estuaries which can provide both the avid angler and the more casual family fishers with satisfying catches. The south-eastern region of the State is particularly well provided for, with waters such as Frederick Henry Bay, Norfolk Bay, D'Entrecasteaux Channel, Derwent Estuary and the Huon Estuary. Fishing in these larger waters is usually more productive if a boat is used although shore-based anglers can take good catches from rock platforms, beaches and jetties.

The most popular target species in these waters is the sand flathead, which is found on shallow, sandy bottom throughout the State. Although sand flathead of over 1.5-kilos are rarely caught in these waters, it is an excellent table fish and relatively easy to catch. The sand flathead lies on the bottom and captures prey by making fairly short dashes and as a result it is necessary for the angler to move the bait over the bottom in search of fish. The best way to do this is to fish from a drifting boat or slowly to retrieve the bait along the bottom if fishing from the shore. It is important that the bait is kept on or near the bottom and on very windy days it may be necessary to use a sea anchor to slow down the drift enough for the bait to reach the bottom without the aid of a huge snapper lead.

A simple 2-hook rig is usually used when drifting, while a running sinker above a single hook is popular when fishing from shore. In either case, it appears likely that the disturbance created by the sinker bouncing along the bottom will attract the attention of any flathead waiting in ambush. Choice of bait is rarely critical when fishing for flathead and any small fish or fish strip will usually be taken with some enthusiasm. Lures are also very effective on flathead when jigged from a boat or retrieved near the bottom when fishing from shore. Lures should have a strong action when worked slowly and spoons, Wonder Wobblers, minnows and soft-bodied plastics are preferred.

Sand flathead are available throughout the year although the best catches are taken in the warmer months. As the location of flathead hotspots can change from day to day it is advisable to do some exploratory drifting or casting early in the day to locate the best fish and then concentrate on an area with repeated short drifts.

A second species of flathead, the tiger flathead, may also be taken in Tasmanian bays and estuaries but usually from slightly deeper waters (over 15 metres). The tiger flathead attain a weight of some 3 kilos and can be quite abundant during spring when they fall victim to anglers using the drift fishing technique.

Morwong, or squeaker perch as they are called locally, are also common in the bays and estuaries and are often taken by anglers drifting for flathead. Although most fish taken from shallow inshore waters are quite small, less than 1 kilo in weight, they provide excellent sport, are fine table fish and are available throughout the year.

Morwong are usually found in schools and often congregate over the margins between sand and reef or rubble bottom. Drift fishing is often effective in locating these aggregations which can then be fished with repeated short drifts or by anchoring. Baits of small fish or fish strips should be suspended just off the bottom on a two-hook rig if drifting or on a single hook with a small, free-running-ball sinker when fishing from an anchored boat.

The sand whiting is another small but keenly sought-after resident of the bays and estuaries which is taken in large numbers during the warmer months. This species is most abundant over sandy bottom in relatively shallow water in the south and east of the State although it does occur in the north-east and north-west. Whiting feed on worms, molluscs and small crustaceans gathered from the sea bed and so it is necessary to fish small baits on the bottom. Drift fishing with a simple two-hook rig baited with marine worms, squid or fish pieces is an effective technique.

Gear for this type of bait fishing need not be complicated or expensive as a handline or light boat rod with a sidecast or threadline reel spooled with 4- to 8-kilo line will handle most drift fishing, while a medium spinning outfit is ideal for shore-based work. Other species the angler is likely to encounter while bait fishing with this type of gear include black bream, flounder, Australian salmon, barracouta, silver trevally, spotted trevalla, cod, yellow-eye mullet, jack mackerel, leatherjackets, wrasse, dogfish and gurnards. However, many of these species are rarely taken by drift fishing and the angler must target a particular species and modify the techniques accordingly to get better results.

Flounder are a good example as, although they are very common in these sheltered inshore waters, they are rarely caught by the average 'chuck and chance it' angler. A light line with minimal lead and a small hook baited with fresh marine worms are what is needed to take flounder consistently. Of course, spearing them at night in the shallows is even more effective while some anglers have had success with soft-bodied plastic lures retrieved slowly along the bottom.

Bream are another target requiring some specialised techniques as they have a reputation for being fussy about baits and on occasions are very particular about the way a bait is presented. Bream are available in most Tasmanian estuaries throughout the year but are most abundant in the southern and eastern rivers during spring. Some of the larger waters are more easily fished from a boat while the smaller rivers are best fished from the shore as a boat may send timid fish off the bite.

Most fishers use soft-actioned spinning outfits with lines of 3- to 6-kilos as the ability to cast a lightly weighted bait is often an advantage. In most fishing situations it is wise to use the smallest amount of lead necessary to get the bait to the fish and this is particularly important when bream are biting timidly. Split shot or a small bean sinker is usually used above a single hook with the sinker running freely down to the hook or onto a swivel about 60 centimetres above the hook. In areas where the bottom is very weedy it is best to use the swivel and trace rig as this allows the bait to remain above the weed even if the sinker settles into it.

Many baits are used for bream around Tasmania and many anglers maintain that particular baits are necessary for particular rivers. Some of the more commonly used baits include live or fresh shrimps, marine worms, prawns, hardyheads (known locally as pretty fish), fish strips, mussels, crabs and dough. The bait should be allowed to wash around snags, rock outcrops, weed beds or channels as flat, featureless bottom is rarely productive. When a bite is noticed it is often advisable to allow the fish to move off with the bait before striking, as a premature strike will simply pull the bait away from a timid fish. On other occasions the bait may be taken with such gusto that a strike is just a formality.

Of course fishing in the bays and estuaries is

A fast-growing method of catching flathead in bays, estuaries and coastal rivers, even from beaches, is to spin for them. They are attracted by a wide variety of lures retrieved across sand flats, along the edges of channels and near weed beds. (Photo Warren Steptoe)

not restricted to bouncing a bait along the bottom as good catches may be taken with lures. Flathead and flounder have been mentioned as lure-fishing targets but the most keenly sought-after species on lures are Australian salmon and barracouta.

Salmon are most abundant in bays and estuaries during the warmer months but may also be taken during winter. Sub-adult fish to about 1.5 kilos, known locally as 'cockey salmon', may be found throughout the State but the larger adult fish, 'blackbacks', are more common in the north-west.

A boat is useful when fishing for salmon as the schools are often very mobile and may only be within casting range of the shore fisher for a few brief but hectic minutes. When a surface school is located, either through bird activity or surface disturbance, it is wise to approach with

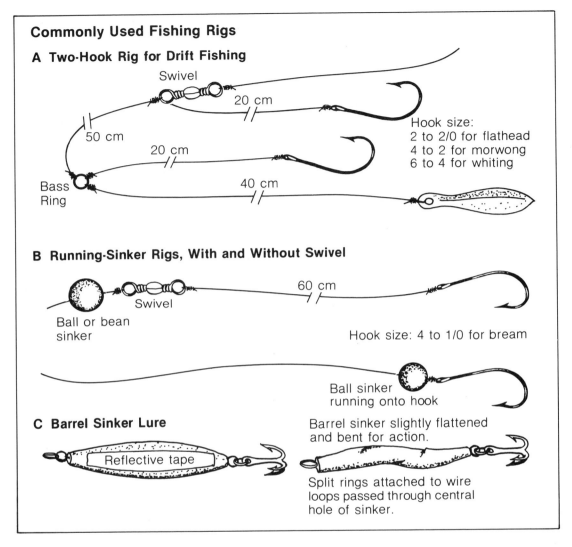

caution as a speeding boat will often put the whole school down. For the same reason it is better to troll around the fringes of the school rather than through the middle. A better technique still is to position the boat in the path of the school with the motor in neutral and cast lures into the school.

Most metal casting lures and minnows are effective on salmon and size is usually more important than shape, action or colour. On many occasions salmon will only take very small lures and home-made barrel sinker lures are both effective and cheap. A light spinning outfit spooled with 2- to 4-kilo line is ideal for throwing small lures from a boat while a little extra length in the rod is handy for shore-based fishing.

Barracouta tend to be most abundant in late summer and autumn when large schools of adult fish are found close inshore. They are rarely as timid as salmon and it is possible to troll in a tight circle in the middle of a school without putting the fish down. In many cases, this surface activity will actually send the fish into a feeding frenzy when anything thrown into the water will be attacked with a great deal of enthusiasm. An equally productive but more fuel-efficient strategy is to cut the motor and jig lures through the depth of the school.

Larger lures with single hooks are used because they are easier to remove from toothy jaws than small lures bristling with treble hooks. A medium spinning outfit spooled with 3- to 6-kilo line is more than adequate although a short wire trace is helpful in maintaining levels in the lure box.

Barracouta may also be taken by spinning or bait fishing from rock platforms and jetties and any such feature in the larger estuaries and bays is well worth a few casts, not only for 'couta and salmon but also for pike, jack mackerel and perhaps a sea-run brown trout.

Hazards, and Safety Measures

Most estuarine and bay fishing is done during the warmer months when a day on the water is quite pleasant. Unfortunately winds are very variable during summer and dramatic changes in wind speed and direction can occur with little warning. Prevailing westerly winds are much more predictable during winter. Anglers should also note that, even in summer, Tasmanian inshore waters are cold and every precaution should be taken to ensure the angler stays out of the water.

If venturing outside it is wise to seek local advice as many of the estuaries have very variable and potentially dangerous bar ways.

ROCK FISHING IN TASMANIA

David Tulip

Rock fishing is not as popular in Tasmania as it is in, say, New South Wales, perhaps because of a greater emphasis on small-boat fishing in Tasmania's many sheltered waterways. In addition, the 'bread-and-butter' fish of mainland rock-hoppers, luderick and bream, are almost totally absent, the former confined mainly to the north-west coast, and the latter being black or southern bream which are rarely taken outside the estuaries.

However, while Tasmania's rock platforms may not provide the variety of fish available in northern States, or, indeed, available to small-boat fishers in Tasmania, there is still plenty to keep all but the freezer-fillers and land-based game fanatics happy around the rocks.

Perhaps before describing the fishing that is available, the exclusion of land-based game should be explained. Although Tasmania has some excellent gamefishing available offshore for southern bluefin, albacore, skipjack tuna, mako sharks and several other species, opportunities to contact them from the shore are very rare. Even the good old standby, the yellowtail king, is far from common, with only isolated catches occurring around the mouth of the Tamar, Freycinet Peninsula and Maria Island.

While there are obviously some possibilities in these areas and around the Tasman Peninsula there are no established land-based gamefishing hotspots, and anyone visiting the State looking for this type of fishing must face the reality that they are engaged in pioneering work!

Despite the apparent lack of gamefish from the rocks, lure casting can be very rewarding, and it is probably now as popular as bait fishing. The main targets are salmon and barracouta, with an incidental catch of pike and snook.

Tailor, again, are rare, and probably confined to the far north-east corner.

Salmon use Tasmanian waters as a nursery area, and can be found in sizes up to about 30 centimetres in most places all year round. The larger adult fish are more common in the warmer months from November to March, and while they too can be found right round the coastline they are most prolific and of largest size on the Bass Strait coast and around Flinders Island.

From the rocks the usual method is to cast a

silver metal lure out as far as possible from a rocky headland, and retrieve at a moderate pace. Favoured lures are Wonder Wobblers, Stingsildas, Halco slices and hexagonals and similar simple patterns. North-west coast anglers have considerable success with clear plastic tubing slipped over the shank of a hook, which presumably looks like a whitebait or similar tiny prey, and this may well succeed when larger lures fail. For the usual run of fish, up to 2 kilos, tackle need only be light to medium, but some of those Bass Strait 'sambos' go to 5 kilos and more, and demand more respect.

Barracouta are a nuisance to anglers seeking more glamorous game fish, but fished for in their own right they are heaps of fun and are excellent eating when in good condition. They are probably second only to flathead as a target in Tasmania, and such popularity speaks for itself! Like salmon, small 'couta are about for most of the year, and the larger ones run inshore in summer and autumn, with March-May probably being the best time in the south-east, while the north-west coast gets a spring run also. Similar methods are used to those for salmon, with nothing more elaborate than a chrome slice usually being necessary, fished near the surface. 'Couta don't like bright sunshine very much, but can still be caught sometimes by fishing wide and deep with a heavy metal lure or diving minnow. Most anglers use a wire trace for 'couta because of their teeth.

Snook, or short-finned pike, are found only in Bass Strait, while the smaller long-finned pike (called jack pike on the north coast) are more widespread.

Bait fishing from the rocks, while widely practised, is not realising its full potential, with most anglers just soaking a bait on the bottom for whatever comes along. The few that use berley, fresh bait and a bit of thought about fish habits usually get good results, and those who do all right on their local rocks should do likewise here—provided they adjust to the local species!

The major bait-fishing targets from the rocks are cod, morwong (locally called 'perch'), silver trevally, warehou ('snotty' trevally), trumpeter, yellow-eyed mullet, blue-throated and purple wrasse ('kelpies') and leatherjackets. In addition, many flathead are caught where the bottom is sandy. Sorry, very little chance of snapper!

Cod are a soft-bodied fish, usually pink or red, lacking the spiky dorsal fin of the various fish called 'cod' in mainland States. They can often be found in large numbers, especially in winter, and are relatively easy to catch, having large mouths and appetites to match. Any fish bait, or even red meat, fished above a sinker resting on the bottom will usually find any cod in the area. They will take slow-moving lures, so having found them with bait you could then have some fun with Mr Twisters or similar. Cod usually average 0.5 to 1.5 kilos.

Morwong are the same species as in Victoria and New South Wales, but perhaps tend to be more accessible to land-based anglers in Tasmania, although probably in smaller sizes. Tackle and methods are similar to those used for cod, but use much smaller hooks—size 4 or even 6—and baits to match. Catches will improve with better quality baits. Try fresh mussels or cockles if you can get them. 'Perch' tend to favour sandy bottoms near rocks rather than solid reef, and with small hooks, whiting and even flounder can provide a surprise or two. The normal inshore run of morwong is well under a kilo but bigger ones are not rare.

Silver trevally and warehou are usually both called trevally (although the warehou is not a trevally) and are known as 'silvers' and 'snotties'. Their habits seem to be similar, both being mid-water feeders and therefore difficult to catch with a bait anchored to the bottom. Best prospects are to berley with crushed mussels and fish a fresh mussel with little or no lead in the trail. Other baits include whitebait and blue pilchards. Both species are most common in late summer to autumn and average 0.5 to 1 kilo, although net-caught silvers to 5 kilos are not rare.

There are two major trumpeter species, one of which, the striped or Tasmanian trumpeter, is a very unlikely catch for a rock fisher these days due to its susceptibility to netting. The bastard or silver trumpeter is still common, and can be caught on a hook despite many claims to the contrary. It is a fussy, delicate biter, an expert at removing a bait with no indication to the angler, but one method to beat this is to lower a small lightly weighted hook baited with fresh mussel down a rock face, and raise it slowly back up again. Many leatherjackets also fall for this method. Trumpeter seem more common inshore in spring and early summer, but are always around. They average 0.5 to 1 kilo, but can be up to 3 kilos, with stripeys reaching 10 kilos or more offshore.

Mullet are a good winter standby, as they are often around in vast numbers, and can be great fun to catch. Unlike sea mullet, yellow-eyes take a bait readily. Again, a No 4 or 6 hook baited with mussel, cockle, scallop, sandworm, bread or almost any bait, fished with as little lead as possible, should do the trick.

Wrasse and leatherjackets are fun fish, and can save a day when there's nothing else about. Some of those kelpies are big and mean, however, and they fight dirty—it depends on your definition of fun! Fresh bait (again, mussels or limpets are usually handy and well accepted) dropped into likely rock holes or clearings in the fringing kelp will usually get instant results. There are no mangrove jacks and rock blackfish are rare, but some kelpies seem to think they are a combination of both—look out!

Most northern and eastern population centres have potentially good rock-fishing areas near them, but specific information on locations is not, to the best of my knowledge, available yet in print. However, the natives are friendly, and many caravan park, motel, service station, pub and general store proprietors are only too happy to advise their customers on fishing spots as part of the service.

A few likely spots to head for? Stanley, Rocky Cape, Mersey Bluff, Eddystone Point, St Helens, Bicheno, Coles Bay, Swansea, Oxford (for Maria Island), Dunalley, Eaglehawk Neck, Port Arthur, Adventure Bay (Bruny Island), Dover—and a lot of others in between.

The West Coast is largely inaccessible, and the few places where civilisation has met the Southern Ocean, eg, Strahan, Granville Harbour, Pieman Heads and Marrawah, can be wiped out most of the time by huge swells, so a phone call to check if any sort of fishing is actually possible may save you a long wasted trip. But do the trip anyway—the scenery alone is worth it!

TASMANIA'S WILD TROUT
Dr Robert D Sloane

The historic Salmon Ponds hatchery near Hobart was the site of the first trout introduction to the Southern Hemisphere. After several unsuccessful attempts, Atlantic salmon and trout ova were brought from England to Tasmania by sailing ship in 1864. Although the salmon failed to acclimatise, the handful of brown trout which were reared and released thrived in the Tasmanian environment and their progeny were later used to stock the other States of Australia and the waters of New Zealand.

Today, more than a century after they first became established, wild trout continue to flourish, with the clear mountain streams and gravelly riffles providing ideal spawning and nursery conditions for the Tasmanian trout.

The Tasmanian fishery is still dominated by the brown trout which has populated virtually all lakes and streams. Sea-run brown trout are well established in southern, western and northern rivers. The rainbow trout inhabits most waters in lesser numbers but is common in Great Lake, Lagoon of Islands, Dee Lagoon, Lake Rowallan and the remote Lake Meston. Some streams do hold reasonable stocks of rainbows, but generally brown trout predominate. A population of wild brook trout occurs in Clarence Lagoon.

The average size of trout varies depending on the physical and chemical properties and the natural spawning facilities of each water. Catches also vary from place to place and from day to day, but generally the angler can choose whether to take light tackle for trout of half a kilo or devote more time to a water which holds real trophy fish of 4 and 5 kilos. The choice of water and tackle is really limitless and caters for all tastes.

Wet Fly

Wet-fly fishing is practised throughout the season on both lake and stream in Tasmania. Early and late in the season large matukas, fur flies and other bulky patterns are popular. During summer small nymph and beetle patterns are favoured. Basic fly patterns include the Red and Black Matuka, Mrs Simpson, Yeti, Woolly Worm, Watsons Fancy, Brown Nymph and the Black Beetle.

In the lake country boat fishing is popular on many waters and sink-tip and sinking lines are often used to good effect. But the real beauty of Tasmania's wet-fly fishing is that trout often move into the shallows and can be caught from the shore; their backs, dorsal fins and tails are often clearly visible as they fossick for food in the shallows. Brown trout are rarely easy to catch when they are 'tailing' like this, but just seeing them excites the heart of even the most experienced angler.

Dry Fly

Tasmanian waters boast prolific fly hatches at various times of the year. Lowland rivers such as the Macquarie and Break O' Day are famous for their prolific 'red spinner' mayfly hatches, particularly in October. The mayfly hatches on Brumbys Creek are delayed and prolonged by colder water and may extend well into autumn. Midges, caddis, beetles, stoneflies, moths and grasshoppers also produce rises on Tasmanian streams at various times of the year.

In the highlands the mayfly 'dun' hatches extend from November to April whenever conditions are favourable. Hatches occur on most highland lakes, notably Little Pine, Arthurs, Sorell, Penstock and Bronte. Warm summer and autumn days produce extensive beetle and leaf-hopper falls on many timber-surrounded lakes, resulting in spectacular rises. Favoured patterns include Red Tag, Greenwell's Glory, Red Spinner, Black Spinner, March Brown and the Zulu.

Spinning and Trolling

The use of spinning gear with artificial lures is the most popular trout-fishing method in Tasmania. Spinning for sea-run trout in the estuaries and lower reaches of rivers is productive early in the season and a small wobbler or Celta used with light tackle can provide excellent sport in Tasmania's many small streams.

In the lake country spinning from the shore is popular on most waters. The large lakes such as Pedder, Arthurs, Sorell and Great Lake are ideal boating waters and drift spinning and trolling are widely practised. Favoured lures vary with the season and from water to water, but local tackle shops always stock the most suitable kinds and are happy to give advice.

Baiting

Although some Tasmanian waters are restricted to fly-fishing and others only to the use of artificial lures, natural bait fishing is permitted on the majority of lakes and virtually all streams. However, fishing is restricted to the use of one rod and line—set lines and handlines are not permitted on Tasmanian inland waters. Early in the season the earthworm is a popular bait on streams and later in the summer the grasshopper is a deadly bait. Wood-grubs, corby-grubs, cockroaches and frogs are also used quite commonly.

Famous Waters

To the tourist angler in Tasmania, Arthurs Lake probably represents the best chance of landing a wild brown trout. Arthurs is Tasmania's most popular and productive trout fishery and boasts an abundance of naturally spawned brown trout averaging a half to one kilo. Local anglers often land their bag limit of twelve trout in a day on this water. Spinning, trolling, natural bait and fly fishing are all effective methods.

Great Lake is the largest of the lakes in the Central Highlands district and lies at an altitude of 1034 metres above sea level. This cool, clear hydro-electric lake supports both brown trout and rainbow trout. Bait fishing is permitted on most areas of Great Lake and set-rod fishing is popular from the shore. Spinning and trolling are also commonplace on this water and the superb rainbow trout are eagerly sought by locals and visitors alike.

Little Pine Lagoon is perhaps Tasmania's best known fly-fishing water and only fly-fishing is permitted here. This small lagoon is shallow and weedy and supports a rich aquatic life. During the spring months trout 'tail' freely in the shallows and these wily fish have gained the reputation of 'untouchables' because they are often very difficult to catch. But Little Pine is probably best known for its mayfly hatches which occur on warm days from December to March. When conditions are just right the dun hatches on Little Pine are probably unequalled on any other still water in the world.

The Western Lakes is a region of countless lakes, lagoons and tarns scattered across the Western Central Plateau between Great Lake and the Cradle Mountain/Lake St Clair National Park. This region provides the ultimate challenge for the angler who enjoys back-packing to little-known waters. Nature regulates the trout stocks here, with some waters supporting an abundance of small trout while others hold small numbers of real trophy specimens exceeding 5 kilos.

Lake Sorell is a 55-square-kilometre water which rivals Arthurs Lake as Tasmania's best trout fishing lake. This is essentially a natural lake and features extensive shallow marshes which provide ideal trout feeding grounds and create a unique fly-fishing environment. Lake Sorell is reserved for the use of artificial lures and also attracts many spinning and trolling enthusiasts. The brown trout here, too, are wild stocks and they are larger than those caught at Arthurs Lake. The Sorell browns are usually 1-2 kilos and larger speciments of 3 kilos are caught. Rainbow trout are also abundant in this water.

Nearby Lake Crescent appears very similar to Sorell, but poorer spawning beds at Crescent result in far fewer trout. Although they are not easy to find, the Lake Crescent brown trout grow as large as 12 kilos and fish of 4 and 5 kilos are not unusual.

The township of Bronte Park is sited near a chain of excellent trout lakes comprising Pine Tier, Bronte, Bradys, Binney and Tungatinah. A number of other fisheries including Lake Echo, Dee Lagoon and Laughing Jack Lagoon can be readily visited from this base. Bronte Lagoon is the feature water of this region. It is a popular fly-fishing water and also produces fine catches for trollers and spin-fishers.

In 1973 the construction of a hydro-electric scheme in south-west Tasmania created a new and spectacular trout fishery. Lake Pedder reached its fishing peak in the late 1970s when the legendary trout reached an average size in excess of 4.5 kilos. Today the usual size of Pedder brown trout is a much more modest 1.5 to 2 kilos, but there are still plenty of 3-kilo fish landed. Trolling is the most popular method on this giant (242-square-kilometre) storage, but the mudeye (dragonfly nymph) migration in summer still attracts fly anglers from around Tasmania.

The Macquarie River flows northward through Tasmania's midlands and is arguably the best of the State's lowland streams. However, many other rivers such as the Leven, Mersey, Meander, North Esk, South Esk, St Patricks and Break O' Day provide excellent trout fishing which rivals the famed Macquarie. In fact, virtually all of Tasmania's lowland streams and their small tributary creeks hold self-supporting wild trout populations, and although stream fish are generally small compared with their lakeland cousins, fat little half-kilo trout provide great sport on light tackle.

Near Cressy and Longford a series of weirs, known as Brumbys Creek, has been created where the cold Great Lake water is dissipated after passing through the Poatina power station. These weirs are regarded by many as the best trout waters in Tasmania, as they offer a unique combination of riverine and still-water fishing and the cold water produces a rich aquatic fauna and prolonged fly hatches.

Tasmania's Seasons

In Tasmania the trout fishing season on most inland waters opens on the Saturday nearest 1 August. Although the weather can be changeable and cold, the early-season fishing can be rewarding. Bait fishing, spinning and trolling are effective from the start of the season in the lake country. Often the rivers are swollen by spring rains, creating ideal backwater wet-fly fishing and worming. This is also the best time of year for sea-run trout in the estuaries, and flooded lake margins also produce excellent wet-fly fishing as the brown trout forage in the marshes and 'tail' in the shallows.

Dry-fly fishing and 'polaroiding' (using sunglasses to cut surface glare) are best on sunny midsummer days and the settled weather produces excellent fly hatches on most inland waters. The grasshopper is an effective bait on the rivers during late summer but great stealth is required when the rivers are low and clear. Generally the weather and water levels dictate the behaviour of Tasmania's trout so the angler should adopt a flexible approach towards water fished and methods.

In the lake country autumn brings mild, clear days and cool, frosty nights. Spinning and trolling for rainbows is particularly effective at this time of year. Warm autumn days also produce spectacular rises to midges and gum beetles and both browns and rainbows fall to the dry fly.

In Tasmania brown trout spawn during May, June and July, whereas rainbow trout mainly spawn from July to September. The closed seasons are designed to protect spawning trout, because the wild fishery is dependent on successful natural recruitment to provide stock for years to come. Remember, all inland waters in Tasmania are closed to fishing during June and July.

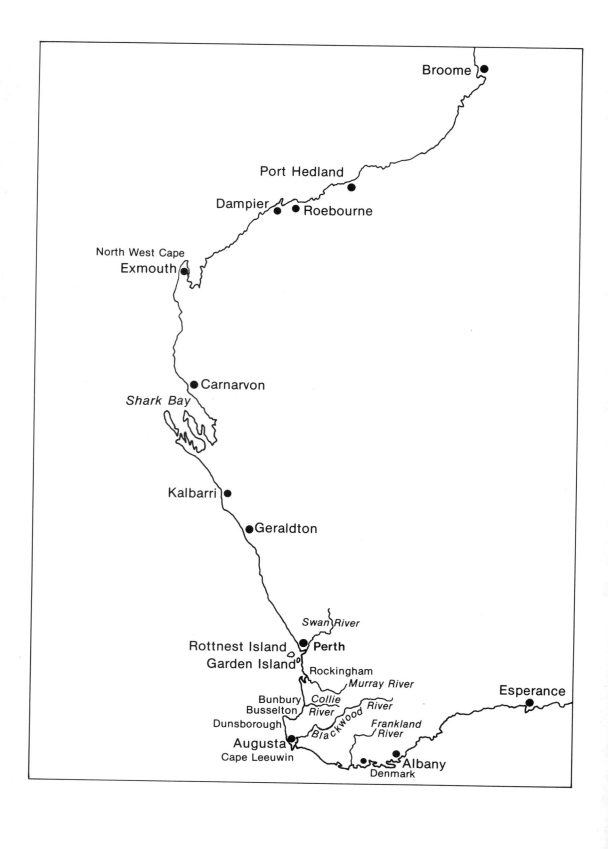

SECTION FIVE

Western Australia

INLAND FISHING IN THE SOUTH-WEST

Neil Coy

Western Australia's south-west holds interesting and varied fishing for both the casual and enthusiast angler.

At the top of the list is the large freshwater crayfish known as marron, which is eagerly sought during the warmer months. Trout, redfin perch and freshwater cobbler also have their adherents who enjoy good fishing in the cooler months, April to October inclusive.

In recent marroning seasons as many as 28 000 people have taken out licences to fish for these delectable creatures in the larger streams and irrigation dams of the region. While drop nets baited with old meat is the preferred catching method in rivers, the locals scatter handfuls of chicken pellets in the water, along shelving shorelines, when fishing the dams. As the marron clamber inshore to feed on the pellets at dusk and after dark, they are stalked by torchlight then scooped out of the water with scoop nets fashioned from chicken wire.

The minimum legal catching size for marron is 76 millimetres carapace length – from tip of beak to rear of head shell. The largest specimens exceed 400 millimetres body length (170 millimetres carapace) with a body weight of about 2 kilos.

These large marron are usually only caught by experienced hunters who guard their local knowledge jealously because, in some south-west towns, a person's worth is sometimes gauged by the size and number of marron he or she catches.

In years gone by these hunters could catch their favourite 'bush tucker' by the sackful but they usually gave the marron a sporting chance by patiently snaring the quarry with a polesnare fashioned with a loop made from piano wire.

Increased fishing pressure over the past 20 years or so has recently warranted a bag limit of 20 marron a day during the legal fishing season, between mid December and the end of

April. Despite continuing restrictions on the catching of marron there does not seem to be enough to go round in some waters. However, since the advent of commercial marron farming in the mid 1970s, the gourmet can now enjoy eating this delicious crustacean at a number of restaurants.

The only other endemic species sought after in the south-west's inland waterways is the local variety of catfish, known as freshwater cobbler. These eel-tailed fish which can exceed 3 kilos and have delicious white flesh, are caught by a few worm fishers in the evenings, along the larger rivers and dams between the Moore River, north of Perth, and the Frankland River on the south coast.

Because the longer rivers rise in the low rainfall wheatbelt zone, the impressive flows of winter are reduced to a mere trickle during the very hot summers. Wholesale land clearing has turned these larger rivers saline and led to severe eutrophication, thus restricting the habitat for inland fish and crayfish.

In former years cobbler, marron and the introduced redfin perch were prolific in the upper reaches of the Murray, Collie, Blackwood, and Frankland rivers. But, as the habitat deteriorates progressively downstream, the marron and redfin are disappearing from their former haunts.

Though a number of fish species were introduced into the south-west during the 1890s the only fish that acclimatised in the long term were redfin perch and Crucian carp.

The most extraordinary acclimatisation was the introduction of Murray cod into Lake Powell, near Albany. Some of these fish, which persisted into the 1950s, weighed in excess of 40 kilos.

Trout were not acclimatised in any number until the 1930s when the late C A 'Sticky' Glew began his experiments with brown-trout fry at the Pemberton schoolhouse. Both brown and rainbow trout fishing is now available for an ever-growing number of anglers who fish the forested, fresher waters between Perth and Albany. These are mainly concentrated close to the Darling Escarpment, the streams and dams around Pemberton, and a few waters in the Albany district.

Contrary to the situation in eastern states, the rainbow is the most prolific trout in the south-west and because of the marginal conditions a temperature-superior strain of 'hot' rainbows has developed. These trout can tolerate warmer conditions for longer periods than other rainbow trout around the world.

Although most of the metropolitan water supply dams abound with trout and marron the closest fishing to Perth, of any magnitude, is more than 100 kilometres to the south-east, in the Murray River near Dwellingup.

The irrigation dams of the Harvey River system, between Waroona and Harvey, offer a variety of fishing, as all six dams hold marron, trout, redfin and cobbler in varying proportions.

Waroona Dam, arguably the State's best trout fishery between 1976 and 1982, has been overrun by redfin, though a few trout are still being caught by the determined enthusiast. Other redfin-dominated waters in this area are Drakesbrook Dam and Harvey Weir. The main trout waters are Samsons, Logue Brook and Stirling dams, the upper reaches of the Harvey River, the Brunswick River, and a few small hill streams.

Travelling south the next bastion of inland fishing is the coal-mining town of Collie, recognised as the redfin and marroning centre of the south-west. On warm evenings in summer the 100-kilometre shoreline of Wellington Dam is marked by the lights and cooking fires of hundreds of people seeking marron. In the cooler months the redfin school in prolific numbers for the bait and spin anglers who catch good bags in the dam backwaters and the rivers close to town. In the gorge below Wellington Dam, there are trout and marron in the cold, artificial flow of summer irrigation water.

Further south there is good fishing for those

with local knowledge in the large Blackwood River system, between Boyup Brook and Sue's Bridge, near Augusta. Despite the deteriorating habitat redfin are still caught upstream from Boyup Brook but marron are not in any number until the vicinity of Bridgetown. Downstream from Bridgetown the river and larger tributaries can hold rainbows averaging 1-3 kilos, if hatchery stockings are maintained.

The Pemberton district is the high citadel of trout fishing in the south-west. The main features are the Warren and Donnelly rivers, Lefroy and Barlee brooks, the commercial trout fisheries at Karri Valley and Treen Brook, and the government fish hatchery in Pemberton itself.

The Donnelly, which abounds with rainbows averaging a kilo, is best fished via forestry tracks from Graphite Road, Seventh Day Road, and the Vasse Highway. In summer many large rainbows drop downstream to the estuary, near the mouth of the river.

The Warren and Lefroy maintain a prolific number of wily brown trout and the current State record of 4.5 kilos was caught near Brockman Bridge by Francis Loutsky, in January 1987. The new dam on Big Brook is proving to be a popular rainbow fishery.

Limited trout fishing is available in the Denmark River and the King, Kalgan and Waychinicup near Albany. Marron and some cobbler are present in most of the other southern coastal streams, with the Gardener River near Northcliffe being the home of the largest marron in the region.

Trout anglers enjoy winter fishing in the dams, with lures and wet flies. There is a little dry-fly fishing in spring and autumn but the best catches on fly are usually at night when the mudeye hatches occur in early autumn.

During spring the larger rivers provide good streamer and lure fishing in the rapids and glides and though fishing is generally quiet over summer the trout become active again in April.

PERTH TO ALBANY-BEACHES, ESTUARIES AND BAYS

Phil Stanley

What the beautiful south of Perth beaches lack in glamour species they make up for in numbers. The Perth to Albany coastline is noted for its small fish rather than the line-stretching monsters of the north.

It's not that there aren't big fish – there are monster mulloway, occasional samson fish, small sharks, the odd big groper and others. Mainly, though, it's the little ones, tommy ruff (herring), silver trevally (skippy), garfish (gardie), tailor and bream that make the south-west coast memorable.

The fish aren't that difficult to catch either. Let's face facts, you can never call catching a fish easy; there are occasions, however, when it's possible to make good hauls of herring, garfish and trevally.

Mainstay of the recreational fishery is the herring. The little fellows are a year-round proposition although their autumn run attracts the most attention. During this run they can be caught throughout most of the day, but they are best pursued morning or evening.

Herring respond well to berley and the major technique is use of a wooden float with a large hole for berley. The float (about 60 grams) casts well – an essential on this coast and, when stuffed full of berley, can attract schools of the tough fighting fish. A long trace (2 metres of 3-kilo line) from the swivel stopping the float should end with a small hook (No 6 or 7 suicide).

Best baits are maggots which dedicated anglers breed themselves, followed by small pieces of prawn or cubes of a freshly caught sand whiting. Squid and octopus, in very small, skinned cubes, can do the job.

Herring will attack a lure, and a piece of green

drinking straw slid over a hook, or white rawl plug, may attract strikes. Small ABU Tobys (4-7 grams) or similar do well although the high leaping herring very often throw a heavier lure. Bait, however, is the best proposition. Fish caught must be looked after as herring are an oily fish and poor handling rapidly ruins their quality.

A berley cage can be substituted for the float when distance is not such an important consideration and anglers have found that floats made from the slow-sinking timber wandoo are outstanding.

Sinking herring rigs also bring the angler into contact with other species; silver trevally provide a happy alternative and can be caught in numbers, particularly in winter.

When the rig is allowed to sink further it comes into the range of sand whiting, a few silver bream and flathead. Surface floats can have a split shot at the end of the long trace which will allow the bait to sink more deeply. Garfish can be caught when the floating rig and bait stay near the surface.

Another small-fish technique that anglers should have in their repertoire is use of a small running sinker for fishing near rock or reef. It's the simplest of rigs, a small ball stopped by a small swivel, then a trace of around 45 centimetres, then the hook with baits similar to those for herring. An alternative, very popular and effective rig, is a small gang of three or four hooks to hold a whitebait or sardine. This bottom or mid-water rig will account for a variety of species—trevally, herring, bream, rockfish, flathead, flounder, tailor, King George whiting, etc. It can be fished from a short or long rod, depending on circumstances.

The third major south-western Australian technique (although it would work throughout the country), is to use a mulie (Western Australian pilchard) rig. This is the standard method of fishing for the other bread and butter fish, the razor-toothed tailor.

Tailor lack the year round reliability of herring and are predominantly caught in summer. Early morning and late evening is best and should anglers encounter a good run, then they are into exciting fishing. A 1-kilo tailor is a tough-fighting and tasty adversary.

The mulie rig is far more complex than that for herring. Key ingredient is a gang of hooks (four No 3 tarpon style are a good standard), fished with a sinker rig.

This rig will also successfully fish for other south-west Western Australian fish. It should be called a 'classic' rig and will readily account for salmon, mulloway, small shark, flathead, bream (occasionally), samson fish, snapper, groper, etc. A couple of key points: the hooks must be sharpened and should just fit the length of the mulie.

An angler thus armed with the makings of these three rigs and suitable rod and reel (around 3 metres *at least* for beach and rock fishing, for estuary, rock and jetty, 2 metres is fine), will be adequately equipped for this coast.

We can now look at the 'wheres' of the south-west coast.

Perth is associated with beautiful white-sand surf beaches and this must be taken into account by fishers. It implies biggish wave conditions and hence long rods and heavy gear. Anglers will find that in winter the best beaches are Cottesloe (Grant Street reef), Swanbourne (right next to the nude beach is a top fishing spot!), Swanbourne Drain, City Beach, Floreat, Scarborough and Trigg. Around Fremantle, South Beach and Port Beach are worth a try.

Man-made structures add significantly to fishing quality. North and South Moles are good in winter along with parts of the new America's Cup Marina, Cottesloe Groyne (especially for herring), Floreat Groynes, the massive Hillary's boat harbour, Ocean Reef marina and Yanchep's marina. All these locations are good in the early morning and evening in summer and autumn, for tailor, herring or garfish.

In the Swan/Canning estuary, a ball-sinker rig can attract tailor in summer (Nedlands to

Fremantle), flathead, flounder, cobbler (specialised baits required), black bream (causeway up river in summer), while the big mulie rig could score one of the monster mulloway that come right up the river in summer.

Cockburn Sound is a haven for small-boat anglers with prolific numbers of herring, skippy and garfish available. Autumn brings an increase in skippy schools and early winter gives a chance of encountering very large pink snapper, which come into Cockburn and Warnbro Sounds to breed. Boat anglers should also try their squid jigs and may score themselves a bonus. Bonito are active in autumn. Near Garden Island samson fish and an occasional shark mackerel (January, February or March) are caught.

Warnbro Sound (Safety Bay) holds promise for small fish, pink snapper and King George whiting near reef areas. Shore fishing in Warnbro Sound is excellent for tailor in summer (particularly January) and herring and other small fish in winter. The variety, at times, can be staggering.

Madora, Golden Bay, San Remo and Silver Sands (all just north of Mandurah) have legendary status for their summer tailor run and some catches of huge mulloway, within easy casting distance from the shore. Big sinkers (up to 120 grams) may be needed to fish into the sea breeze in the evening.

Mandurah sits at the sea entrance to the huge Peel/Harvey estuary. The estuary, a top crabbing location, attracts attention from king prawners in April and May. The river near the town bridges abounds in small fish, with chopper tailor in summer and varieties of small fish in winter (bream, herring, trevally, garfish, with cobbler and occasional mulloway adding interest). Ocean fronts near the resort town are very popular in early summer mornings for tailor anglers. Small boats can do very well in the bay on tailor in the evenings.

Just south of Mandurah, a long stretch of flat beaches holds exciting beach fishing. Tim's Thicket, White Hills, Preston Beach, Myalup and Binningup are attractive locations. Summer is tailor time with herring and whiting available throughout the day.

Preston, Myalup and Binningup have bitumen road access although a four-wheel-drive allows exciting exploring of the kilometres of sand beaches. Anglers fish Tim's Thicket and south for the autumn salmon run. These beaches are also noted for large numbers of small sharks and rays. There is no ready small-boat access along this stretch of coast.

At Bunbury, the Leschenault Inlet is nursery for large numbers of fish (King George whiting especially), crabs and prawns, and in the Collie River are ever-present mulloway and black bream. Ocean beaches fish well for salmon (autumn), tailor, flathead, herring and occasional big mulloway.

The Cut, a man-made structure, is a wonderful fishing platform. Shipping channels just offshore have been known to provide outstanding mulloway fishing on occasions.

Busselton has its famous jetty, a long structure that attracts thousands of anglers to the pretty town. There's always something being caught from the old jetty that curves its way a kilometre out to sea. Herring are the mainstay with blue mackerel, bonito (autumn), tailor (summer), squid, some crabs and many other species caught. It's the perfect place for the young, the old, the inexperienced and the competent.

Geographe Bay is a superb stretch of protected water for small-boat anglers who can come into contact with schools of herring, whiting, gardie, skippy and an occasional jewfish or snapper in deeper waters.

Eagle Bay and Castle Rock, near Dunsborough, offer the first good rock fishing south of Perth. In most weather the rocks are safe platforms. Bunker Bay has good shore fishing.

From Cape Naturaliste, the coast changes significantly and heralds a whole new approach to fishing. The straight beaches north of Dunsborough give way to rocky headlands and small bays. Rock fishing takes on greater

Dinghy fishing can be productive on close-in reefs near metropolitan Perth. One of the species taken is silver trevally ('skippy'). (Photo Phil Stanley)

importance, as does the safety aspect of it. Techniques described early in the chapter are still suitable, with the exception of changing from a star sinker for surf beaches to a spoon sinker for reef areas.

From the ocean rocks, main species sought are groper, blue morwong (queen snapper), some tailor (although numbers decline as you travel east), salmon, and rock fish. Canal Rocks, Yallingup and Smith's Beach are favourite salmon-chasing venues in autumn and good for herring, garfish and trevally almost year round.

Beautiful bays at Wyadup, Injidup and Smith's Beach allow excellent light-rod fishing, with Canal Rocks, Torpedo Rocks and Sugarloaf Rock dangerous with a swell running.

Massive schools of herring at Cowaramup in early winter are responsible for bonanza hauls.

At Margaret River shore fishing at Conto and the mouth of the river can result in catches of herring, trevally, whiting, salmon (in season), from protected areas and from more exposed areas add groper, sweep, some pink snapper, morwong, shark and rock fish.

Hamelin Bay has good launching facilities and some protection for small boats. Skin divers find the area a treasure for jewfish, snapper and jumbo crayfish. Some lovely protected reefs and rocks are available for light-rod anglers, particularly just south of the caravan park. King George whiting figure more prominently in this area with big numbers of herring and trevally.

Augusta is a jewel on the south-west corner of the State with a magnificent estuary (Hardy Inlet) full of whiting, bream, garfish, herring, skippy, flathead, flounder and other estuary species. It's a haven for dinghy anglers and further offshore the bay promises good small-boat fishing. Ocean rocks provide excellent small fish.

At Black Point the mouth of the Donnelly River and the mouth of the Warren River have shore fishing which is largely untouched. Some believe that the Warren River area is the most prolific fish producing in all Western Australia—and that's saying something. Rock fishing is limited by difficult access and dangerous conditions, but beach fishing for silver bream, trevally, tailor, salmon, mulloway, herring and whiting is outstanding, while sharks, flathead and other species are often encountered. Snapper, groper and samson fish can be caught from fishable rocks.

Walpole is a diamond on a jewelled coast. The Nornalup Inlet, fed by the Frankland Deep rivers, holds garfish, trevally, King George whiting, bull herring, black bream, occasional mulloway, chopper tailor (right up the Frankland). Beach fishing for trevally, silver bream, tailor, King George whiting, mulloway and seasonal species like salmon, is popular.

Rock fishing is possible at Cliffy Head, Long Point and Point Nuyts (all dangerous but particularly the last).

Peaceful Bay is a beautiful little spot conducive

to small-boat fishing, although often choppy just offshore. Beach, reef and protected rock fishing are available for trevally, silver bream, King George whiting and salmon.

Parry Beach, William Bay, offers scenic locations and magnificent places to visit, but also gives anglers the opportunity of catching salmon, herring, whiting, skippy, silver bream and rock fish.

Denmark, situated on the shore of the delightful Wilson Inlet, has plenty of fishing for flathead, salmon trout, King George whiting, bay snapper, cobbler, prawns and crabs.

Ocean Beach and Back Beach can be fished for salmon, tailor, big trevally, silver bream, whiting and herring. Some huge yellowtail kingfish and samson fish are caught. The squeaky, fine white sands of our southern beaches, like Ocean Beach, are a delight to feel underfoot.

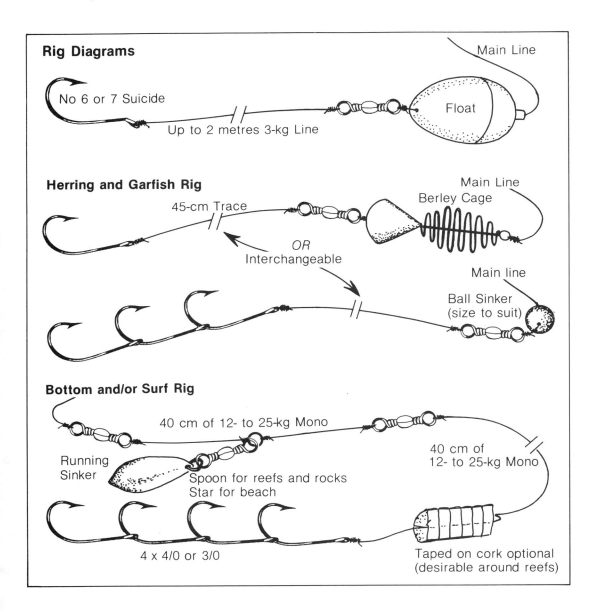

At Lowlands (specialist four-wheel-drive only) there is superb scenery, like much of the Albany, Denmark precinct. Here skippy, salmon and silver bream are found.

Bornholm offers, for fit people and fit four-wheel-drives, year round fishing for salmon, shark, skippy, herring and snapper.

Horton's Beach is a good family fishing beach (swimmers should watch out for undertow). While hang gliders soar from the cliffs towering above the beautiful beach, fish for herring, flathead, skippy, and silver bream.

The waters around Cosy Corner produce herring, salmon, skippy, rock fish and occasional tailor.

Closer to Albany the Sand Patch is renowned for year-round salmon schools. Anglers descending the 100-metre cliffs should take plenty of gear and line around 10 kilos for mulloway, groper, skippy, bull herring and silver bream.

In King George Sound small boats can often be used when fishing for salmon, groper, snapper, leatherjacket, herring, King George whiting (this is the spot where the King George were named!), trevally and squid.

In Oyster Harbour (a dinghy is usually big enough), fishing is great for King George whiting, squid, crabs, bream, skippy, leatherjackets and others. Well worth a try for trevally, herring, squid, leatherjackets and bream are the town jetty and meatworks outlet pipe.

Gull Rock is a fairly protected rock for skippy and herring. Ledge Beach with protected reef fishing can turn on salmon, skippy, herring, whiting and silver bream.

Nanarup, still close to town, provides conventional vehicle access for silver bream, herring, trevally, whiting, salmon, flathead and some tailor.

On Western Australia's south-west coast, wherever you choose to fish, you will see why beach and estuary fishing are so popular—the sheer beauty, the proliferation of small fish, the peace.

Rock Fishing Safety

Many, many lives have been lost on this coast—it's one of the potentially fiercest in the country. Some platforms face the predominant south-west swells. King waves are a common occurrence. On this Cape Naturaliste to Esperance coast local knowledge is required to fish the exposed 'big rock' areas. Here are a few simple rules:

1 Watch the weather and water.
2 Ensure you have adequate footwear providing a good grip.
3 Beware of black, wet or sloping rocks and rocks that form a wall at your back.
4 Don't tempt fate when trying to de-snag gear or gaff fish.

PERTH TO ALBANY– SALTWATER RIVER FISHING
Phil Stanley

When rainfall was dished out, Western Australia was left from the major carve up, and the resultant lack of rivers means Western Australian anglers and tourists are poorly off in terms of saltwater river fishing. There are a few good ones and some fine nurseries, but basically, the rivers should be considered estuaries. Despite being the wettest part of the State, the rivers flow for only part of the year.

The predominant fish in most of the saltwater river sections are black bream. They live all their lives in the brackish water, move down towards the mouths of the rivers in winter, when the freshwater flow is greatest. Another angling species is mulloway. Some huge specimens travel well up river in summer and fish of 15 kilos are not an uncommon occurrence within sight of the centre of Perth.

Cobbler (estuary catfish) are caught on blood

worms in the rivers and, when the salt reaches up river, chopper tailor are often caught. Flathead and flounder towards Fremantle are regularly caught, although they don't like the fresh water when it comes down. They will take a whole river prawn, a whitebait on a gang of hooks and small lures, but conditions are difficult for lure use.

River prawns are drag netted from November to March and king prawns dab netted in April/May and sometimes June. Blue manna crabs are caught in the rivers, more often in summer. Mullet are not an important angling species in our rivers even though good populations exist.

A few whiting are taken, although they have decreased in numbers. Yellowtail and trumpeter are often hooked and when the river is particularly salty blue mackerel, herring, silver bream and trevally are no surprise, especially near river mouths. Small sharks (in particular, metre-long Swan River whalers) attract interest if spotted but, though apparently common, are rarely seen.

Fishing Locations

The Swan and Canning Rivers have black bream (Belmont, Maylands jetties, Garratt Road Bridge – well up the Swan River; in winter, as far south as Nedlands, Claremont, Freshwater Bay; the Narrows Bridge and Canning Bridge are top black-bream locations)

... flathead, flounder (yacht club at East Fremantle, Rocky Bay, Blackwell Reach in summer; flathead further upstream in summer)

... tailor (Nedlands, Claremont, Mosman Bay, summer evenings for trollers; limited jetty access in this area)

... mulloway (Blackwell Reach, Mosman Bay, November/December; well up towards Belmont in January, February, March)

... river prawns (drag netting along the river near Kwinana Freeway, Deep Water Point – Applecross, Nedlands, Claremont, Heathcote, etc, in November, December, January then gradually towards Peppermint Grove as the season progresses)

... cobbler (towards the old Swan Brewery)

... king prawns (Rocky Bay and East Fremantle late April early May, as they head to sea on dark nights and run out tides).

At Mandurah, the Serpentine and Canning rivers produce bream (well up river), mulloway, mullet, a few whiting, river prawns, cobbler and blue crabs. The Channel (at Mandurah itself), particularly the bridge, has garfish, chopper tailor, herring, cobbler, mulloway, yellowtail, king prawns and crabs in season.

Collie River (Bunbury), after the superb Leschenault Estuary, a favourite spot for black bream and mulloway (see the chapter, 'Perth to Albany-Beaches, Estuaries and Bays').

Margaret River offers limited fishing for black bream.

Blackwood River (see Hardy Inlet, in the chapter, 'Perth to Albany-Beaches, Estuaries and Bays') has excellent black-bream fishing, cobbler, some mulloway.

At Donnelly the salt areas have mulloway, large black bream, mullet, sometimes trevally, herring, flathead and others.

Warren River has fewer mulloway and bream than in the Donnelly. The Warren is more noted for its freshwater fishing upstream and beach fishing at its mouth.

The Frankland and Deep rivers flow into the picturesque estuary at Walpole and are both very good for black bream, with estuary species (tailor, flathead, mulloway, etc), often going well up river.

Kalgan (Albany) is a beautiful river which provides black-bream fishing. Big gleaming bronze fish to 2 kilos can be taken by casting towards shore from a dinghy, or from accessible shore spots. Nippers and whole fresh prawns are often best fished towards the banks.

SMALL-BOAT FISHING

John Curtis

Small-boat angling has, in the past few years, seen somewhat of a boom in Western Australia. With more and more people having an increased leisure time, many are turning to the water for their recreation. Sales of new and second-hand boats under 5 metres are booming. Some 65 per cent of all smaller craft purchased in Western Australia are for use as fishing boats, or fishing is the prime reason for purchase.

Western Australia is a relatively dry section of the continent, and most of its navigable and fishable waters are located in the south-west. Rivers such as the Blackwood, Donnelly, Margaret, Deep, Frankland, Denmark and Swan are only navigable for short distances, but still provide excellent small-boat angling. Most of these rivers flow into large estuaries or inlets and these in turn provide the majority of inshore angling activity.

From Esperance in the south-east of the State, right through Kununnurra in the north there are ample locations for small-boat anglers to enjoy their pastime, without too many problems. Western Australian rivers are in the main slow, and there aren't many that develop 'bars' to cause the problems experienced in the eastern States, when anglers are heading out to sea.

With Western Australia's extensive coastline the variety of species available to the small-boat angler is enormous, whether it is inshore, estuarine or river fishing.

In the south of the State the species that are available to small-boat anglers include Westralian jewfish, pink snapper, samson fish, blue groper, blue and black morwong, skipjack trevally, salmon, King George and sand whiting, flathead and flounder, tarwhine and black bream. Pike, garfish and leatherjacket are often found over the weedbanks and rock formations and tailor are also occasionally caught.

Offshore anglers often encounter large southern bluefin tuna and yellowfin tuna, as well as sharks of all sizes and species. Crabs and rock lobsters are also often sought by boat anglers in the estuaries of the south, along with prawns. There are licensing restrictions on the capture of some of these species and a quick check with the local Fisheries Department officer, will save embarrassment later.

Esperance in the south-east offers small-boat anglers numerous locations in the Recherche Archipelago to fish for these species. The islands of the archipelago provide sheltered fishing, almost regardless of the weather, but care should be taken at all times. A local group of volunteers from the Civil Defence organisation operates a limited sea search and rescue facility.

West of Esperance the species encountered remain the same and locations such as Hopetoun, Bremer Bay and Cape Riche, offer small-boat anglers limited access to them. The Wellstead Estuary at Bremer Bay offers small-boat anglers limited fishing, but as the estuary is closed by a sandbar which very rarely opens to the sea, the size of the fish is also limited. For offshore fishing, the coastline around Bremer Bay is excellent. Launch facilities are available in Bremer Bay itself, and there are several beach-launching sites, where a four-wheel drive vehicle is needed on the hard sand.

Albany offers unlimited small-boat angling, from the car topper to larger trailer craft. The King and Kalgan rivers feed into Oyster Harbour and the black bream fishing is excellent in both. Oyster Harbour itself provides limited estuary fishing for smaller species of fish, as does Princess Royal Harbour. Offshore boating enthusiasts will find the islands in King George Sound (the home of King George whiting) good value.

West of Albany the area does not offer a lot of good fishing from small boats due to the limited access to the water. However, Torbay

Inlet and the adjacent area has quite good inshore fishing. At Denmark, the Denmark River flows into Wilson Inlet and estuarine anglers can have a field day among good fish. Small snapper, mulloway, salmon, herring and skipjack trevally, whiting, black bream and tarwhine are all caught in the inlet. There is a sandbar across the inlet which prevents access to the ocean, but this is broken by the local shire on a regular basis and then the fishing improves dramatically.

The Nornalup Inlet at Walpole has both the Deep and Frankland rivers feeding it, along with a lot of smaller rivers and creeks. The area is renowned for its small-boat fishing in the estuary and many Perth anglers trail smaller boats here for their annual holidays. It is also very popular with anglers from the inland towns in the south-west of the State. Ocean fishing around Walpole is limited to the inshore areas as prevailing weather conditions make it too hazardous to venture too far from shore.

Broke Inlet is located west of Walpole and offers similar fishing to that found in the Nornalup Inlet. Offshore the Broke Reefs offer small boats reasonable fishing. Windy Harbour is aptly named. It lies at the base of Point D'Entrecasteaux but is still subjected to very strong winds. It is not well protected from swells and launching boats in the area is difficult.

Augusta is situated on the mouth of the Blackwood River, and the estuary and river fishing in this area are excellent. Offshore fishing is dependent upon weather a little, but when the winds and swells permit, the fishing is excellent. Upstream from Augusta lies Molloy Island and Alexander Bridge. The river is navigable upstream from Alexander Bridge and it is possible to take trout when water conditions are right.

From Cape Leeuwin through to Cape Naturaliste, the opportunity for small-boat angling is somewhat limited, but 'around the corner' Geographe Bay is sheltered by the cape and allows access to excellent small-boat fishing. Offshore fishing is also good with the bottom comprised mainly of weed, sand and broken coral. There are very few 'lumps' to be found in the bay and boat anglers will find that a good supply of 'berley' is required, as the preferred method of fishing the area is to anchor and berley the fish up to the boat.

The estuaries at both Bunbury and Mandurah offer the opportunity for small anglers to enjoy excellent fishing. At Bunbury there are annual runs of mulloway and King George whiting as well as samson fish. In the estuary at Mandurah, succulent blue manna crabs and prawns are the most sought after. Both locations have excellent launch facilities dotted around them, and the local anglers will readily direct visitors to good fishing locations. The Peel Inlet at Mandurah is one of the few estuaries in Western Australia to develop a 'bar', and this only occurs at certain times of the year. Care should be taken when crossing it. Offshore fishing in both locations is excellent with several reef systems located just a few kilometres offshore, all producing good fish.

Mandurah is almost considered part of the Perth metropolitan area, and from here north through to Two Rocks offshore fishing from small boats is good. Access to the ocean is from many ramps located throughout the metropolitan area, as well as the Swan River. The offshore fishing in the metropolitan area consists mainly of drift fishing, or anchoring and berleying. The offshore reef systems extend right along the metropolitan coast and this draws anglers at every opportunity. Along the northern section of this coast, Direction Banks lure anglers with the chance of catching extremely large Westralian jewfish. The Banks are located some 25 kilometres offshore and it is recommended that a 'pairing' system (two boats in contact) is used when fishing the area.

Main access to these local waters is via either the Swan River at Fremantle, or the two marinas located in the northern suburbs at Ocean Reef and Hillary's. For anglers fishing the sheltered waters of Cockburn Sound, launch facilities are located at Coogee, Kwinana and Rockingham.

Around Rottnest Island the numerous reefs that have claimed ships also provide boat anglers with excellent fishing. Trailer boats regularly fish around the island for a wide variety of species while, offshore from the island, the Rottnest Trench allows gamefishers a chance at larger species.

North of Perth, the small-boat fishing opportunities start to become a little limited, mainly due to the lack of launching facilities. To some extent this problem is being alleviated by the building of new ramps at most popular holiday locations.

Places such as Guilderton, Ledge Point, Lancelin, Cervantes, Green Head and Seabird allow access to good fishing along the offshore reefs. Jurien Bay has recently had a new launch facility for small boats installed and this now allows anglers to enjoy extremely good fishing from the reefs and sand patches offshore. The bay has recently become very popular with game fishers for the numbers and size of the samson fish it produces.

Small-boat angling around Dongara and Geraldton is also good, with excellent catches being made regularly. These towns harbour quite large crayfishing fleets and therefore the facilities available to the small-boat angler are excellent. It is from here north that a change starts to take place and there is an overlap of northern and southern species. Small-boat anglers specifically set out to catch pelagics such as mackerel, while the capture of other gamefish is often achieved.

Kalbarri is where the action for small-boat anglers really starts to warm up. The estuary offers good fishing for the smaller species, but offshore is where all the action is. Mackerel seem to school along a ridge running north-south, which is just a metre or so high. This ridge is located about three kilometres offshore and during the summer school holidays a procession of small boats trolls lures and baits, seeking the mackerel and also large yellowfin tuna.

Shark Bay provides excellent fishing for the small-boat angler, but there is a lot of local knowledge needed to be successful. Tailor, mulloway, pink snapper, spangled emperor, many species of trevally, mackerel and tuna can be caught in the bay. Launching facilities are limited and four-wheel-drive launching across the firm sand is the most convenient.

Carnarvon offers small-boat anglers limited access to offshore fishing, but excellent and virtually untapped inshore fishing south of the town among the mangrove creeks and bays and inlets of the northern end of Shark Bay. For larger boats heading offshore, Bernier and Dorre islands offer excellent fishing for bottom species as well as the pelagics.

North of Carnarvon, small-boat fishing is restricted, mainly due to the rocky coastline, but at Coral Bay the reefs offer excellent opportunities to catch the northern species. Reef- and bottom-dwelling fish that are caught in northern waters of Western Australia include turrum, golden, goldspot, lowly and giant trevally; narrow-barred, broad-barred, shark and spotted mackerel; cobia; coral trout; queenfish; red-throat, spangled and red emperor; yellowfin and longtail tuna; and the variety of sharks is almost as big as this list. Hammerhead, tiger and whaler sharks of many differing species are all taken regularly.

Exmouth is noted for its gamefishing and the opportunities for small-boat fishing are limited to the inshore waters on the west of the peninsula. Inside the Ningaloo reef it is possible to catch the species listed above. On the eastern side of the peninsula the sheltered waters offer small-boat anglers much the same species but generally they are a little smaller as the area is a nursery. On the eastern side of the Exmouth Gulf the waters adjacent to the Australian mainland have been relatively unfished, but there is every reason to believe that this area could hold the rarely caught bonefish.

North of Exmouth the fishing opportunities are generally restricted to the waters adjacent to

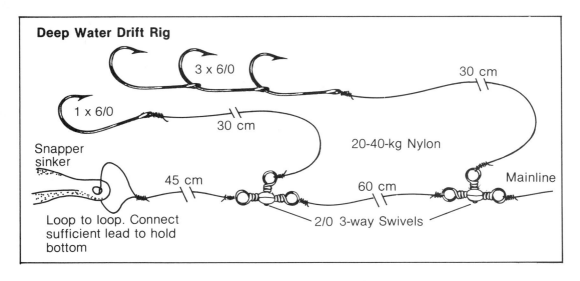

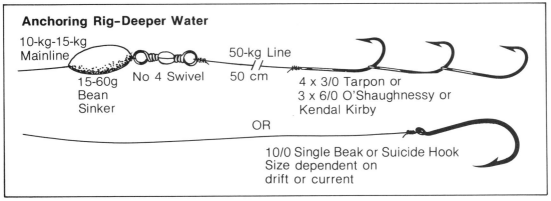

settlements. Locations such as Onslow don't have a lot of small-boat fishing available. The Mackerel Islands are a group of islands situated some 25 kilometres offshore from Onslow. Thevenard is the largest island of the group, and all-in fishing holidays including food and the use of a small dinghy can be arranged at this idyllic location. The fishing around the islands for the small-boat angler is superb. Species contained in the list above can all be caught as well as small marlin and sailfish.

Around the mining towns of Dampier and Port Hedland the opportunities for small-boat angling are too numerous to list. Dampier offers more for the light-tackle gamefishing enthusiast, while Port Hedland offers more for the bottom fisher. The area between both of these locations is virtually unfished and anglers with access to a small boat, and unlimited time, will enjoy exploring and fishing these waters.

Located offshore from Dampier, the many islands allow access to excellent fishing, while along the coast adjacent to both of the iron-ore ports, the creek fishing for threadfin salmon, mangrove jack and even barramundi offers a completely different angling challenge to the small-boat angler.

Rigs for the Small-Boat Angler

Rigs for the small-boat angler are relatively simple. The major differences occur when the

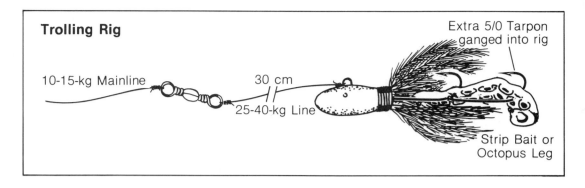

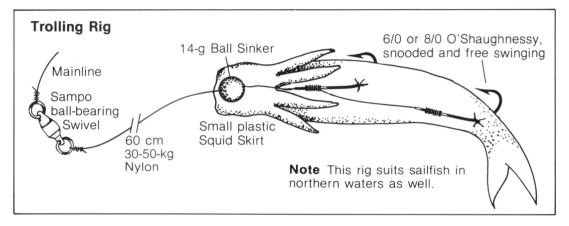

style of fishing is altered. If anglers sit at anchor and berley, a smaller weight is required to reach the bottom. When anglers drift fish, the rig remains basically similar, but additional weight is used to keep the rig near the bottom.

Hook styles are similar to those preferred by shore-based anglers, although there is a tendency to use a slightly larger hook when boat fishing than would be used from shore.

With the numbers of pelagics available to small boat anglers in Western Australia, trolling is very popular. Using a lure requires a slightly different rig from that used when trolling a bait.

The opportunities for small-boat angling in Western Australia are almost unlimited. This form of angling is taking off in a big way as small-boat anglers start to obtain more enjoyment from their fishing. Because they can be launched almost single handedly, the small boat is opening up new areas for angling. The challenges that this form of fishing offers are only now being realised, as bigger and bigger fish are caught in the inshore and closer offshore waters of the State.

GAMEFISHING
John Curtis

Gamefishing in Western Australia is a growing sport. It has undergone a subtle change in the last few years, with more and more smaller boats participating. The challenges offered by this form of fishing are almost as limitless as the species available in Western Australian waters.

Gamefishing in Western Australian waters can be divided into three distinct areas: Cape Naturaliste to Jurien Bay in the south of the

State (probably the southern limit of gamefishing in Western Australia); Exmouth (an established gamefishing area and recognised world wide); and the Pilbara coast (incorporating Dampier and Port Hedland, and Broome with the Rowley Shoals).

Cape Naturaliste to Jurien Bay

This section of the Western Australian coastline would not be a gamefishing region at all, if it were not for the Leeuwin Current. This stream of warm water flowing down the coast brings with it numerous species of gamefish. The occurrence of sailfish, marlin and broadbill swordfish washed up on southern coastal beaches around Albany, in what are regarded as cool waters, testifies to its spread.

With the start of the Naturaliste Gamefishing Club, anglers dedicated to gamefishing opened up a new area around the cape after which the club is named. The main species sought by these anglers are marlin and oceanic sharks such as mako and blue sharks.

The area is also noted for the large samson fish which are found around the 'lumps' and coral 'bombies' of the area. Migratory tunas also play an important part in the gamefishing scene of this region, with several larger specimens having been caught in recent years.

Offshore from Perth, the waters around Rottnest Island provide gamefishers with ample opportunities to catch samson fish, mackerel, bluefin and yellowfin tuna, mahi mahi (dolphinfish) and blue and black marlin. A large underwater canyon coming in from the Continental Shelf, just west of Rottnest, with its associated upwelling of nutrient-laden water, provides the main source for this action. In recent years the installation of Fish Aggregating Devices (FADs) has seen an improvement in the numbers of fish being captured.

There is a growing tendency for Western Australia's gamefishers to 'Tag and Release' most of their fish, and the results of this program are opening what was previously a closed book on the movements of gamefish in the region.

At Jurien Bay, north of Perth, the occurrence of marlin, tangled in rock lobster marker ropes, started Perth-based gamefishers thinking about the potential of the area. With satellite photographs, colour enhanced to differentiate the water temperatures, it was found that the Leeuwin Current was located fairly close inshore at Jurien Bay.

The waters adjacent to Jurien Bay are relatively shallow and behind a reef area, known by the locals as the second bank, it settles out at around 50-60 metres deep. It is here that the current seems to have most effect and is where gamefishers concentrate their efforts in seeking out marlin. Large schools of baitfish frequent these warmer waters and these baitfish are in turn pursued by pelagics upon which the marlin feed.

Species such as broad- and narrow-barred mackerel, shark mackerel, yellowfin and southern bluefin tuna, bonito, and samson fish are all caught regularly around this area, and as such offer excellent light-tackle gamefishing. Marlin captures, however, are infrequent, and seem to depend on the proximity, and temperature, of the Leeuwin Current.

Exmouth

Exmouth is located at the tip of the Exmouth Peninsula. The main purpose of the town is as a communications base. It has long been recognised as a gamefishing area, and in the past few years a tourist industry has developed around the fishing to be found in its offshore waters.

Cairns is the home in Australia for giant black marlin, but Exmouth is also gaining a reputation for their capture. Along with the black marlin, which are generally smaller than those caught on the east coast, blue and striped marlin are also captured regularly.

Along with the variety of marlin available, sailfish, cobia, wahoo, a variety of mackerel species, mahi mahi, and all sizes and species of trevally are caught. The reason for this activity is believed to be that in this area, the Australian Continental Shelf is at its closest point to the mainland. The associated upwellings and the interaction of the cool and warm waters attract the game species. The Exmouth Gulf on the eastern side of the peninsula is also a breeding ground for numerous species of fish, and this provides a ready food chain for the gamefish.

Exmouth's annual gamefishing competition, 'Gamex', attracts anglers from all over Australia each October/November. Marlin are the most sought-after prize, but each year exceptional captures of other species are made.

More gamefishing records are broken or established in the waters adjacent to Exmouth than anywhere else in Australia. Some examples which readily spring to mind are Peter Brock who captured a world record giant trevally in 1982 on 10-kilo line. The fish weighed in at 39.8 kilos. Perth-based angler Ian Cornelius set a world record for yellowfin tuna with the capture of a fish of around 9 kilos on 2-kilo line, and Perth veteran angler Jack Clugston set an Australian record for a blue marlin in the 37-kilo line class with the capture of a 275-kilo specimen.

In January 1984, a government-sponsored survey was conducted in the area, to discover what potential it held as a tourist destinaton. The results were very encouraging. Four experienced gamefishers trolled lures and baits from the local charter boat *The Gun*, and raised, captured, tagged and released dozens of marlin in a one-month period.

This effort places Exmouth at or near the top in potential for light-tackle fishing and it will come as no surprise to Western Australian anglers to see world gamefishers start to exploit the potential of the area.

The Pilbara Coast, Broome and Rowley Shoals

Each year, on the first weekend in August, gamefishers from all over Australia gather in Dampier to participate in the King Bay Light Tackle Classic. With the number of participants, and continued successes, it is doubtful that there is another gamefishing competition in Australia that can compare with this one. Numerous Perth-based anglers either sail or tow their fishing rigs to the northern town, to participate in the event.

The attraction of the area is the large number of sailfish which congregate around the islands offshore. They are there almost all year round, but tend to become more active at this time. They are not large by world standards, averaging around 20-25 kilos, but what is lacking in weight is made up for by sheer numbers.

Sailfish are not the only game species located in the area. Very big trevally, wahoo, mackerel and an assortment of other gamefish are also taken during the competition. Large sharks are a feature as well, with tigers predominant.

The Dampier area is basically a light-tackle sportfishing location. Line classes of 2, 4, 6 and 8 kilos allow anglers to fish for the more predominant species, and still enable them to release unwanted fish without harm.

Port Hedland is a relatively unknown angling location, but there are numerous opportunities for gamefishers to test their skill, and patience, on the fish found. Being mainly shallow waters offshore, a deep channel has been dredged to accommodate the bulk carriers which visit the port regularly. It is around the markers, adjacent to the channel, that the main angling activities are centred.

Trevally, cobia, mackerel and tuna are all captured around these markers which act as FADs to the piscean populations. They are a ready home for the lure-thieving trevally, who wrap lures with monotonous regularity around the barnacle-encrusted pylons. Mackerel are a little more civilised and show more respect for anglers by generally making long straight runs in open water.

With the pylons of the channel markers attracting numerous schools of baitfish, schools of longtail tuna are attracted to this ready source of food, and can be taken on smaller lures.

Sailfish are often seen free jumping here, but with the supply of other gamefish available, not a lot of anglers fish specifically for them. The area has a lot of potential as a small-boat light-tackle gamefishery and it is worth taking the time to explore it.

Broome doesn't have a lot to offer the gamefisher except that it is the centre of the charter-boat fleet operating along the southern Kimberley coast. Charters are also booked for the Rowley Shoals from various operators in Broome.

The Rowley Shoals consist of a series of coral atolls spread over some 80 kilometres of ocean, roughly halfway between Broome and Port Hedland. They lie some 165 nautical miles offshore, and are thought to be the remains of a long extinct volcanic ridge. The northern reef is Mermaid, Clerke lies in the middle, and Imperieuse is the southern atoll in the chain. They are roughly circular, with a central lagoon fringed by protecting reefs.

As a gamefishing proposition they are ideal, offering most oceanic species – marlin; yellowfin, longtail and dogtooth tuna; wahoo; numerous trevally species; queenfish and sailfish.

The Rowley Shoals has recently been declared an 'A' class reserve by the Western Australian Government and this should assist in maintaining the pristine conditions found there. Anglers who are also keen divers will find the underwater scenery almost mindblowing, with the nearly endless variety of small reef-dwelling fish. Large potato cod and maori wrasse are also resident in the lagoons and these species are protected by law.

The area is a gamefisher's dream and, with care and consideration from all who visit, it will remain so. Possibly there is no other location like the Rowleys to be found anywhere else in the world. It is unique to Australia.

ESPERANCE TO CUVIER – ROCKFISHING
John Curtis

Touring anglers, travelling by road from the east, often head north towards Kalgoorlie from Norseman on their way to Perth. From there, they travel further north to the oft-reported locations of Kalbarri, Steep Point, Carnarvon, Quobba and Cuvier, and even Exmouth. All want to sample the excellent fishing that can be found along this section of Western Australia's extensive coastline.

In so doing they are missing out on some of the best rock fishing available in Australia. This can be found by leaving the Eyre Highway at Norseman and heading south some 200 kilometres to the quiet coastal town of Esperance, whose boast is, 'The best beaches in Australia'. This is no idle claim. If you're looking for kilometres of clean white sand, caressed by the clear, cool blue waters of the Southern Ocean, with hardly another soul in sight, and the opportunity to catch big fish, then this is it.

What can the itinerant angler expect from this area? The climate is surprisingly mild, with summer temperatures averaging in the high twenties, and dropping to the low 'teens' of an evening. During this time of the year the prevailing winds are easterly, with a south-easterly sea breeze during the afternoon. Despite its relatively cool climate, Esperance can experience some very hot days.

Fish species often caught in the area are salmon all year round (just their size varies), herring (tommy tuff, mulloway, whiting, flathead, tailor, skippy (white trevally), garfish, pike and gummy sharks. These species seem to be taken more regularly from the gutters and holes along the beaches, generally early morning or evening.

For the rock-hopper the coastline boasts a number of quite prominent rock platforms which jut out into the Southern Ocean, and afford the angler a chance at catching pink snapper, sweep, blue and black morwong, blue groper, samson fish, and, on odd occasions, bonito and southern bluefin tuna.

Close to the town, on the western side, there are a number of locations which are accessible by conventional vehicle. All provide quiet and safe swimming areas for the family, along with good fishing for the above species. A little further west are the Nine, Ten, Eleven and Fourteen Mile beaches. These spots are a combination of sandy beaches, rocks and reef.

Cape Le Grande, Hellfire Bay, Wylie Bay, Lucky Bay and Rossiters all provide excellent rock and beach fishing from numerous, easily reached areas.

If you don't have the luxury of a four-wheel-drive, don't be disappointed. There is a good bitumen road out to the Le Grande National Park and other locations in the area, with excellent roadside scenery.

Further east are Dunns, Wharton, Alexander's, Kennedy's, Duke of Orleans Bay, Tagon and Cape Arid which provide anglers with fishing challenges often only dreamed about. Rock-hoppers will fall in love with the sloping rocks of volcanic origin dropping into the deep water, which vary in hue from pale green to almost black. The beauty of the area is that it produces good catches continually, and the capture of large fish is not uncommon.

The small town of Hopetoun is quiet and relaxing for the visiting angler. Excellent rock fishing is available in this little town at numerous locations but the best is approximately three kilometres west of the town along a rough dirt track to the salmon anglers' camp, where salmon, skippy, groper, snapper and Westralian jewfish can all be caught at various times of the year.

At Bremer Bay rock-hoppers will delight at the number and variety of species available from the rocks around the area. Being on the south coast, its headlands jut southwards and provide an east-west aspect. This means that there will always be places to fish, despite the weather.

Whalebone Point, Doubtful Island Bay and Hood Point all provide excellent rock fishing. From Hood Point around to Peppermint Beach low cliffs offer plenty of action for the rock-hopper.

The cliffs around Cape Knob also provide excellent angling for the itinerant angler, with an excellent view across Dillon Bay on the east side of the cape. It is an excellent groper spot.

Locations such as Reef Beach, which is aptly named, provide the land-based angler with some exciting tussles with big sharks. Here, a live salmon that is swum out invariably ends up being a meal for a predator. The area has a history of excellent captures, and numerous angling clubs from Perth have a weekend at Reef Beach on their calendar.

Albany is the next major town located along the 'Leeuwin Way' and anglers will always remember it, not only for the variety of fish that can be caught in the area, but also for the climate and beautiful scenery. The area offers numerous rock-fishing locations, but it must always be remembered that 'sneakers' or king waves are ever ready to remove the unwary angler from the rocks. When fishing from the rocks anywhere in the south-west, *never* take your eyes from the ocean for an instant.

Many areas around Albany are popular rock-fishing platforms as the coastline lends itself to this style of fishing. Places such as the Salmon Holes, the Sand Patch, and Jimmy Newell Harbour produce excellent captures for the visiting angler almost any time of the year. Species encountered include small (and larger) sharks, salmon, skipjack trevally, tailor, herring and an occasional blue groper.

West of Albany towards Torbay there is a set of high coastal cliffs. Access to the area is limited and it is not regularly fished. The only really popular location is the Sand Patch which produces a wide variety of species. The fishing platform is located at the base of a steep limestone and sand track. A minimal amount of tackle and gear is the answer to fishing this spot, as the walk-out after a good session can be almost murder! Many a good fish has been left on the side of the track as an angler has had to forgo it, just to get himself back to the top. Not a spot for the unfit!

At Cosy Corner, access to the rocks for salmon, herring, skipjack trevally, and groper is relatively easy and safe for children. It is protected from the southerly swells by a headland, which makes fishing a lot safer.

There is some good fishing to be had from the rocks around Forsyth Bluff and Torbay Head. West Cape Howe is situated on the other side of the peninsula and all spots are fishable, with care, for salmon, groper, herring, skipjack trevally and other small species.

Lowlands Beach provides excellent rock fishing at the western end and is the last readily accessible spot for rock fishing until Nullaki Point, adjacent to Wilson Inlet. The rocks on the south-east end of Back Beach are reached via a track which takes in the spots of Lights Beach, Madfish Bay and Sphinx Rocks. All provide above-average rock fishing, but again care must be taken when fishing from these more remote locations.

Parry Beach at the south-west end of William Bay has some good rock fishing for skipjack trevally, salmon, mulloway, groper and tarwhine. Access is good and from this spot fishermen often battle with large sharks on heavy tackle with honours going each way.

At Augusta there is excellent small-fish angling available from the rocks between Dukes Head and Point Matthew. Groper Bay, Ringbolt Bay and Sarge Bay all offer good fishing prospects as well, particulaly for skipjack trevally.

In addition to skipjack trevally, anglers are able to catch plenty of herring, salmon, samson fish and the occasional tailor. This location is dangerous in heavy weather and all care should be taken.

Cape Leeuwin is the south-west corner of Western Australia. From here anglers head north along the coast to Cape Naturaliste. This section of the southern coastline is a rock angler's dream come true. Many locations offer excellent fishing but care should be taken at *all* locations because of larger than average swells which will readily remove the unwary angler from a fishing platform.

Fish that can be captured from the many rock platforms include the usual smaller species of salmon, herring, skipjack trevally, tailor, sweep, and pike. Larger fish often caught along here include mulloway, samson fish, sharks, southern bluefin tuna, groper, yellowtail kingfish, snapper and Westralian jewfish.

Deepdene, Cape Hamelin and Cosy Corner (not to be confused with the Cosy Corner near Albany), all have good rock fishing. To reach Elephant Rock and Honeycomb Rock from Cosy Corner is relatively easy and these spots are very popular. Hamelin Bay is a little more readily accessible and has a number of good fishing locations within easy walking distance of the township.

North from Hamelin Bay to the estuary of the Margaret River, at Prevelly, much of the coastline is inaccessible.

For Western Australian anglers, Cowaramup Point, Cowaramup Reef, Moses Rock, Big and Little Injidup, and Wyadup are synonymous with excellent reef and rock fishing. Canal Rocks is one location that almost regardless of the swells is fishable somewhere. The main feature of this spot, as its name suggests, is the natural cutting through the rocks which provides some exciting fishing. North from Canal Rocks, Torpedo and Slippery rocks are favoured fishing platforms, although, as their names indicate, *care* must be taken when fishing from them.

From here to Cape Naturaliste the coastline consists of rocky beaches interspersed with high sheer cliffs. From Cape Naturaliste the coastline heads south-east. This section is protected from the prevailing weather, which makes fishing here much more popular with anglers, particularly during the cooler months of the year. Bunker Bay, Rocky Point, Eagle Bay, Gannet Rock, Sail Rock, Castle Bay and Bird Rock are all very popular fishing spots, generally safe enough to fish in all weather conditions, and offer many species of fish.

From here northwards there are only limited opportunities for rock and reef fishing, until anglers reach the southern limits of Perth. Rock fishing in and around the metropolitan area consists mainly of fishing from the rock groynes adjacent to the various harbour entrances or from the rock platforms installed for control of beach erosion. Fishing from these locations should never be frowned upon as they have provided some excellent captures of very large fish.

Offshore from Perth lies Rottnest Island and this saves the sanity of large numbers of Perth-based rock anglers. The island offers unlimited fishing for the rock-hopping enthusiast, and being an island there is always a lee shore. In the winter months the West End is visited regularly by salmon fishers. Large salmon feature regularly on the menu in Perth households after a trip here, and it is one of the few locations in Western Australia where yellowtail kingfish are captured. Although they are not very big, and their numbers few, the challenge of landing one from the rocks draws anglers regularly.

Herring are the mainstay of anglers visiting the island, and can be caught all year round. In addition there are skipjack, tarwhine, flathead, King George whiting, sand whiting, pike, tailor and mulloway in numbers sufficient to ensure that even the most inexperienced angler can take home a feed of fish.

Bickley Point, Jubilee Rocks, Henrietta Rocks, Vera Rocks, and Parker Point all face roughly south-east and are a little more protected than other locations from the prevailing south-westerly winds and swells. All spots offer some form of reef or rock fishing, are not too far from the main settlement, and can be reached by walking or riding a bicycle. For the angler who is a little fitter, locations in Salmon Bay provide excellent angling from the rocks and reefs. Jeannie's Lookout, Salmon Point, Fairbridge Bluff, Nancy Cove and Kitson Point are only a few kilometres' ride from the settlement, and all offer good fishing.

West of Narrow Neck is known as the 'West End', and reef and rock fishing are almost unlimited. From South Point, through Wilson Bay, on to Radar Reef, with its popular herring location known as the 'Tennis Court', Fish Hook Bay, Cape Vlamingh, around the corner to Cathedral Rocks, Eagle Bay and King Head, the area is surrounded by reefs.

The northern shoreline of the island is also well protected from the prevailing wind and swell, and offers a little more relaxed fishing from locations such as Mabel Cove, Hayward Cape, and Celia Rock on the western end of Marjorie Bay.

Abraham Point on the western end of Rocky Bay, Crayfish Rock at Ricey Bay, Charlotte Point, Armstrong Point, North Point, are other good reef- and rock-fishing locations.

Along the northern and eastern shore of the island the locations of Parakeet Bay, Geordie Bay, Point Clune, Fay Bay, Longreach Point, The Basin, Bathurst Point, and Mushroom Point are all within good walking distance of the settlement, and offer rock and reef fishing in protected waters.

North of Fremantle, where the Swan River meets the Indian Ocean, reefs extend along sections of the beachfront. From the Cable Station at Leighton to North Cottesloe reef, anglers chase tailor, herring and skipjack trevally from the low coastal reef formations. At Cottesloe the groyne affords access for disabled anglers and it is a popular spot with elderly anglers. The prime location for the 'retired' brigade is the Grant Street reef.

The reefs from Trigg Island north are low and flat and are best fished at low tide. They peter out at Marmion. Sorrento Beach is broken by the three sand erosion control groynes. These groynes are popular spots, particularly in winter when the first north-westerly storms bring out the snapper anglers.

From the Ocean Reef marina north there are several isolated reef formations which allow anglers ready access to reasonably deep waters close to shore. The townsites of Burns and Quinns Rocks are popular spots for reef anglers and the surrounding coastline is the regular haunt of mulloway and herring anglers. One of the more popular spots is the 'Kingie Hole', located just south of Quinns Rocks.

Pippindinny is a few kilometres north of Quinns Rocks and the reefs along this stretch produce some of the largest tailor to be taken in the metropolitan area. The freighter *Alkimos* is a ready landmark for both reef and boat anglers as it lies stranded on the shore here. The reefs adjacent produce a variety of fish.

Between Yanchep and the Two Rocks marina lie two spots that are very popular with outer metropolitan anglers. The groyne at Club Capricorn and 'The Spot' produce large tailor, skipjack, tarwhine and mulloway regularly.

Just north of Guilderton, at the mouth of the Moore River some 80 kilometres north of Perth, two of the more popular fishing locations are the Two Mile and Five Mile reefs.

A few kilometres north of Cervantes, there are a few isolated patches of reef and rocks which are worth fishing. Adjacent to the mouth of the Hill River a few small reefs regularly turn on good tailor, mulloway, herring, garfish, tarwhine and skippy. It is worth spending some time in Jurien Bay fishing from the groynes and rock walls of the harbour. Samson fish and pink snapper are caught regularly during the cooler months of the year, from both locations.

Port Denison is the port for Dongara where the major industry is crayfishing. The rock walls and groyne which protect the harbour are a top location for rock anglers. North of the town, the Seven Mile and Nine Mile beaches are both good for reef fishing. The offshore reefs come quite close to the shore here and allow anglers ready access to reef fishing in protected waters.

Jews, Flat Rocks, Lucies, and Drummonds are all top fishing spots, located near 'S' Bend. They are renowned among Perth's angling community. It is one of the few locations in the State where Westralian jewfish can be caught regularly from the beach and rocks, hence its popularity. It is not only the jewfish which draws anglers to this area – good hauls of herring, tailor, cod, small sharks, whiting, skipjack trevally and tarwhine can be taken regularly.

At Geraldton, rock and reef fishing for herring, skipjack trevally, mulloway, tailor, small sharks, and whiting, is restricted to the harbour breakwater.

On the North-West Coastal Highway, the turn-off to Horrocks and Port Gregory is at Northampton. Rock fishing at these locations is somewhat limited, but the road leads on towards better reef fishing at spots such as Lynton, Sandalwood Bay, Halfway Bay, Lucky Bay and Weygoe. Weygoe Reef extends from the northern end of the beach, and anglers are able to walk onto the reef and fish the front and back of it. Large swells often make this spot unfishable and care should be taken. The reef has a narrow gap through which a large amount of water flows when the tide is running or the swell is up. This assists with drifting baits out considerable distances but a wary eye should always be kept on the water for a rogue swell.

Anglers are able to balloon from this spot when there is an easterly wind blowing and it is not uncommon to catch narrow- and broad-barred, as well as spotted, mackerel from here. Pink snapper, an occasional spangled emperor, mulloway, Westralian jewfish, sharks of all sizes, tailor and whiting can also be caught from this reef, particularly during summer months.

From Weygoe, northwards towards Kalbarri, a four-wheel-drive track extends along the coast to spots that produce large fish regularly. Natural Bridge, Castle Rock, Layer Cake Gorge, the Shell House, Goat Gulch, Madmans Rock,

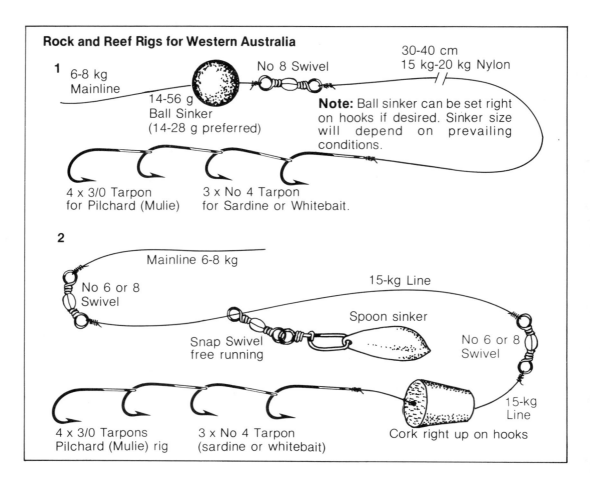

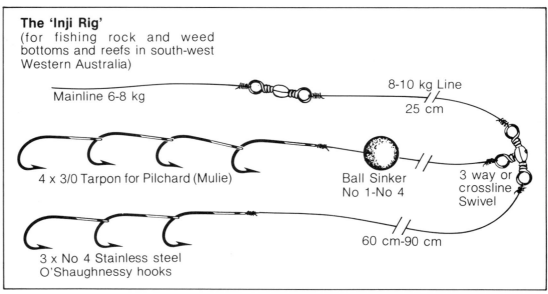

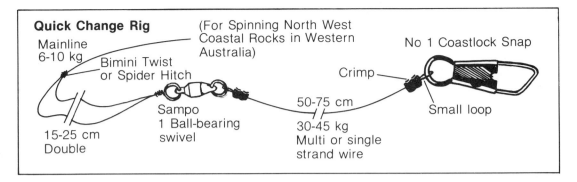

Eagle Gorge, Pot Alley Gorge, and Mushroom Rock are all top fishing spots. Species caught are cod, groper, tailor, snapper, Westralian jewfish, spangled emperor, Spanish mackerel, samson fish and many more, all being taken at different times of the year.

Most of these spots are also accessible from Kalbarri in a conventional vehicle. In most cases, however, it involves a long walk from the car to the selected spot. Closer to Kalbarri itself, Red Bluff often evokes a lot of interest with rock-hoppers, with good catches of the smaller species. A little closer to town the Blue Hole, Chinaman's Rock and the reef on the southern side of the estuary, all provide excellent fishing.

On the north side of the estuary, Oyster Reef provides plenty of action, in particular Frustration Rock. This spot is aptly named, as not only do anglers lose a lot of tackle to the reef, but also a lot of fish.

The Zuytdorp Cliffs extend northwards for some 200 kilometres and end at Steep Point. Access to 'The Point' is via North-West Coastal Highway, turning off at the Overlander Roadhouse. The track is accessible on odd occasions to conventional vehicles, but the use of a four-wheel-drive is strongly recommended.

Species of fish that are caught from Steep Point, the most westerly point of the Australian mainland, read like a *Who's Who* of the fishing world. Small marlin, sailfish, yellowfin tuna, northern bluefin or longtail tuna, shark mackerel, narrow- and broad-barred mackerel, trevally of several kinds, tailor, snapper, spangled emperor, amberjack and cobia. Steep Point is also one of the few locations in Western Australia where large yellowtail king fish can be caught although, from the rocks, the task is pretty daunting.

It is a very popular spot with anglers from all over Australia, and is coming under increasing angling pressure all the time. There are *no* facilities out on the point and so all provisions, including water, must be carried in.

If you visit the area, don't spoil it for others. Remove all of your rubbish, including plastic bait bags, discarded line, etc, and don't leave fish frames to rot on the rocks. There have been threats of closing access to the area, and so prevent angling activities, if it becomes too dirty and untidy.

At Carnarvon, reef and rock fishing is limited, but when the coastline north has so much reef and rock fishing on offer, nobody is really upset. The Blowholes are located some 70 kilometres north of Carnarvon and the area adjacent is renowned for its excellent reef and rock fishing Australia wide. When there is a large swell running, the Blowholes are quite spectacular, shooting jets of water 25 metres into the air.

Two kilometres north of the Blowholes is the 'Old Boundary' of Quobba Station. This section of the coastline is probably even more well known by Australian anglers than is Steep Point. Mention locations such as High Rock, the Two Mile, the Ledge, Garth's Rock, Camp Rock, the 17 Mile, the North 17 Mile, the Caves and Red Bluff to rock fishermen anywhere and they will

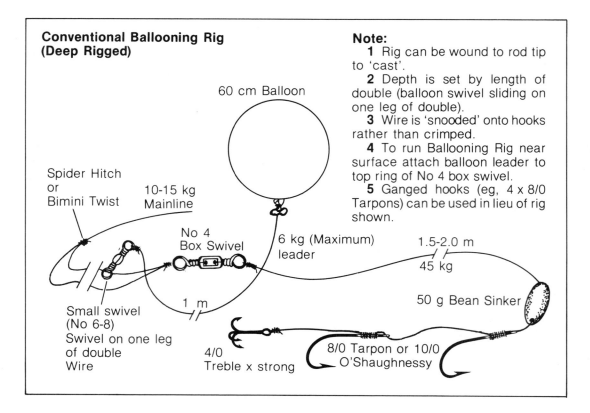

have heard about them, or more than likely fished them.

These places are located on the pastoral lease of Quobba Station. Meikle Meecham is lessee of the property and is another dedicated fisher. Because of the popularity of the area, he has installed several transportable huts on the property, adjacent to the homestead. Itinerant anglers are able to have almost all of the comforts of home here, with fabulous fishing to boot.

Accommodation is available to cater for large parties of up to twenty anglers, as well as smaller parties. The accommodation consists of several cottages, shearing quarters and a camping area.

Accommodation details are available by writing to Quobba Station via Carnarvon.

The fishing from the area is possibly the best there is on offer in Australia. A list of species that can be caught at the various locations includes: narrow-barred, broad-barred and shark mackerel; longtail (northern bluefin) tuna; striped tuna; golden, gold-spot, bludger, turrum and giant trevally; queenfish; tailor; cobia; sailfish; samson; yellowtail kingfish; amberjack; swallowtail and spotted dart; snapper; spangled, red, and red-throat emperor; spotted cod; and Spanish flag. This list doesn't include any of the numerous species of sharks.

These species are able to be taken on a variety of lures, and virtually any minnow pattern will work. High-speed spinning with metal lures is also very successful, but, be warned, you will need a good supply of any kind of lure.

The other very popular method of fishing the area has been ballooning. There are now two methods, with the use of balloon gas (a mixture of helium and nitrogen — safe and inert) possibly being the more productive. Ballooning rigs are sent out, and then most anglers continue to spin until a strike is signalled from their balloons.

A word of warning about ballooning. DO NOT USE HYDROGEN GAS! This gas is

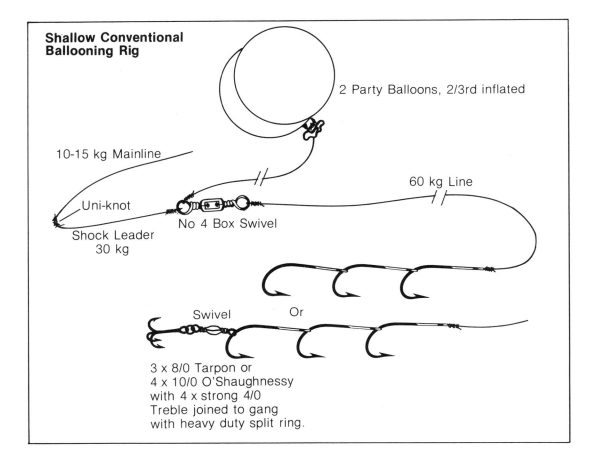

volatile, and it only requires a spark to ignite it. Static electricity generated by clothing, or nylon fishing line, can be just sufficient to provide this spark.

For the enthusiast, another method of angling becoming more and more widely used is saltwater fly-fishing. The locations around Quobba are ideally suited to this style of fishing, and excellent captures are being made on fly-fishing tackle.

The area has claimed many lives over a number of years and there is a large sign on the Blowholes road into the area—*King Waves Can Kill*, which is no idle warning. Take extreme care at all times when fishing here. The Carnarvon Rotary Club has installed a set of heavy stainless-steel wires on the top of High Rock to try and encourage anglers to use a safety rope, but still anglers are lost.

Situated on Quobba's northern boundary is Gnaraloo Station. There is limited accommodation also available at the station, but information on the accommodation is limited. The area does not have the high cliffs of Quobba, but there is still good fishing available from the low reefs and rock platforms. Species that can be captured are similar to those at Quobba.

The Cape Range extends down the length of the Exmouth peninsula and virtually divides it in two. To the western side the Indian Ocean pounds the Ningaloo Reef and allows anglers to fish from sections of the reef in relative safety, while on the eastern side the sheltered waters of the Exmouth Gulf provide some limited reef and rock fishing.

The best locations for reef and rock fishing are

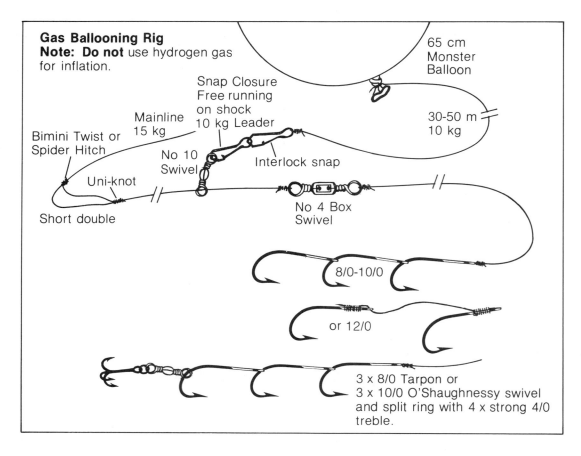

along Bundegi Reef, which is situated at the northern end of the peninsula. Rising tides provide the best action along this reef as the predators come in to feed. Huge trevally haunt the shallow-water reef area and several record fish have been taken from the 'Oysters' adjacent.

Rigs for Reef and Rock Fishing

In the south of the State, it is recommended that anglers dispense with wire traces, and use heavy nylon instead. If fishing in the north, where the fish tend to have a set of razors in lieu of teeth, wire becomes a necessity. Fishing from the rocks and reefs for sharks also necessitates the use of wire traces. The length of these will vary with the size of shark being sought, as their tendency to roll up in a line requires the use of extra lengths of wire and heavy nylon traces.

Hook sizes and styles all depend a lot on the species being sought, as well as the type of bait being used. Types preferred by Western Australian anglers are the forged patterns such as Tarpons, O'Shaughnessy, and Beak, which are far stronger hooks than the wire patterns like the Limerick, French, and Kendall Kirby. These wire patterns are satisfactory to use when fishing for the smaller species, but if larger fish are sought, then a stronger hook is required.

A small sharp hook will always penetrate the gristle and bone of the jaw of a fish far more readily than a dull blunt hook. Hooks must always be kept sharpened. To the rock angler this is important as a snag on a reef could, and often does, remove the sharpened point of a hook. Check them regularly.

Anglers using lures in the northern part of the State are advised to use a simple, quick-change style of rig which will allow ready changing of lures. These can be prepared in advance and don't take up a lot of room in a tackle box.

Ballooning rigs vary according to the type of inflation. If ballooning gas is used, then the rig will be a little different from that used for normal ballooning, as this requires a longer leader for the balloon. Several variations on the rigs are available to suit the prevailing conditions and various locations. It is possible to get a ballooning rig out over quite extensive inshore reefs using a little skill and not have the rig snag up.

There are no shortages of top rock and reef fishing locations throughout Western Australia. Touring anglers could spend years trying them all out and still not have covered all their seasonal variations.

There is always something different happening in Western Australian angling. The State's anglers are a pretty gregarious lot, and will willingly show visitors the 'ropes'. All that is asked is that you obey the commonsense laws of angling, take no risks with the sea, and most importantly, enjoy your fishing.

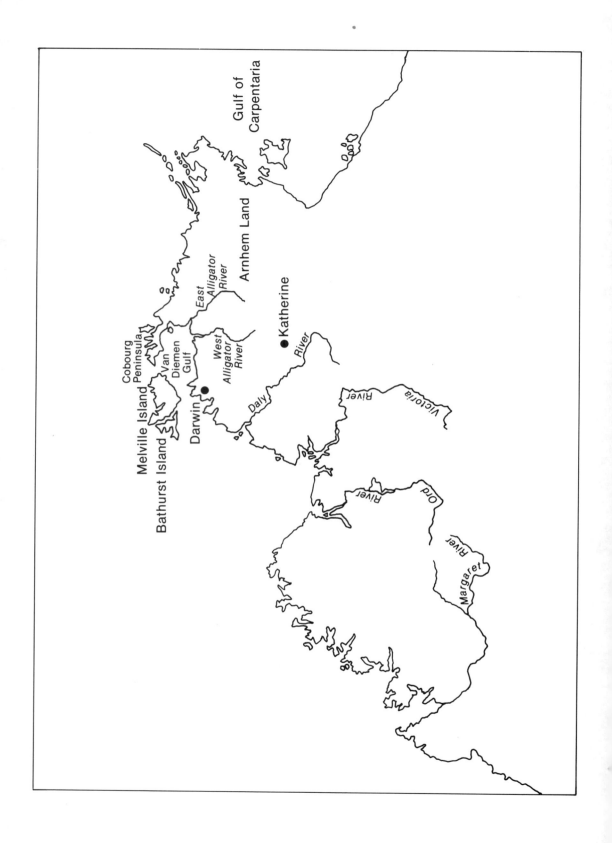

SECTION SIX

Northern Territory and North-West Western Australia

ESTUARY AND RIVER FISHING

Alex Julius

The Northern Territory and northern Western Australian coastlines contain hundreds of estuary and river systems. Because of the essential remoteness of much of the country, the quality of estuary and river fishing is better than anywhere else in Australia.

The climate of the region is tropical and for that reason the seasons are distinct, ranging from a wet season from January to at least the end of March, to a dry season for most of the rest of the year.

During a good wet season, the rivers flood, roads become impassable and much of the coastal region becomes inundated with water. As the floods recede with the commencement of the dry season, the country becomes more accessible. As the dry season progresses, the upper reaches of most rivers break up into lagoons and distinct waterholes.

The dominant and most sought after fish in the north's rivers and estuaries is the barramundi, a species often described as Australia's premier native sportfish. More than any other fish, its availability and the locations where it can be caught are governed by the seasons.

During the wet season, most dirt roads and bush tracks are impassable and fishing is mostly restricted to water near bitumen roads. Wet season barra are usually caught from small boats by anchoring and casting lures to creek mouths where there is floodwater run-off, or fishing in channels on the floodplains. There is also always a chance of catching fish from causeways, culverts and drains which traverse the major rivers and their tributaries — again, along the bitumen.

Saltwater creek and estuary fishing can be excellent during the wet season, but usually only near centres of population where there is good road access. Once again, accessibility is the key to success.

From Easter well into May is the post-wet season and one of the best times for barramundi, particularly in rivers as floods recede and the fish congregate around freshwater creek run-offs to feed on prawns and small fish. As in the wet season, anchoring and casting is the usual method.

Late May through to the end of October is the main dry season, when bush roads are passable and freshwater lagoons as well as the rivers can be fished. In the saltwater estuaries and some tidal river locations, casting to snags, rock bars and tidal run-offs can be very productive. However, trolling is generally the best method in the lagoons because the water is at its coolest and the barramundi tend to stay deep. Most fish are caught by trolling close to banks or weedbeds, or over submerged snags or rock bars.

The build-up to the wet season, usually late September through to December, offers many options. Water temperature in the lagoons is rising and the barra become increasingly active. Good fishing is still to be had by trolling lures, but casting at snags and fishing at night with surface lures is also worth while.

During the build-up, the salt water is at its most productive, and again most fishing takes place in estuarine creeks and inlets. Other species likely to be encountered are mangrove jack, threadfin salmon, golden snapper (fingermark bream), black jewfish, trevally species, estuarine rock cod and queenfish.

With the exception of jewfish, these species and barramundi can be readily caught on lures or saltwater fly. Bibbed, swimming minnow-pattern lures are favoured, but sinking, lead-head rubber lures are also consistent fish takers. Poppers also work well.

For barramundi and most other species, a short monofilament trace of about 25 kilo breaking strain is adequate. However, a wire trace is advisable for queenfish.

All species take bait. Live bait is the best, particularly mullet or prawns. For barra, hook sizes should vary from 2/0 to 6/0, depending on the size of the bait. In fact, only for jewfish should hooks larger than 6/0 be used.

Dead mullet, pilchards, fish bait or squid will also catch most creek species, including, at times, barramundi. Generally, bait is fished right on the bottom with just enough lead to withstand the current. However, on snaggy or rocky bottoms, it is often advisable to suspend the bait below a small float.

Tides are critical in the tidal rivers, estuaries and creeks in the north. The situation is complicated by the incredible variations in tidal movement. At Darwin, for example, the tidal range can be up to eight metres on big spring tides to less than a metre movement on dead neap tides.

The last half of a falling tide is usually the most productive, particularly for barramundi and mangrove jack. However, barramundi also often bite well on the first of the incoming tide. The best tides are intermediate between springs and neaps. In some places, especially at the mouths of small saltwater creeks, the top of a big tide will fish well for barramundi, threadfin salmon, jewfish and queenfish.

Besides barramundi, species likely to be

The most sought after fish in the rivers and estuaries of the Northern Territory and in North-West Western Australia is the barramundi. Its availability and the locations where it can be caught are governed by the season. (Photo Alex Julius)

encountered on inland waters are saratoga, sooty grunter, tarpon and archer fish. Saratoga tend to be near patches of water-lilies and pandanus palms, and take small barra-type lures. Sooty grunter, tarpon and archer fish prefer very small lures, particularly small lead-head rubber lures. As in the salt water, all species take fly.

A light, fast-action rod between 1.8 and 2.0 metres, coupled with a small bait-casting or threadline reel, will cover most situations. Handlines to 30 kilos are also quite functional when bait fishing.

Hazards, and Safety Measures

Crocodiles The country we are talking about is the natural habitat of Australia's largest predator, the saltwater crocodile. Anglers should be vigilant at all times and keep out of the water.

Box Jellyfish October to May inclusive is when the box jellyfish is prevalent in northern waters, particularly off the Northern Territory coastline. Take care with small children. Apply vinegar to box jellyfish stings.

Tides Because of the huge tidal movements across much of the Northern Territory and the north-west Australian coastline, care must be taken when fishing in and around river mouths and shallow estuaries. Many a careless or inexperienced boat angler has been stranded high and dry on a creek or river bed with no deep water in sight for hundreds of metres, or even kilometres, and the incoming tide still hours away.

Floods The Top End of the Northern Territory and northern Western Australia are subject to floods every wet season. The intensity of monsoons over specific areas governs the extent of flooding. Fortunately, all highways are now sealed and bridged across rivers. Only severe floods prevent access between main centres.

On the dirt roads, it's a different story. Check with local authorities on road conditions before undertaking bush trips in the Wet.

SMALL-BOAT AND LIGHT GAME
Alex Julius

Some of Australia's best light-tackle sportfishing is found in the coastal waters of the Northern Territory and northern Western Australia. Queenfish, Spanish mackerel, longtail tuna, trevally species, threadfin salmon, cobia and barracuda are common, and the occasional lucky angler manages to tangle with a sailfish or even a marlin.

Queenfish can be taken year round, usually near rocky headlands and exposed reefs at creek and river mouths.

Spanish mackerel are most abundant in the latter half of the year. They also frequent waters around rocky headlands and exposed reefs, but prefer to feed above shallow reefs next to deeper water.

Longtail tuna can be caught alongside Spanish mackerel in June, July and August, but they depart inshore waters earlier than the mackerel schools and are often found in deep water following schools of baitfish.

Trevally are less migratory, usually inhabiting shallow reef country subject to strong tidal flows. The giant trevally is the main species encountered, but golden trevally, big-eye trevally and others are also prolific in northern waters.

The barracuda is another shallow reef dweller, occasionally encountered in numbers. Most are caught by anglers pursuing other species.

Cobia, or black kingfish, are far from common but can turn up anywhere, from the widest offshore reefs to shallows well inside estuaries.

Sailfish and marlin are quite common along the Arnhem Land coast, particularly around Nhulunbuy. However, little is known of their movements near Darwin and few are taken by local anglers. In north-west Australia, their numbers increase the further south one travels.

Spanish mackerel are most plentiful in the waters of the North-West and the Territory in the second half of the year. They are a popular target for small boat fishers. (Photo Alex Julius)

All northern sportfish can be taken on lures, mainly by trolling but also by casting. A basic selection should include bibbed, swimming minnow patterns, both deep- and shallow-diving and in a variety of sizes; surface poppers; metal spoons; jigs; and spinning lures in a variety of sizes. Saltwater flies also work well. Tropical sportfish can be taken on a variety of baits. Floating pilchards on ganged, three-hook rigs work well. Garfish, either trolled or floated on ganged hooks, also work, as do whole small mullet or local squid. Live bait, of course, works particularly well.

Most tropical sportfish have sharp teeth or abrasive mouths, and it is essential to use wire trace.

Two basic outfits will suffice. A short, solid, fast-taper game rod with quality high-speed runners, coupled with a reliable overhead geared reel capable of holding at least 400 metres of 6–10-kilo line is ideal for trolling. A quality, medium-sized threadline reel, 6–8-kilo line, and fast-taper rod 2.0-2.3 metres long, is all that is required for casting.

Small-boat reef fishing is very popular in northern waters. A number of species are prevalent throughout the year, including golden snapper, saddletail snapper, red-finned emperor, red emperor, estuarine rock cod, coral trout, moonfish, mangrove jack, bream and black jewfish.

By far the most sought after is the golden snapper, known also as spotted-scale sea perch and fingermark bream. This fine table fish attains a weight of 10 kilos, but is usually encountered at 2-5 kilos. It prefers shallow inshore and estuarine reefs, although it is not uncommon to strike a school in deeper water offshore.

The saddletail snapper, often called redfish because of its deep red colouring, is a superb table fish which inhabits both inshore and offshore reefs. It averages 1-2 kilos.

The red-finned emperor and red emperor are

Black jewfish inhabit a variety of waters, including deep holes in tidal rivers and around creek and river mouths. They have an affinity for sunken wrecks in Darwin Harbour. (Photo Alex Julius)

rarely found close inshore, preferring deeper reefs. The red emperor is highly prized, usually weighing in at 2–4 kilos, but occasionally caught at up to 10 kilos. The red-finned emperor rarely exceeds 3 kilos.

Estuarine rock cod and coral trout are wide-ranging reef species. Both are non-schooling and anglers usually meet them while fishing for other reef species. The coral trout in particular is a highly regarded table fish.

Moonfish prefer inshore reefs and estuaries but are occasionally found offshore. Schools of 1–2 kilo fish are quite common.

Mangrove jack and bream are strictly estuarine and rarely venture far from shallow reefs, rock bars or mangroves. The mangrove jack takes an artificial lure readily and is sometimes caught by anglers fishing for barramundi.

The black jewfish is one of the Top End's biggest reef fish. It can exceed 50 kilos, but schools of 5–15 kilos are most common. It inhabits a variety of waters, including deep holes in tidal rivers and river and creek mouths, and by rock ledges and rocky headlands. The black jewfish has a particular affinity for sunken wrecks such as those in Darwin Harbour.

Reef fish take a variety of baits, including local squid, pilchards, mullet, tuna and mackerel. Small live mullet, fished on the bottom, work well.

For most reef fish, a 25–40 kilo handline and extra-strong 5/0–7/0 hooks are more than adequate. However, 50-kilo plus line, or even cord line, and extra-strong 10/0 hooks are required for jewfish.

SECTION SEVEN

The Environment

ESTUARIES AND BAYS
Peter Saenger

Estuaries and sheltered bays are the most popular fishing locations in Australia. Recent surveys of recreational fishers show that between 26 to 35 per cent of all fishers indicated estuaries and sheltered bays as their primary fishing location. Around Syndey alone, over 800 000 hours of fishing effort is spent by sportfishers each year in estuaries and sheltered bays, predominantly for relaxation and recreation. Several factors contribute to the popularity of estuaries and sheltered bays including sheltered and often extensive waterways, accessibility (in most weather conditions and with short travelling time) and such landscape features as river views and bank vegetation. At least of equal importance, however, is the generally successful fishing that is to be had in these areas.

Estuaries are generally shallow, sheltered and fertile. They are the meeting place of rivers and the sea. Here sea water is mixed with fresh water, and nutrients and silt brought down by the rivers are deposited. As a result, estuaries are changeable – tides change on an hourly pattern, freshwater flows change on a daily pattern, temperatures change on a monthly pattern, while other factors change at more variable intervals.

Individual organisms have adapted to these fluctuations and the estuarine systems themselves show a degree of resilience. Different species come and go, the life cycles of many species are adjusted to the seasonal change in estuarine conditions. For example, mangroves grow rapidly when sea water is diluted while seagrasses grow rapidly when fresh water input is low.

Seagrasses and algae are common subtidally and mangroves and saltmarshes abound in the intertidal areas. The high production of plant material can support a variety of other organisms, apparently by the breakdown of detritus, ie the plant material is not used directly but the breakdown of the plant litter provides a rich food source for various invertebrates and, in turn, for other species such as fish and crustaceans. Because of this abundance of food, many estuaries are not only highly productive of a few species, but they are able to support a great diversity of species.

However, in addition to these features, estuaries show varying salinities (salt content), ranging from fresh to fully salt waters. As the brackish waters of an estuary gradually decrease upstream to the progressively fresher waters of a river, there is a gradual replacement of the plants and animals as a result of their tolerance for varying degrees of salinity. During a 'fresh' following heavy rains, many fish are concentrated at the mouths of the estuary while during normal conditions of flow, these species are spread along the length of the estuary, as shown in the graph.

The salinity patterns of an estuary can also result in distinctive differences between adjacent estuaries. Such characteristics as the catchment area, the inflow of freshwater and the type of sediments give each estuary a characteristic flavour, and the discharge of waters with a particular flavour is used—like a chemical roadmap—by many species of fish to relocate individual estuaries. Most fish do not breed in estuaries; on reaching sexual maturity, they move downstream and often congregate at the mouths of estuaries. Spawning takes place at sea and after a short planktonic phase, the tiny juveniles find their way back into the estuaries, gradually move upstream, and remain in the estuary until reaching adulthood.

Even major events such as intense floods appear to disrupt the system for only short periods. Many fish and prawns are flushed out of the system along with some of the finer sediments with their invertebrate infauna. Recovery takes about two years and leads to a rejuvenation of the entire system.

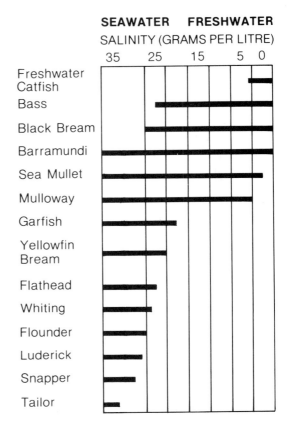

As a result of the abundance of food, the physical shelter and the biological shelter (from predators and parasites) they provide estuaries form ideal conditions for juveniles of many species of fish and crustaceans. In fact, of the total commercial catch in New South Wales, 66 per cent by weight and over 70 per cent by value is estuarine dependent at least at some stage of its life cycle.

Historically, many Australian estuaries were the points of human settlement. Initially, they formed a focal point for shipping which was soon followed by storage, processing and supply facilities. Adjacent lowlands proved suitable for early agricultural activities while the estuaries themselves were used as efficient waste-disposal systems. Ironically, the natural productivity of the estuaries ensured the supplies of fish, shellfish and crustaceans to sustain the settlements which now threaten that productivity.

With increasing populations along Australia's coastline and with a corresponding increase in recreational usage, all the coastal resources are coming under increasing pressures. This is particularly evident in estuaries near large urban centres where the historical uses are being supplanted by the newer demands for further urban development as well as leisure and recreation.

All estuarine uses have some resultant impact although, clearly, some are less intense than others. In order to maintain estuarine values in terms of their productivity and the services they provide, it is essential that some activities be regulated while others will need to be relocated to non-estuarine areas. However, as a first step towards such rationalisation and management, information on the state of Australia's estuarine resources is required to facilitate a balanced and planned approach. The Australian Recreational and Sport Fishing Confederation is presently undertaking such an inventory.

In conclusion, estuaries are known to be valuable and productive for a number of reasons: they are the major nursery areas of numerous fish and crustaceans and they provide opportunities for fishing in a sheltered and safe environment. With a little care and forward planning, these highly productive systems will continue to provide these opportunities for years to come.

NATIVE FRESHWATER RECREATIONAL FISHERIES OF EASTERN AUSTRALIA
Stuart J Rowland

The Environment and Possible Causes of Decline

Australia is one of the driest continents on earth. The mainland is characterised by low topography, an absence of high mountain ranges and permanent snowfields, low rainfall, limited run-off, high summer temperatures and high evaporation. There are few large, permanent, natural freshwater lakes, and the discharge of most river systems is dependent on an often variable and irregular rainfall. During severe droughts many rivers dry up to form a series of waterholes, yet at other times floods can inundate thousands of square kilometres.

Australia's aridity and variable climate, and the relative scarcity of freshwater habitats, have had several major influences on the endemic fish fauna. First, the recent evolutionary history of most freshwater fish has been confined to riverine habitats, and secondly, during the last 100 years there have been substantial man-made changes to many of the river systems in south-eastern Australia.

Murray-Darling River System

The Murray-Darling is Australia's largest river system. It drains approximately one million square kilometres or one-seventh of Australia's land mass and the total length of the Murray, Darling and Murrumbidgee rivers is over 7000 kilometres. The volume of water carried by the system is very low compared to similar-sized systems throughout the world.

Most tributaries of the system rise in the Great Dividing Range, fall quickly to the western slopes and then flow through the flat arid inland regions. Ephemeral swamps, billabongs and extensive floodplain areas are typical of the system; however, there are now 146 man-made water storages on the various tributaries and the flow in the system is highly regulated.

Coastal Drainages

South-eastern drainage This drainage is characterised by rivers which are short and have a relatively large run-off. Some rivers such as the Yarra, Manning and Tweed flow directly to the coast, while others such as the Clarence have more extensive upper reaches which, in part, flow parallel to the coast. The maximum flows in the southern rivers occur in winter and spring, and during summer and autumn in the northern rivers.

North-eastern drainage The rivers in this system all have large annual discharges, and include the Burnett, Fitzroy, Burdekin, Herbert, and North Johnstone rivers. The maximum flow in all rivers occurs in summer during monsoonal rain; the flow in other seasons is low. The Dawson, Fitzroy, Burdekin and Burnett rivers regularly dry up to form a series of waterholes.

Freshwater Fish

Evolution and biological adaptations Australia is a very old continent and has a very distinctive, endemic freshwater fish fauna; most of the popular angling species, with the notable exception of the barramundi are found only in this country.

The evolution of these freshwater fish has resulted in some remarkable biological adaptations to the variable regimes of droughts and floods that are characteristic of most of our drainages. For example:

Golden perch spawn only when there is a flood or substantial rise in water level and water temperatures are about $23°$ C or above. Floods produce an increase in both habitat and food for larvae and juveniles. Consequently golden perch spawn only when conditions are suitable for the survival of larvae. Floods or 'freshes' are also thought to trigger spawning migrations and possibly spawning in silver perch, barramundi, Australian bass, sooty grunter and jungle perch.

Golden perch and silver perch undergo extensive upstream spawning migrations during floods in spring and summer; this is an efficient dispersal mechanism which compensates for the downstream movement of the pelagic eggs and larvae.

Many native fishes can withstand water temperatures as high as $37°$ C and dissolved oxygen concentrations as low as 2 milligrams per litre; extreme conditions which can occur during summer.

Buccal incubation in the spotted barramundi (also commonly known as saratoga or Dawson River barramundi) is a mechanism which alleviates the effects of high turbidity and low levels of oxygen in the Fitzroy system.

There is circumstantial evidence that the spangled perch becomes torpid during prolonged dry periods.

Recreational Fisheries

Despite its vast size, the Murray-Darling river system has a relatively poor fish fauna, consisting of only about 24 native species. Included in these are some very popular angling species (see table). The most famous is the Murray cod, Australia's and one of the world's largest freshwater fish, growing to at least 113.5 kilos. Its size and excellent edible qualities make it the most sought-after native inland fish. Other popular native fishes are golden perch (also known as yellowbelly, callop and perch), silver perch (known as grunter or bream), and catfish (known as tandan or jewfish). Spangled perch are common in the north-western area of the system, and are sought by some anglers.

Trout cod and Macquarie perch are both fine angling fish found in the upper reaches of some southern tributaries of the system. These fish are now rare, and the trout cod is an endangered species.

Fish of the Coastal Drainages

The coastal drainages of eastern Australia support two of our finest sport fishes, the barramundi in the north-eastern drainage and the Australian bass (often known locally as perch) in the south-eastern drainage (see table). Bass are also found in the southern part of the north-eastern drainage. A distinctive feature of the freshwater fish fauna in these drainages is the number of angling species that are known, or thought to be catadromous, ie fishes that live principally in freshwater and migrate to brackish or saltwater to breed. These are the barramundi and bass, plus the freshwater mullet, freshwater herring, Australian grayling, jungle perch, long-finned eel, and short-finned eel.

Other fish keenly sought by some anglers are catfish, spangled perch, sooty grunter, golden perch and spotted barramundi; the last two are found naturally only in the Fitzroy river system. The superb angling fish mangrove jack and tarpon, although essentially estuarine, often penetrate well into freshwater reaches of the northern parts of the south-eastern drainage and the entire north-eastern drainage. Other fish that are sometimes sought by anglers in the north-eastern drainage, and are thought to be capable of breeding in freshwater, are long tom, snub-nosed garfish, and archer fish.

There are a number of endangered and threatened species in the eastern drainages. The eastern freshwater cod is found only in some southern tributaries of the Clarence River system, New South Wales, and is considered to be endangered. There is a prohibition on the capture of this species. The taxonomic status of the small population of cod in the Mary River system, Queensland, is unknown, and these cod are also considered to be threatened. Several small populations of the threatened Macquarie perch are found in two river systems of the south-eastern drainage near Sydney; one or both of these populations may not be conspecific with *M. australasica* of the Murray-Darling river system. The taxonomic status of golden perch in the Fitzroy system is also uncertain.

Species known to have been translocated from the inland to the coastal drainages are Murray cod, trout cod (these species are now hybridising in Cataract Dam near Sydney), golden perch, silver perch and Macquarie perch. The effects of these translocations on the native fish fauna in the eastern drainages have not been determined.

Decline of Native Fish

Although large fluctuations of fish populations occur naturally, particularly in harsh environments such as that of the Murray-Darling river system, historical, anecdotal and scientific literature, as well as catch statistics from inland commercial fisheries clearly indicate that there has been a decline in the abundance and distribution of most inland native freshwater fishes. The decline of some of the important angling species, Murray cod, trout cod, Macquarie perch, and to a lesser extent golden perch and silver perch has been dramatic since the early 1950s. Golden perch, silver perch and catfish became extinct upstream of Yarrawong Weir on the Murray River soon after its completion in 1939.

Unfortunately, there is little quantative information on the populations of freshwater fish in coastal drainages; however, some species that were once very common, such as eastern freshwater cod, cod in the Mary River system, and Australian grayling, are now rare. Freshwater cod are extinct in the Richmond and Brisbane river systems. There is much subjective evidence suggesting that there have been significant reductions in the abundance of barramundi, bass, jungle perch and freshwater mullet in some or all river systems.

Possible Causes of the Decline

This discussion centres on the fish of the Murray-Darling river system because more is known about their biology, and this river system has been subjected to far greater environmental change than most systems in the coastal drainages.

Reduced larval recruitment
The larval stage is the most critical of a fish's life cycle. Experiments conducted at the Inland Fisheries Research Station, Narrandera, New South Wales, have shown that low densities of zooplankton, and delays in the initial feeding of golden perch, silver perch and Murray cod larvae result in greatly reduced survival. Research has also shown that although Murray cod spawn annually in the wild when water temperatures reach about 20^0 C during spring, relatively strong populations are only established when the breeding seasons coincide with floods; a similar relationship exists for golden perch.

The floodplain areas of the Murray-Darling river system are highly productive and when they are inundated, large blooms of zooplankton and aquatic insects develop; hence providing the essential food items for the larvae and juveniles of native fish.

The construction of dams, weirs and levee banks has dramatically reduced the frequency, extent and duration of flooding. The southern tributaries, in particular the Murray and Murrumbidgee rivers, no longer flood annually in spring following the snow thaw, and much of the system does not flood at all except under extraordinary circumstances. Consequently optimum conditions for the survival of the larvae of native fish now rarely occur.

It is possible that a similar relationship exists between flooding and recruitment of the larvae of native freshwater fish in coastal drainages.

Other adverse effects of flow regulation
Reduced incidence of spawning The regulation of flow reduces the reproductive potential of species, such as golden perch and silver perch, that require a flood or rise in water level to actually induce spawning. This is probably a major factor preventing the establishment of large populations of such native fish in impoundments; the water level often falls during late spring and summer as irrigation demands are met and the main stimulus to spawn is removed. The spawning of barramundi, bass, mullet, herring, jungle perch and sooty grunter may be suppresssed by reduced flows in coastal drainages.

Reduced water temperatures Water is released from the base of most large impoundments and so stratification in spring and summer results in greatly depressed water temperatures downstream. For example, temperatures during summer in the Goulburn River below Lake Eildon are 10^0-15^0C cooler than those of inflowing water and would consequently remain below the critical spawning temperatures of most native fishes. The water temperature in the Murray River, above its junction with the Darling River, now rarely reaches 23^0C; golden perch, silver perch and catfish spawn at temperatures of 23^0-24^0C. The depression of water temperatures below impoundments has reduced the habitat available for the spawning of native fishes.

Alteration of seasonal flows The maximum flows in the southern tributaries of the Murray-Darling river system used to occur in late winter and spring; however, these flows are now impounded by large dams and weirs for release to irrigation areas in summer and autumn.

Rapid reductions in water level The water level in some inland rivers falls rapidly when weirs are closed to divert water for irrigation purposes. Spawning sites of some species, including Murray cod and catfish, may be in relatively shallow water, less than one metre, and so rapid decreases in water level can lead to dessication and predation of eggs, as well as reducing available spawning habitat.

Barriers to migration Dams and high-level weirs act as permanent barriers to migration of fishes (with the exception of eels). Unfortunately very few weirs in the Murray-Darling river system have fish ladders, despite the success of the ladder in Lock 15 (Euston Weir) which was built in 1937; large numbers of native fish have

The distribution and status of the principal native freshwater angling fishes of the inland and coastal drainages of eastern Australia

Drainage	Fish		Recreational Fishery	Status	General Comments
	Common name	Scientific name	*** keenly sought ** popular * sought by some anglers	A-abundant C-common U-uncommon R-rare E-endangered	
Murray-Darling	Murray cod	*Maccullochella peeli*	***	U	dramatic decline in abundance since 1950s
	trout cod	*Maccullochella macquariensis*	* **	E	only some small populations – ENDANGERED
	golden perch	*Macquaria ambigua*		C	reduced abundance and distribution; still relatively common
	Macquarie perch	*Macquaria australasica*	*	R	only 1 large population (Dartmouth Dam); some small populations
	silver perch	*Bidyanus bidyanus*	**	U	reduced abundance and distribution; patchy distribution
	catfish	*Tandanus tandanus*	**	A/C	reduced abundance in rivers; still common in some impoundments and lakes
	spangled perch	*Leiopotheropon unicolor*	*	A/C	found north of Menindee/Condobolin
	river blackfish	*Gadopsis marmoratus*	*	C/R	greatly reduced abundance in NSW; common in Victoria
South-eastern drainage	†Australian bass	*Macquaria novemaculeata*	***	C	reduced abundance in some systems
	eastern freshwater cod	*Maccullochella ikei*	-	E	one, small population – ENDANGERED
	Macquarie perch	*Macquaria australasica*	*	R	taxonomy uncertain; several small populations
	†catfish	*Tandanus tandanus*	*	A/C	no apparent change in abundance
	†freshwater mullet	*Myxus petardi*	*	C	reduced abundance in some systems

The distribution and status of the principal native freshwater angling fishes of the inland and coastal drainages of eastern Australia

Drainage	Fish		Recreational Fishery	Status	General Comments
	Common name	Scientific name	*** keenly sought ** popular * sought by some anglers	A-abundant C-common U-uncommon R-rare E-endangered	
	freshwater herring	*Pomatolosa richmondia*	*	A	no apparent change in abundance
	Australian grayling	*Prototroctes maraena*	-	R	once common, now RARE
	river blackfish	*Gadopsis marmoratus*	*	C	common in Victoria
	†long-finned eel	*Anguilla reinhardtii*	*	A	no apparent change in abundance
	short-finned eel	*Anguilla australis*	*	A	no apparent change in abundance
North-eastern drainage	barramundi	*Lates calcarifer*	***	C/U	uncommon in southern systems; decline in abundance
	spotted baramundi	*Scleropages leichhardti*	*	C	only natural in Dawson-Fitzroy system, has been translocated to other systems
	cod	*Maccullochella sp.*	*	U	only found in Mary River system; decline in abundance
	jungle perch	*Kuhlia rupestris*	*	U/R	reduced abundance; patchy distribution
	sleepy cod	*Oxyeleotris lineolatus*	*	C	excellent eating; poor sport
	golden perch	*Macquaria ambigua*	*	C	only found naturally in Dawson-Fitzroy system
	spangled perch	*Leiopotherapon unicolor*	*	C	no apparent change in abundance
	sooty grunter	*Hephaestus fuliginosus*	**	A/C	no apparent change
	mangrove jack	*Lutjanus argentimaculatus*	***	C/U	no apparent change
	tarpon	*Megalops cyprinoides*	*	C	no apparent change
	long tom	*Strongylura kreffti*	*	C	no apparent change
	snub-nosed garfish	*Arrhamphus sclerolepis*	*	C	no apparent change
	archer fish	*Toxotes chatareus*	*	C	no apparent change

† *Also found in parts of north-eastern drainage.*

regularly used this ladder.

Yarrawonga Weir is a high-level weir which prevents the recruitment of native fish to the Murray and Ovens rivers above this site. Such barriers reduce the amount of suitable habitat available to native fish. Golden perch and silver perch do not establish large, self-maintaining populations in impounded waters (exceptions in New South Wales are silver perch in Burrinjuck Dam and golden perch in Keepit Dam) and so recreational fisheries for these species depend on the stocking of hatchery-reared fry.

Dams and high-level weirs have disastrous consequences for the fish which descend to the coastal drainages to spawn; unless a weir has an effective fish ladder, such fish cannot complete their life cycles. Dams and weirs have probably contributed to the dramatic loss or decline of the Australian grayling in many rivers in the south-eastern drainage, and to the reduced abundance of barramundi, bass, mullet and jungle perch.

Desnagging

Instream cover is probably the most important component of the habitat of most native freshwater fish. Important angling species that rely on cover are Murray cod, golden perch, Macquarie perch, river blackfish, barramundi, bass, sooty grunter, jungle perch and mangrove jack. All of these fish can live in relatively shallow water provided ample cover is available, in the form of logs, tree roots, overhanging vegetation, rocks, clay banks and undercut banks.

River 'improvement' programs involving desnagging and channelling result in extensive loss of native fish habitat. Potential spawning sites of species such as Murray cod, river blackfish, and possibly trout cod that spawn adhesive eggs onto firm surfaces are also removed or destroyed. The large scale removal of vegetation from river banks, eg the logging of river red gums and cedar, has greatly reduced the main source of instream cover of many rivers.

Siltation

Siltation has destroyed some habitat of native fishes including the spawning habitat of Macquarie perch, trout cod and river blackfish. Local anglers and residents claim that there has been extensive siltation in the lower reaches of rivers such as the Murray, Darling, Murrumbidgee and Lachlan.

Many rivers and creeks in the coastal drainages have been greatly altered by siltation and much fish habitat has been lost.

Introduced fishes

Overseas studies have shown that the introduction of exotic fishes can have dramatic effects on native fish faunas and environments. Introduced fishes have flourished in Australian inland waters and there is no doubt that some species have contributed to the demise of some native fish.

The salmonids have been implicated in the decline of river blackfish, trout cod and Macquarie perch in the cooler, upper reaches of the southern tributaries of the Murray-Darling river system.

English perch, also known as redfin, have been implicated in the elimination of Macquarie perch from Lake Eildon. They are an aggressive, schooling and often prolific fish, and were extremely abundant in the southern rivers of the Murray-Darling river system around the 1950s. Their diet is very similar to that of larval and juvenile native fish, and small fish become a major part of the diet of larger English perch. Circumstantial evidence strongly suggests that English perch contributed to the decline of Murray cod and other native fishes during the 1950s, probably through competition with, and predation of larvae and juveniles.

The common carp, also known as European carp, underwent a massive population explosion in the Murray-Darling river system during the 1970s; however, this was well after the dramatic decline of many native species. Carp are omnivorous and generally bottom feeders. It is therefore possible that carp compete with catfish, and there is circumstantial evidence that they have displaced catfish in some waters. There is also evidence that carp have adversely affected the environment in some areas by increasing turbidity and destroying weedbeds. During the late 1970s, the incidence of a parasite called anchor worm on native fish, as well as carp in the Murray and Murrumbidgee rivers was very high; however, during this time anchor worm was not present on native fish, particularly Murray cod above Yarrawonga Weir where there were no carp. Carp may be an important host and carrier of this parasite.

The mosquito fish is widespread in inland and coastal drainages. It eats fish eggs and young fish, and nips the fins of larger fish. Mosquito fish have been responsible for the extinction and reduction of small fishes in other countries, and they have been shown to affect adversely the survival and growth of juvenile golden perch and silver perch in farm dams.

Cichlids are popular aquarium fish and several species have become established in some coastal rivers. They are abundant near Brisbane, and have the potential to establish large self-maintaining populations north from the Clarence River system. Further expansion of their distribution may pose serious threats to the popular native angling fishes.

Australia once had a 'disease free' status, but recent outbreaks of bacterial and viral diseases on goldfish, trout and English perch in eastern Australia have placed this status in jeopardy. These outbreaks act as loud warnings of the potential threat posed by diseases carried by introduced fishes, be they long-established exotic species or the imported aquarium fish. The effects of these diseases on native fish are unknown.

Overfishing
There is little evidence to suggest that overfishing has contributed significantly to the general decline of the native fish that are widely distributed throughout the Murray-Darling river system. It is possible, however, that heavy fishing pressure in localised areas during spawning migrations of Macquarie perch reduced populations of this species. There is also evidence that jungle perch and the small population of eastern freshwater cod suffered from relatively heavy pressure by anglers during the 1970s.

Species that are locally abundant and/or migrate to form large spawning aggregations, such as barramundi and bass, are susceptible to heavy fishing pressure, as are species such as Murray cod that are extremely active and aggressive during the breeding season.

Pollution
Freshwater environments have been subjected to many types of pollutants—pesticides, herbicides, fertilisers, sewage effluent, agricultural, industrial and mining wastes, heavy metals, toxic chemicals and so on. In general the effects of most pollutants on native fish are unknown; however, pesticides such as DDT and Dieldrin that were used extensively until recent years are known to be lethal to aquatic fauna and have long residual lives. They may accumulate in body tissue and DDT is known to reduce the hatchability of fish eggs.

Historical reports suggest that chemicals, including cyanide from mines, may have caused massive kills of the eastern freshwater cod in the Clarence River system in the early 1900s, and so contributed to the demise of this species.

Summary

Australia's endemic freshwater fish fauna has evolved in riverine habitats that are subjected to harsh climatic conditions. The variable and often irregular rainfall may produce long droughts or extensive floods. Our native fish are adapted to live and reproduce under these extreme environmental conditions. Over the last 100 years, in an effort to conserve and utilise water, we have substantially and rapidly altered the freshwater environments in south-eastern Australia. The abundance of many native fish has declined, and some are now rare and endangered. The construction of dams, weirs and levee banks and the subsequent regulation of flow has resulted in a substantial reduction in the frequency, extent and duration of flooding, and the alteration of the thermal regime in many rivers. These changes have adversely affected the reproduction of native fish by reducing larval recruitment and the incidence of spawning. Dams and weirs on coastal rivers disrupt the life cycles of many species. Desnagging, siltation, barriers to migration, competition with and predation by introduced fishes, overfishing and pollution have also contributed to the demise of our native recreational freshwater fishes.

SECTION EIGHT

Australia Underwater

QUEENSLAND DOWN UNDER

Ray Oakey

When one says 'Go Fish Australia' to the underwater enthusiast, he or she knows that the quarry at least will be seen if not captured. Divers have three ways of enjoying fishing. The most common of course is spearfishing, but in recent years the hobbies of aquarium fishing and the capturing of marine specimens on film have become immensely popular. Modern equipment has enabled the divers to keep marine fish successfully in the living room and technology has produced sophisticated waterproof cameras capable of being submerged to great depths.

Queensland offers the diver a wide range of venues. Divers in south-east Queensland may be found hunting the large mulloway off Hastings Point or the morwong, mangrove jack or sweetlip around the bomboras of Cudgen Reef. These reefs, in far northern New South Wales, are easily accessible to the rock-hopper, but boats would be an asset if the current is running.

The Gold Coast reefs off Tweed Heads are well worth the sometimes hazardous crossing of the Tweed River bar. Fido, Five Mile and Nine Mile reefs are plateaus rising to about 10 metres and are particularly good for large pelagics such as cobia and Spanish mackerel.

Moreton and North Stradbroke islands provide excellent diving. In this area a mixture of southern fish and the coral species of the Barrier Reef gather. More than 50 spearable species have been recorded at Flinders Reef and Smiths Rock. Stradbroke Island's Flat Rock has deep drop-offs and fishes well. Visibility in these areas very rarely falls below 10 metres and more often than not is 20 metres or more. This clarity is particularly good for the photographic fisher, making it easy to spot the many species of nudibranch that are prolific.

One cannot go past Moreton Island without mentioning the highly successful Frank Curtin artificial reef. Constructed of old whaling vessels, tugs, car bodies, tyres and other materials, the reef has become a haven for a large population of fish. It was built by the Underwater Research Group over several years and is a popular dive site for photographers and aquarium collectors. Spearfishing is banned on the inside of Moreton Island and the fish have become very confident with divers. Likewise the huge Queensland groper, tuskfish and coral trout are at home with divers at the Roy Rufus artifical reef in Hervey Bay. Both artificial reefs have been resounding successes and will provide a nursery for the surrounding reefs for years to come.

Just an hour's drive north of Brisbane the Sunshine Coast is 50 kilometres of headlands and bays which are ideal for the rock-hopper. The rocky reefs support enough fish and crayfish to keep the sparo happy. The only problem with this area is that water clarity during summer tends to be a bit of a problem close in. Boats are required to reach the clearer waters of the Gneering Shoals off Mooloolabah. The odd coral trout may be found around the ledges of both the Inner and Outer Gneerings.

Probably Australia's most valuable marine asset is the Great Barrier Reef—the Mecca for divers. There are many ways to fish the reef. Day trips, extended cruises or camping drop-offs are available through numerous charter-boat operations. Drop-offs are the most economical way of spending a fishing holiday on the reef, especially if a small power boat is taken on the trip. For a reasonable fee, approximately $120, a chartered boat will drop a group of people and their gear on one of the islands, then return at the end of their holiday to collect them and their freezer or esky full of fish.

Before any trip to the Barrier Reef is organised it is recommended that a permit be obtained, as the whole of the reef is a marine park. It is controlled and managed by the Great Barrier Reef Marine Park Authority (GBRMPA). The islands and reefs are subject to periodical restrictions and closures, and stiff penalties may be incurred for infringements.

GBRMPA has divided the reef into sections, Capricornia, Central and Far North. The oldest and most established marine park is Capricornia which covers the islands and reefs of the Bunker and Capricorn groups. Heron, Lady Elliot and Lady Musgrave islands are probably the most popular diving areas.

Heron Island's bombora is known world wide and the photographer should not miss the spectacular fish surrounding it. These have been hand fed for many years and are large in numbers and size. Naturally, spearfishing is prohibited.

For those who would prefer to get away from the touristy atmosphere, Northwest, Masthead and Tryon islands are excellent camping islands with large reefs and plenty of fish. All forms of underwater fishing are permitted in specific areas. Again check with GBRMPA for details on each reef.

The Central district covers all reefs off the coast from Rockhampton to Mackay, and includes the Kepple, Percy and Whitsunday Island groups as well as the Swain Reefs. The islands are reasonably accessible by small power boats and are well serviced by the charter-boat industry. Many good catches of trout, red emperor, cod and wrasse may be speared here. The Swain Reefs have long been regarded as a Mecca for the serious diver, and there are kilometres of shallow coral reefs to be explored. These reefs do have some barren areas so spend the time and talk to the charter operators. A number of charter vessels have set up their own bag limits to restrict the numbers taken on these trips, which is a good thing.

It is said in the Far North that there are so many reefs, bomboras and cays, that a person diving seven days a week for a lifetime would still not see it all. Look at any map and one would have to agree. It is difficult to comprehend the quantity and quality of the fish, especially on the reefs further from the major cities and towns. It is quite fantastic to see a Queensland groper the size of a family car sit in front of a diver and wave his pectoral fins, or a giant turrum glide past. This is the magic that awaits those who dive the wreck of the *Yongala* off Townsville, or the Ribbon Reefs and Lizard Island to the north of Cairns.

SPEARFISHING IN NEW SOUTH WALES

George Davies

Spearfishing in New South Wales offers the ardent underwater enthusiast a wide diversity of fish species, in waters from the cooler south to the semi-tropical coral areas of the north.

While many of the species taken by underwater fishers are regularly taken by anglers, others rarely form a part of such catches. The Australian Underwater Federation has always carefully monitored populations of sedentary species that it considered vulnerable to spearfishing pressures, and successfully recommended legislation to protect the giant Queensland groper, estuary cod, the largest of the wrasse, the blue and brown groper, and the smaller 'living jewels', the blue devil and elegant wrasse which are extremely rare and exist in only select locations.

Some species captured have a wide distribution throughout the State. These include red morwong which are protected with a bag limit of five per person per day, luderick, bream, pike, sweep, trevally, salmon, rock blackfish, silver drummer, sergeant baker, red rock cod, crimson banded wrasse, yellowtail kingfish, bonito, and leatherjacket species including the black reef, spined, deepbodied and yellowfin. Others not so common but regularly included in catches, are flathead, blue morwong, bluefish, silver trumpeter, sea sweep and tawhine. The snapper, although having a statewide distribution, is possibly one of the most elusive of all species and actually to capture one is considered a major achievement.

The brown-banded morwong is the most prolific of southern species; however, captures have been recorded as far north as the Solitary Islands. The blue-throated wrasse and zebra-fish are confined to the south and both species hybridise freely with the crimson-banded wrasse in the first instance and the rock blackfish in the second, producing a hybrid commonly called the banded rock blackfish. The long-snouted boarfish, while generally considered southern, has been captured as far north as Seal Rocks, and the dusky morwong so common to South Australia and Western Australia, is quite rare but has been recorded from Port Stephens and Swansea.

Northwards from the Broughton Island–Seal Rocks areas, the incidence of tropical species increases noticeably. Yellow spotted surgeon and sawtail surgeon which are the most prolific of species in the north, extend into southern waters where small catches are recorded. The more popular of the northern pelagics are the Spanish mackerel and the cobia, while both samson fish and rainbow runners are regularly taken.

Of the fish that frequent the northern reefs, the more prized are the mangrove jack, moses perch, pearl perch, spangled emperor, blue-spotted groper, maori cod and foxfish, and to a lesser degree the brown and spotted sweetlip, the brown unicorn and a number of species of parrotfish.

Although several large yellowfin tuna have been recorded they are rarely captured by spearfishers. There is only one recorded spearfishing capture of a marlin in Australia and the possibility is that this fish was sick or exhausted after escaping from a game fisher.

Spearfishing is often considered more hunting than fishing. The successful spearfishers have a physical fitness that enables them to dive to depths of 30 metres and experience in identifying species by their movement in the water. They know the particular habits of the fish and can stalk them until in range, and they know the territory and locations in which to expect to find the various species and can approach without disturbing them.

Spearfishing competitions encourage conservation by limiting captures to one of each species rather than quantities of a particular fish. This system enhances the hunting skills of competitors as they develop new techniques and physical endurance to meet the challenge of yet another species perhaps a little deeper and more elusive.

Major spearfishing competitions held annually in New South Wales are the Australian Pacific Coast Championships at Shoal Bay during Easter, Metropolitan Zone Championships in Sydney, Canada Cup at Terrigal, and the South Coast Championships and the Tri-state Championships between Victoria, New South Wales and ACT at Eden.

National Championships are hosted by States in turn, and each year the Tripartite Championships are held between Australia, New Zealand and New Caledonia. Australia has competed in a number of world Spearfishing Championships including those held in Malta, Tahiti, Cuba, Chile, Spain, Italy and Peru, and was most successful in winning the Individual Title in Tahiti and taking second place in the National Teams.

Sharks have always provided the extra thrill to the underwater hunt, but despite the perils of contact with dangerous marine life the greatest danger to underwater hunters will always be the sea itself, which has little sympathy for the inexperienced or for those who, from familiarity, ignore the rules. It is crucial that safety rules be strictly adhered to at all times, as second chances are the exception.

VICTORIA UNDERWATER
Andrew Rawlings

Spearfishing in Victoria can be divided into three zones: the New South Wales border to Wilson's Promontory (Eastern Zone), Wilson's Promontory to Cape Otway (Central Zone), and Cape Otway to the South Australian border (Western Zone). While the Eastern Zone shows quite a few similarities to the New South Wales spearfishing areas, the other two zones vary only marginally and are uniquely Victorian.

Except for the Wilson's Promontory area, Victoria doesn't have many islands or offshore reefs. Generally the fish are in shallower water (down to 14 metres) than they are in New South Wales or Western Australia. The best time to dive at most spots is low tide. The best skindiving months are January to June inclusive when the water is warmer and the visibility better.

The underwater visibility on most parts of the Victorian coastline is quickly reduced by wind and rainfall and will take a few days to recover. The main exception is the Port Phillip Heads area around Portsea, Queenscliff and Point Lonsdale. A vast amount of water flows in and out through the Heads so weather effects on this water are less noticeable.

Because of the strong currents, the diving is usually done when the current is turning at the high-water (flood) slack between the high and low tide times and sometimes at the low-water (ebb) slack between the low and high tide times.

Most of Victoria's bad weather comes from the south-west and there are only a few spots left for diving when it arrives. Some of these are Wilson's Promontory (especially the eastern side), Port Phillip Heads, Cape Schanck, Pyramid Rock and the western part of and other small bays of Port Phillip Bay.

The major concentration of boat diving is around Port Phillip Heads. If the weather permits boat diving makes access to some ocean sites easier but most dive sites are accessible from the land anyway. However, there are many parts of Wilson's Promontory where the only practical access is by boat.

There are no restrictions on the use of scuba or hookah to get fish but of course these are banned from underwater fishing competitions when only snorkle (breath-hold) diving is permitted.

The water temperature is cool to cold so a wetsuit is needed if you intend to stay in the water for more than a few minutes.

Most Victorian fish are reef fish but there are some excellent pelagic fish.

The commonest reef fish are blue-throat and black wrasse, leatherjackets (a dozen or more species), magpie and dusky morwong, sea sweep and zebra fish. In recent years the eastern brown-banded morwong has become much more common as it has moved across the State from the east.

The commonest pelagic fish are Australian salmon, trevally, and the yellowtail kingfish.

Some of the more uncommon species are eastern blue morwong, western blue morwong, (queen morwong), whiting, sergeant baker, deep-bodied leatherjacket, jackass morwong, eastern beardie and groper. As in New South Wales, the snapper is a very difficult fish to get because it is so flighty.

The best way to learn which fish is which is to attend a few underwater fishing competitions. Many clubs have their own competitions while the two Australian Underwater Federation regions in Victoria run their own series of competitions and regional championships, and take it in turn to host the Victorian Underwater-fishing Championships.

Some of the competitions allow the use of boats and cars while others are land-based. There are various junior, ladies, senior, veteran and open categories with prizes for the place-getters.

Some of the prizes are sponsored by skindiving equipment suppliers, eg, the 'Champion' Trophy is for the highest number of species weighed-in by a pair of divers in two specified competitions. The most sought-after trophy is the Hannan Memorial Trophy for the highest number of species caught by a team of four divers over all the boat competitions (usually four) in a season.

Our best competitors can dive well over 20 metres but because most fish are in shallower water, you don't have to be that good to compete.

A detailed knowledge of species, such as where to find and how to catch the best fish, is needed to make the most of underwater fishing trips.

The marine reserves in the Port Phillip Heads area generally prohibit underwater fishing; however, parts of the Wilson's Promontory Marine Reserve allow it.

Possibly the best diving in the State is around Wilson's Promontory where there is deep-diving around granite boulders. Cape Woolamai is similar. Most of the Central Zone is sandstone and limestone coastlines with a flat intertidal platform and then a zone of reefs of 6 to 14 metres deep.

There are volcanic basalt rocks on Phillip Island, the adjacent part of the Mornington Peninsula, and much of the coast between Warrnambool and Portland.

Relatively recent lava flows in the Port Fairy area have created a shallow coastline with lagoons.

The Western Zone is the one for crayfish. Here they are much easier to take by hand than in the Central Zone. There are minimum sizes (depending on sex) and it is illegal to take them in some months (also depending on sex).

Abalone are common on parts of the coastline. There are strict minimum sizes and bag limits per day.

Except for some harmless species, sharks are rarely seen by divers in Victoria. You are more likely to be pestered by a friendly seal.

The best way to find out about underwater fishing, gain experience, learn about currents and slack water, fish species, spearfishing and dive spots is to join a club. They have social activities, social dives, meetings and competitions.

ABROLHOS ISLAND ADVENTURE
Graham Anderton

The Abrolhos Islands lie some 80 kilometres off the Western Australian fishing port, Geraldton, 400 kilometres north of Perth. These coral-limestone islands are grouped into four main clusters. The Southern group lie closest to the mainland, to the north is the Eastern group. Still further north is found the Wallaby group so named because of the numerous small kangaroos found on the islands. The remaining island is North Island, some 150 kilometres out from the coast. Apart from East and West Wallaby, (which are some 20 metres above sea level) most of the islands consist of limestone outcrops. Low-lying scrub frequently adorns these barren outcrops which are the home of countless sea birds. Except for the occasional seal or turtle the islands would appear quite desolate.

During the crayfishing season these islands become a hive of activity. Crayfishers make their homes in little shanties from May to June to take part in what has become a multi-million dollar industry.

Below the surface the islands are never desolate. Myriads of fish both tropical and of the southern variety abound all year round. These include the famous Westralian jewfish, coral trout, baldchin groper, cod, tuna, mackerel, samson fish, yellowtail kingfish, mulloway, pink snapper and north-west snapper (spangled emperor).

It is not uncommon to see large humpback whales during the latter part of the year. Packs of sharks have frequently been seen in the southern group by many alarmed divers and fishers.

While drift fishing using bottom rigs on the fat kelp bottom, or trawling, may be very productive, the Abrolhos Islands are more a diver's paradise. On the coral drop-offs it isn't uncommon to see a dozen or so coral trout just waiting for the spearfisher. Meanwhile, frequent baldchin cruise past making an easy target. On the sand edges or around limestone 'bombies', Westralian jewfish abound. These fish may reach up to 16 kilos or more, with several making an excellent day's catch, and spearing such fish can attract some of the pelagics like yellowtail kingfish, samson fish, mackerel or big tuna. Often schools of sky-pink snapper swim warily in the distance and the odd shark comes in to see what all the commotion is about.

How does one get to the Abrolhos? It is best, of course, if you know someone like a crayfisher (no camping is allowed on the islands) or someone with a large boat. Failing this, charter boats can be arranged from Geraldton and operate through most of the year. Information can be gathered from either the Perth or Geraldton tourist bureaux. During the crayfishing off-season many of the carrier boats that deliver supplies and pick up catches also do charters to the islands.

When and if you do get to the islands, do your best to preserve the surroundings. Already both the crayfishing and scallop industries are doing enormous damage. For the most part, the many shacks that litter the islands are a complete eyesore. Refuse until recent times (and sometimes even now) was often discarded adjacent to the dwellings. Even the chemical toilets required under Health and Fisheries regulations are damaging the limestone and coral outcrops by eating away the underlying material. Apart from this, craypots dislodged, entangled, or placed upon coral, leave the coral broken and dead. Wash from the jet-boats in the shallow areas is badly affecting the soft corals. Scallop

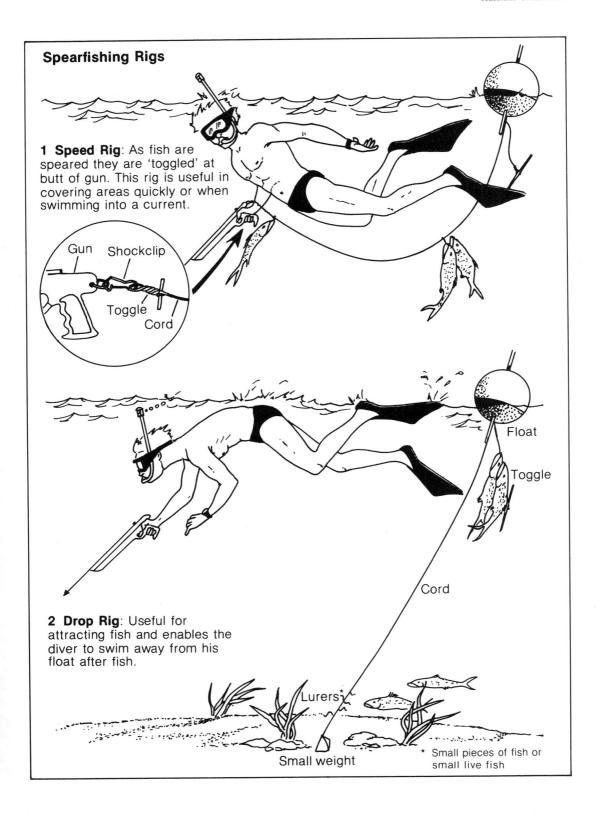

trawling is doing great damage to many fish species. Make sure when you go to the islands you do your best to preserve their ecology. Simple things like bagging your rubbish and anchoring in sand can help.

For spearfishing off the islands either speed or drop rigs work. Although there are no major tidal currents, a speed rig enables the diver to cover a large distance. Drop rigs are good for attracting many of the fish varieties.

UNDERWATER WESTERN AUSTRALIA

Trying to describe the underwater fishing scene of Western Australia in a short chapter is like trying to practise snorkelling in the bath—you can do it but it's not very satisfactory.

The Western Australian coastline stretches some 12 500 kilometres from the warm tropical waters of the north to the cool temperate southern oceans and the marine and fisheries environments show dramatic variations with the changes in latitude.

The length of the coastline, the State's small population and the very remoteness and inaccessibility of some of the northern and southern regions all combine to make the underwater scene in Western Australia probably the most interesting and exciting of any Australian State.

Even today, large sections of the north-west coast are rarely visited by divers and the same can be said about the rugged coastline along much of the State's south. In fact, most of the State's diving and underwater fishing is concentrated on the south-west coastline, generally within a few hundred kilometres of Perth. This area, especially the coast and reefs around Perth, has been the focus of underwater fishing for many years yet still provides exciting and challenging diving for the serious competition spearfisher or the weekend diver.

Boat diving is the standard around Perth itself and the top dive site is Rottnest Island lying 19 kilometres offshore from Fremantle. Rottnest provides year-round dive action in virtually any weather. Like many of the offshore reefs in the Perth region, the underwater habitat of Rottnest comprises limestone ledges which offer plenty of hiding places for sedentary reef species. In addition, swirling offshore currents around the island attract plenty of bait and naturally, pelagic fish follow the bait. Thirty-kilo kingfish are not uncommon during the summer months. The deeper reefs off the island are still home to cod in excess of 100 kilos.

The predominant species hunted in the Perth region include blue groper, Westralian jewfish, kingfish, pink snapper, queen snapper, harlequin cod, fox fish, tiger cod, sea sweep and leather-jackets. Large schools of buff bream (silver drummer) and big dusky morwong abound in the area but are left alone because of their poor eating qualities.

South of Perth the coastline changes with long lines of cliffs and deep water close to land facilitating shore diving. While limestone ledges still comprise part of the underwater topography, granite boulders become increasingly more the main underwater feature as you continue south. Fish species are similar to those encountered at Perth.

Heading north from Perth boat diving is once again more or less a prerequisite. Long stretches of sandy beach offer little for the underwater fisher, and most of the action occurs on reefs which may be anything up to 10 kilometres offshore.

Geraldton, about 400 kilometres north of Perth is the jumping-off point for the Abrolhos Islands about 50 kilometres offshore.

North of Geraldton, Kalbarri is a popular dive spot for Perth underwater fishers with extensive reefs providing exciting fishing.

As you progress north the underwater scene

Members of the underwater fraternity often prefer to photograph some of the ocean's colourful and ugly inhabitants. This close-up of a moray eel is a sight unlikely to be seen by above water fishers. (Photo Ray Oakey)

becomes increasingly more tropical and from Exmouth north you are definitely in tropical waters. Wrasse, parrotfish, cod, trout, mackerel, trevally and sweetlip are all common. Unlike Queensland with its Great Barrier Reef, the north-west of Australia doesn't have a large offshore coral reef chain. The only reef as such exists just south of Exmouth at Coral Bay. Nevertheless, the north-west does have plenty of coral diving, most of the reefs being a mixture of limestone and coral.

As mentioned, the underwater hunting scene is largely centred on Perth and there is a keen band of spearfishers who dive regularly and also compete in organised competitions. Western Australian spearfishing competitions have evolved in such a way as to reflect the need for conservation of fishing resources and competitors are only allowed to weigh in one fish of each species. Species eligible for competitions are all fine table fish and each fish has a minimum weight considerably higher than State minimum legal size restrictions. The emphasis of the competitions is on the number of different species you can catch and generally top divers weigh in between 12 and 14 species while 10 species is considered average. Competitions run four to six hours.

Perth divers have developed a novel way of finding their fishing spots. Most divers' boats are generally five or six metres and centre console models are the most popular. The boats are equipped with a glass panel in the bottom about 30 centimetres square from which to view the reefs beneath the boat. When a suitable area is found the anchor is dropped and the reef is fished for a short while before the process is repeated.

Competition divers in Western Australia generally prefer homemade wooden guns with reels attached to provide 20 metres of tethering line between spear and gun. This allows big fish to be played from the surface if a poor shot doesn't kill the fish outright.

Along the whole coast there are suitable areas for both shallow and deep diving. Reefs generally come to within five metres of the surface and descend to 30 metres and more. Average divers work depths between six and 15 metres while good divers can work to depths of 25 metres.

The Western Australian coast is renowned for its crayfish or rock lobster populations and also its abalone in the southern regions. The taking of lobsters of any species requires a current recreational fishing licence. This allows the licence holder to catch eight rock lobsters per day and no more than 16 rock lobsters can be transported by boat or held on any day.

No licence is required for the taking of abalone, but a bag limit of 10 per day is enforced for brownlip or greenlip abalone (or a combination of the two). Roe's abalone has a bag limit of 20 per day. Minimum sizes apply to both lobsters and abalone and should be checked with Fisheries Department officials to ensure you are complying with the latest regulations.

SECTION NINE

Rigs and Safety

HOOKS
Richard Allan

There are two old fishers' sayings: 'Big fish can be caught on small hooks but not small fish on big hooks', and, 'Any shape will do as long as it's sharp'.

The latter adage is most apparent within the pages of this book. Different hook shapes are suggested by several contributors for ganging (or linking), a very versatile and effective hook set-up.

The ganging of hooks probably evolved when long strip baits were being used. Often a small 'keeper' hook was tied—or even left running free—on the line above the main hook. Its purpose was to prevent the bait folding down the shank and covering the hook point. It worked but many big fish were lost when they sometimes were hooked on the small hook. Thus two hooks, linked through the eye, overcame this problem. The size and strength of the hooks chosen depended on the length of fish fillet, octopus tentacle, whole squid, etc, being used for bait and the size of the fish being sought. This enabled the bait to be presented in a more attractive manner without the untidiness of a clumpy mass around the point of the hook.

The use of whole garfish as bait required extra hooks to fit their length and was probably devised in the forties by Queensland tailor fishers. Angling writings of that period on the linked-hook rig mentioned Limerick, O'Shaughnessy or Carlisle hooks.

Limerick is a hook with a half round bend. It is straight, that is, *not kirbed* (the point offset to the left) or *reversed* (the point turned to the right) when viewed from the bottom of the shank.

O'Shaughnessy is also a straight hook, very similar to the Limerick. It is forged, is stronger, and has a flatted shank. But it is also made in a kirbed shape (that is, the point is offset to the left).

Carlisle is in the simplest terms a long-shank kirbed hook. At one time it was probably the most popular for ganging for use with garfish.

To link or gang these hooks, the eye of one is prised open with a sidecutter, small screwdriver, etc, just enough to allow the barb of the next hook in the gang to pass through. The eye is closed with pliers. The alternative method is to squeeze down the barb on each hook in the chain, except the first one, and pass it through the eye of the hook to which it is linked. The barb is raised to its original position by means of a screwdriver, old knife, or other fine-edged tool. There is the possibility of weakening or breaking off the barb when this is done.

Some suggest that if a kirbed hook such as a Carlisle is used, the kirb should be straightened—in effect, this turns it into a Limerick or straight O'Shaughnessy shape.

At the same time, there are users who turn down all the eyes on their hooks, and others who suggest only turning down the eye to which the line is to be tied. Some leave all eyes straight.

The most used hooks for ganging (on the basis of sales) now are either Mustad 4200 or Mustad 4202. Mustad 4200 is a Kendal Kirby (that is, with the point offset to the left) with a straight eye which is closed. The Mustad 4202 is an identical hook except it is made with an open eye already turned down.

To 'gang' the Mustad 4200, the eye is prised open (a small pair of sidecutters is the most convenient tool for this) and after inserting the next hook, it is closed by use of pliers. Or the risk may be taken of weakening or damaging the barb by squeezing it down with pliers and re-raising with a slim-edged tool.

If the eye is required to be turned down on the Mustad 4200 it should be done after the eye is opened, prior to ganging. Whenever I do this, I find the easiest method is to hold the eye with the pliers and place the bend of the hook on the palm of my other hand. A gentle downward pressure with this hand will produce the bend of approximately $30°$-$45°$ required at the eye.

To gang the Mustad 4202 hook requires only the insertion of the next hook and the closure of the eye. This can be done with firm pressure from pliers, but I have found that holding the eye on a hard surface, such as a fire brick, and gently tapping the open side with a hammer closes the eye neatly. Heavy hammering can distort the closure, preventing the hook moving freely on the shank of the other hook.

There are some who contend that all hooks except the top (the one on which the line is tied) should be straight, arguing that it allows the garfish or pilchard to lie straight, and swim naturally during retrieve; but the turned-down eye can be pressed into the flesh of these fish without much effort. However, the top hook should be turned down, as this creates a better angle of penetration for the point of the hooks when striking or during the fight with the fish.

For garfish and pilchards, the size of the hooks ganged ranges from 3/0 to 6/0, the number varying with the size of the bait. Usually for pilchards three of size 4/0 or 5/0 are adequate, but large sea gars may require five, even six, hooks size 6/0.

Smaller hooks may be linked or ganged. In some southern States a popular hook for a two- or three-hook rig is the Mustad Tarpon 7766, especially when using whitebait or similar small fish for salmon, or large prawns, bottle squid and so on.

Whether two, three or up to six hooks are ganged, they are very practical for many baits, especially soft fish, which they hold well for repeated casting. But they also present such baits as fish fillets, octopus tentacles, squid, etc, in a more attractive manner. And in most instances, a rig of ganged hooks dispenses with the need for weighty wire traces which can become kinked or can spook fish.

I have lost count of the different species I have caught on a ganged-hook rig. They include nuisance rock fish, most of the pelagics, flathead, bream, snapper, mulloway, and even some large sharks.

A Bit About Berley
Richard Allan

Berley (called 'chum' by United States anglers and 'ground bait' by some Europeans) is perhaps the secret of consistent catches of marine fish.

Gamefishers lay berley trails by means of special berley buckets, containing chopped-up fish, attached to their boats; reef fishers (sometimes referred to as bottom-bashers) attract fish with a berley-bomb which sinks to the bottom and slowly disintegrates. Such 'bombs' can be purchased from bait suppliers for use also by small-boat fishers on sand patches and even by shore anglers who suspend them off the rocks where they are fishing.

Some boat and shore-based fishers deep-freeze fish frames, old bait, prawn heads, and even minced-up household scraps, in small plastic containers which they drop into the water where they are fishing. Others suspend the berley mix in an onion bag – or just fish frames without the bag – in the wash off the rocks. There are beach fishers who use berley bags in the surf, and others who use berley sinkers. The successful luderick fishers use a steady stream of mashed weed or cabbage, sometimes mixed with sand. Those who catch more rock blackfish often have a contact in a bakery and purchase stale bread. This is soaked in water and the slop is used to attract and hold the fish in the vicinity of the bait.

Without a doubt, berley is the secret of more bream. The mixture can be household scraps put through a mincer, perhaps 'spiced' with pilchard or sardine oil, or left-over bait of any kind; minced mullet, an oily fish, can be substituted for the oil. This is also successful on close-in shallow reefs for snapper and many other species; it can have snapper rising to the surface for the berley and other fish, including pelagics such as tailor, will appear.

Garfish, yellowtail, bream and mullet and others generally can be attracted with soaked bread crumbs, which can have pilchard or sardine-flavoured canned cat food added. Even pollard, bran, or plain instant potato mix is handy to hold these fish.

Crushed crabs, sea urchins and limpets are used by groper seekers and this berley also attracts bream, snapper, trevally, pike, etc.

One all-round, easy-to-prepare berley is boiled rice mixed with pilchard, sardine or canned dogfood. It works in estuaries and off the rocks for almost all fish, provided it is used so that it spreads near the anglers' bait.

Cat and dog biscuits, crumbled and soaked, are favourites of some fishers, as are laying and growing pellets for poultry. Chicken-growing pellets, for example, used in their dry state, will hold schools of tailor in an area.

Whatever the concoction, a steady supply in the water is necessary. There are those who contend too much berley will put the fish 'off the bite' by overfeeding them. I dispute this, having caught yellowtail, snapper, bream, even tailor, with the rice or old pilchards I have been berleying stuffed in their throats.

One point about flavouring the basic berley ingredients with fish or fish oils is not to use the flesh or oil of a fish which is a predator of the fish being sought. Research by marine biologists overseas shows that even a minute amount of the scent of a predator will send small fish into flight or to form tight balls from panic.

My own experiments, conducted spasmodically over the years, tend to confirm the research: rice containing salmon or tailor flesh or tuna oil is far less effective as a berley for yellowtail, sweep, garfish, etc. For that reason, the safest 'flavours' or additives are prawn, pilchard, mullet, yellowtail, etc, which are not predators of other fish.

Not only will berley attract fish, it will hold them for long periods. A bonus, if you like, is that the activity, and the vibrations created by hordes of small fish, often attract more prized fish, such as mulloway, snapper, tuna, salmon, and kingfish. If, suddenly, the smaller fish which have been around disappear, don't be surprised if a mulloway, snapper, kingfish, tuna or even a shark, appears.

The use of berley pays dividends – more fish at the end of a fishing session.

SMALL-BOAT SAFETY

Dick Lewers

No one, today, can walk on water.

Truthful though that statement may be, there are many boat owners and would-be owners who would fail to recognise the implication of it. If you're into boating and have a grain of commonsense, and because you can't walk home if you have to abandon ship, pay heed to what follows. It could save your life.

Whether you own a canoe, a runabout, or a cabin cruiser, you rely not only on that craft to bring you back to your launching ramp or mooring, but also on your skill as a skipper, sea conditions, weather conditions, and the behaviour of others.

Before you take to the water – even before you have bought the boat – attend a boating course. You may think that you know it all, but a boating course run by the Australian Volunteer Coastguard or the Royal Volunteer Coastal Patrol, will soon show that you have more to learn. You will be taught the rules of the road, nautical knots, chart and compass reading, boat and motor maintenance, radio procedure, boat handling and launching, anchoring, and many other subjects.

Before buying the boat, be perfectly satisfied that it is the right boat for the work you want it to do. Talk to other boat owners with needs similar to yours. Visit several boat dealers and compare their comments on different craft and motors. If possible, talk to the manufacturers of both. Reading fishing and boating magazines and books will help cement your ideas.

If your boating needs take you on to the open sea, install a two-way radio, and learn the correct procedure for using it. Even on enclosed waters, such a radio can save your life, so consider its purchase one of your highest priorities.

Before launching day arrives, check to ensure that your boat complies with the regulations as laid down by the marine authority in your State. Check the on-board location and condition of all safety equipment and make sure that you know how to use it.

Check your fuel supply, and ensure that you have followed the rules for mixing the correct ratio of petrol to oil. Confirm that you have sufficient water and food on board, not only for the proposed trip, but for any emergency that could prevent you from returning home as planned.

Study charts of the waters you are going to fish, and familiarise yourself with any hazards that could endanger you and your crew. Buy in a good First Aid kit, know what its contents can do, and learn resuscitation techniques; you could be the one to save someone's life.

When launching day arrives, ensure that a neighbour or someone at home knows where you are going, and can clearly describe your boat should you be the subject of a search and rescue operation. Check the boating weather forecast before leaving home and be prepared for the conditions to be different when you arrive at your destination.

If the weather report tells of high winds, storms, rough seas, and deteriorating conditions, stay at home. *Do not countenance bravado*. Not only could you endanger your own life, but you could place at risk the lives of those sent to find you should a mishap occur.

On arrival at the boat ramp, but away from it, remove all tie-downs, tie a rope to the bow, check that the bungs are in place, then proceed in a determined but unhurried way to launch your craft. Don't dither. Have someone hold the boat while you drive the trailer away to its parking place. Lock the car.

Once afloat, trim the boat by careful placement of equipment and passengers, and move away from the ramp to allow comfortable launching and recovery by other waiting craft. If it is a small rowing boat, have each passenger step into the centre of the boat and sit down. If it is necessary to change positions, only do so in calm water and then with care.

If you have a radio on board, at the first opportunity after launching call Coastguard, Coastal Patrol, or a known base station, and tell them the name of your boat, the number of people on board, your destination, and your estimated time of return. *Do not* forget to sign off with that base station upon your return to the ramp, or an expensive search and rescue operation could be mounted.

Out on the water, behave responsibly. Observe the speed limits and the rights of others, and do not allow your passengers to act the goat. Passengers should not dangle their legs over the bow when your craft is under way; if they fell overboard they could be swept against the propeller and seriously injured or killed.

Limit the amount of alcohol taken on board. The skipper has enough problems without having to contend with a drunken passenger. Do not throw your empties, plastic bags, or other rubbish over the side. Plastic bags float and can block your water intakes leading to overheating and eventual seizing of the motor. The bag you threw over the side in the morning could be the one to damage your motor in the afternoon.

When you are at the wheel while under way, don't daydream. Keep a careful lookout for storm clouds, wind on the water (evidenced by white caps on waves), bomboras, floating debris, other boats, marker buoys, pylons, jetties, and shallow areas. Frequently check your fuel gauge and other instruments you might have installed.

In sheltered waters practise dropping and picking up an anchor, approaching a mooring or jetty, recovering an object tossed overboard, or just simply crossing the bow waves left behind by other vessels. By attacking these smaller bow waves both head on and at an angle, you will gain an idea of how to handle bigger waves.

Practise putting your boat into reverse, but do so with caution, and only in calm conditions. While large cruisers may be able to handle such a manoeuvre in rough weather, small boats can be swamped as the waves roll over the stern.

Do not venture on to the open sea until you understand and can confidently control your boat. Then, in your early boating life, only do so on fine days when the seas are calm. As your confidence increases, enlarge your experience by enjoying rougher seas while still exercising caution.

Finally, it is your duty to assist, as best you can, any other boat that is in trouble. Unless you know exactly what you are doing, however, do not place your own craft at risk. It is better that one boat be lost than two. If in doubt, call for help from a larger boat, and stand by to give what assistance you can when it arrives. The mere fact that you are standing by will be of considerable comfort to those people on board the disabled craft.

Happy boating.

ALSO FROM ABC BOOKS

BLUEWATER AUSTRALIANS Peter Fry

'The short-handed sailing movement expresses a romantic rediscovery of the ancient relationship between human beings, the sea and small boats', says Peter Fry in this book, which looks at the Australian experience in ocean sailing and also at questions of building and design. Fry's own interest in ocean sailing prompted two ABC Radio series, one of which formed the basis for this book, which includes interviews with many experienced Australian sailors, including women.

QUEST FOR THE CUP — THE AMERICA'S CUP CHALLENGES 1851-1987 Alan Marks

ABC Sporting Commentator Alan Marks has been involved with yachts since his childhood and he co-ordinated the ABC's coverages of the America's Cup from Newport, Rhode Island, from 1970 to 1983 and from Fremantle, Western Australia, in 1987. In this book he gives detailed accounts of all the challenges, from the first race in 1851 to the most recent challenge between *Stars and Stripes* and *Kookaburra III*.

A NAVY FOR AUSTRALIA Alun Evans

Since the days of the First Fleet Australia has been inevitably dependent on the sea — first for much-needed supplies, later for trade. As the country's potential wealth was recognised the questions of defence became more important and with it the safety of the ships which made trade possible. *A Navy for Australia*, written by a former RAN Commander, is an engrossing story of the development of the Royal Australian Navy.

THE BOAT BOOK Peter Trott

Based on an ABC Television series, this book is a comprehensive guide to preparing an MB24 (8-metre) sloop for the water, starting with basic bodywork and ending with the launch. The author, a yachtsman and boating writer, offers ideas about materials to suit particular needs, both physical and financial, and gives step by step details of the fitting out.